From Underground to Independent

Asia/Pacific/Perspective
Series Editor: Mark Selden

Crime, Punishment, and Policing in China
    edited by Børge Bakken
Woman, Man, Bangkok: Love, Sex, and Popular Culture in Thailand
    by Scot Barmé
Making the Foreign Serve China: Managing Foreigners in the People's Republic
    by Anne-Marie Brady
The Mongols at China's Edge: History and the Politics of National Unity
    by Uradyn E. Bulag
Transforming Asian Socialism: China and Vietnam Compared
    edited by Anita Chan, Benedict J. Tria Kerkvliet, and Jonathan Unger
China's Great Proletarian Cultural Revolution: Master Narratives and Post-Mao Counternarratives
    edited by Woei Lien Chong
North China at War: The Social Ecology of Revolution, 1937–1945
    edited by Feng Chongyi and David S. G. Goodman
Little Friends: Children's Film and Media Culture in China
    by Stephanie Donald
Social and Political Change in Revolutionary China: The Taihang Base Area in the War of Resistance to Japan, 1937–1945
    by David S. G. Goodman
Islands of Discontent: Okinawan Responses to Japanese and American Power
    edited by Laura Hein and Mark Selden
Women in Early Imperial China
    by Bret Hinsch
Local Democracy and Development: The Kerala People's Campaign for Decentralized Planning
    by T. M. Thomas Isaac with Richard W. Franke
Hidden Treasures: Lives of First-Generation Korean Women in Japan
    by Jackie J. Kim with Sonia Ryang
Postwar Vietnam: Dynamics of a Transforming Society
    edited by Hy V. Luong
The Indonesian Presidency: The Shift from Personal towards Constitutional Rule
    by Angus McIntyre
Nationalisms of Japan: Managing and Mystifying Identity
    by Brian J. McVeigh
From Underground to Independent: Alternative Film Culture in Contemporary China
    edited by Paul G. Pickowicz and Yingjin Zhang
Wife or Worker? Asian Women and Migration
    edited by Nicola Piper and Mina Roces
Social Movements in India: Poverty, Power, and Politics
    edited by Raka Ray and Mary Fainsod Katzenstein
Biology and Revolution in Twentieth-Century China
    by Laurence Schneider
Contentious Kwangju: The May 18th Uprising in Korea's Past and Present
    edited by Gi-Wook Shin and Kyong Moon Hwang

From Underground to Independent

Alternative Film Culture in Contemporary China

Edited by Paul G. Pickowicz and Yingjin Zhang

ROWMAN & LITTLEFIELD PUBLISHERS, INC.
Lanham • Boulder • New York • Toronto • Oxford

ROWMAN & LITTLEFIELD PUBLISHERS, INC.

Published in the United States of America
by Rowman & Littlefield Publishers, Inc.
A wholly owned subsidiary of The Rowman & Littlefield Publishing Group, Inc.
4501 Forbes Boulevard, Suite 200, Lanham, Maryland 20706
www.rowmanlittlefield.com

P.O. Box 317, Oxford OX2 9RU, UK

Copyright © 2006 by Rowman & Littlefield Publishers, Inc.

British Library Cataloguing in Publication Information Available

Library of Congress Cataloging-in-Publication Data

From underground to independent : alternative film culture in contemporary China /
edited by Paul G. Pickowicz and Yingjin Zhang.
    p. cm. — (Asia/Pacific/perspectives)
  Filmography: p.
  Includes bibliographical references and index.
  ISBN-13: 978-0-7425-5437-5 (cloth : alk. paper)
  ISBN-10: 0-7425-5437-6 (cloth : alk. paper)
  ISBN-13: 978-0-7425-5438-2 (pbk. : alk. paper)
  ISBN-10: 0-7425-5438-4 (pbk. : alk. paper)
  1. Experimental films—China—History and criticism. 2. Documentary films—China—
History and criticism. I. Pickowicz, Paul. II. Zhang, Yingjin. III. Series.
  PN1995.9.E96F76 2006
  791.43'611—dc22

                                                                          2006009574

Printed in the United States of America

♾ ™ The paper used in this publication meets the minimum requirements of American
National Standard for Information Sciences—Permanence of Paper for Printed Library
Materials, ANSI/NISO Z39.48-1992.

Contents

Preface   vii

1 Social and Political Dynamics of Underground Filmmaking
in China   1
Paul G. Pickowicz

2 My Camera Doesn't Lie? Truth, Subjectivity, and Audience
in Chinese Independent Film and Video   23
Yingjin Zhang

3 "A Scene beyond Our Line of Sight": Wu Wenguang and New
Documentary Cinema's Politics of Independence   47
Matthew David Johnson

4 "Every Man a Star": The Ambivalent Cult of Amateur Art
in New Chinese Documentaries   77
Valerie Jaffee

5 Independently Chinese: Duan Jinchuan, Jiang Yue,
and Chinese Documentary   109
Chris Berry

6 Trapped Freedom and Localized Globalism   123
Tonglin Lu

7 Chinese Underground Films: Critical Views from China   143
      Chen Mo and Zhiwei Xiao

8 Film Clubs in Beijing: The Cultural Consumption of Chinese
      Independent Films   161
      Seio Nakajima

      Appendix 8.1: List of Films Screened at the First Independent
      Film Festival, Organized by the Film Movement Society   189

      Appendix 8.2: List of Films Screened by Culture Salon   194

      Appendix 8.3: List of Films Screened by Formula 3   198

      Appendix 8.4: List of Films Screened by Studio Z   203

Appendix
      The Chinese Underground Film Collection at the
      University of California, San Diego   209
      Jim Cheng

Filmography   245

Bibliography   249

Internet Resources   259

Index   261

About the Contributors   267

Preface

Chinese underground filmmaking attracted international attention in the early 1990s, but media coverage of it has occurred mostly outside China and has been frequently filtered through Eurocentric lenses. On the academic side, a few scholarly works in English from the 1990s could not do justice to the immensely rich materials produced by Chinese underground films, whose social, ideological, and aesthetic significance calls for in-depth investigation.[1]

This book seeks to advance research on Chinese underground films in several ways. First, it brings together a group of committed scholars in Chinese studies and film studies whose expertise in a wide spectrum of subjects is combined to shed light on the changing dynamics of Chinese film culture since the early 1990s. As suggested in the book's title, *From Underground to Independent*, the dynamics in question may point to a direction away from "underground" and toward semi-independence or "in dependence" in the new century, but the sheer variety of *alternative* film culture in contemporary China itself provides sufficient opportunities for different, at times contradictory, configurations of cinematic products. Second, this book encourages *interdisciplinary* scholarship and investigates the objects of its study from various methodological perspectives, ranging from historical and literary to sociological and ethnographic. Apart from critical readings of individual works, this book explores alternative film culture through personal interviews, firsthand on-site observations, and media interrogations, from traditional print media to the visual media of film, television, and video, including the new digital media of the Internet. Third, several chapters in this book concentrate on Chinese independent *documentary* filmmaking of the past fifteen years, and this concentration foregrounds a crucial part of alternative film culture in contemporary China that has been previously obscured by an almost exclusive attention to the "sixth-generation" directors of *fictional* films. Fourth, this book facilitates further research by providing a survey of the existing scholarship in Chinese and an introduction to the rare collection of Chinese underground films at the University of California, San Diego (UCSD), as well as a filmography and a bibliography that contain Chinese characters for easy reference.

Understandably, this book does not claim to be comprehensive in its coverage of Chinese underground and independent filmmaking. For instance, while presenting a critical analysis of Jia Zhangke's *Unknown Pleasures* (2002), this book does not include a study of Jia's first aboveground feature, *The World* (2004), nor does it focus on other prolific independent directors (e.g., Wang Xiaoshuai and Zhang Yuan) or important recent works (e.g., Wang Bing's *West of the Tracks*, 2001; Li Yang's *Blind Shaft*, 2002).[2] Nonetheless, even though comprehensive coverage is beyond its scope, this book does challenge conventional wisdom and contains thought-provoking, sometimes eye-opening discussions of alternative film culture in contemporary China.

Two terminological clarifications are warranted here, the first concerning "underground" (*dixia*), "independent" (*duli*), and other related terms used to describe this alternative film culture, the second concerning its delicate positioning vis-à-vis politics. First, the reader is advised to keep in mind that there is a range of opinion (even constructive debate, as summarized in Chen and Xiao's chapter) about the precise language that should be used when characterizing *nonstate filmmaking* in China. In general, "underground" is a term

Two homicidal migrant miners looking for their next victim in Li Yang's Blind Shaft (2002)

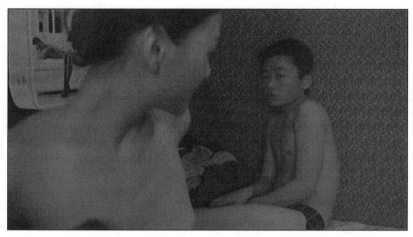

A country boy's first sexual encounter in Li Yang's Blind Shaft *(2002)*

preferred by overseas media and embodies expectations of the subversive function of this alternative film culture in contemporary China. A majority of young filmmakers themselves, however, favor "independent," a term that has gained more currency in Chinese media and scholarship, not necessarily due to censorship pressures. More often than not, "independent" means a cinematic project's independence from the state system of production, distribution, and exhibition, rather than to its sources of financial support, for filmmakers increasingly depend on the private (*minying*) sector and foreign investment, thereby revealing their status of "in dependence" as joint or coproducers, or even contracted media workers (as elaborated in Berry's chapter). From time to time, "avant-garde" (*xianfeng*) and "personal filmmaking" (*geren dianying*) are also used to emphasize the aesthetic styles of the young generation, although these terms describe more than the mode of production and cover a larger group of directors who may actually work, at least occasionally, within the state-owned studio system. Personal filmmaking is thus connected to such terms as "sixth generation," "post–fifth generation," and "newborn generation" (*xinsheng dai*), all of which designate a large, diverse group of directors working assiduously in "postsocialist" China, a new historical period that witnesses fundamental contradictions as well as exhilarating opportunities.[3]

Second, fundamental contradictions in postsocialist China have engendered honest differences of opinion about the "political" thrust of underground and independent works. Here, differences may have emerged form different conceptions of "politics." Does a film have to be openly dissident or explicitly subversive of party authority and power to qualify as "political"? Some scholars, especially those overseas, say yes. Others define the "political" differently, and thus find the political in even the most self-indulgent and narcissistic works. Understandably, even Chinese directors themselves are divided as to their self-positioning to postsocialist politics. While some may thrive on political controversy by astutely acquiring and cashing in on their "political capital" overseas (as did Zhang Yuan in the 1990s), others insist on the "apolitical" nature of their work, strategically distancing themselves from the previously cherished roles of intellectuals as spokespersons of the nation and the party. In response to the unsettled question of the political in underground filmmaking, the contributors will be "talking to each other" in this book in order to stake out alternative positions in this stunning development of Chinese culture. It would be misleading and perhaps a bit dishonest to pretend that we have all the "answers" at this preliminary stage of study. Rather, our aims are to promote various approaches and, through internal dialogue in this book, to give the reader a sense of the excitement and challenges associated with exploring a dynamic new cultural phenomenon in contemporary China.

A brief summary of individual chapters follows. In chapter 1, "Social and Political Dynamics of Underground Filmmaking in China," Paul Pickowicz situates underground filmmaking in the political economy of postsocialist China and correlates underground filmmaking to similar trends of personal expression and narcissistic self-fashioning in popular culture in general and urban youth fiction in particular. In chapter 2, "My Camera Doesn't Lie? Truth, Subjectivity, and Audience in Chinese Independent Film and Video," Yingjin Zhang urges the reader to go beyond Chinese independents' repeated claims to truth and objectivity by analyzing their styles, subjects, and points of view and by exploring questions of subjectivity and audience in the production and circulation of underground films in China and abroad.

After two overviews of crucial issues, the next three chapters deal with independent Chinese documentary. In chapter 3, "'A Scene beyond Our Line of Sight': Wu Wenguang and New Documentary Cinema's Politics of Independence," Matthew Johnson zooms in on Wu Wenguang and uses his career as a pioneer of "new documentary cinema" to illustrate the processes of divergence and convergence in China's official, semiofficial, and unofficial mediascapes since the early 1990s. In chapter 4, "'Every Man a Star': The Ambivalent Cult of Amateur Art in New Chinese Documentaries," Valerie Jaffee argues that the ideal of amateurism constitutes a core component of Chinese independent filmmaking, and this argument informs her meticulous analysis of three documentary works, one each from Wu Wenguang, Zheng Dasheng, and Zhu Chuanming. In chapter 5, "Independently Chinese: Duan Jinchuan, Jiang Yue, and Chinese Documentary," Chris Berry extends this discussion to two other significant documentarists and details the noticeable effects of a three-legged system (the party-state apparatus, the marketized economy, as well as the foreign media and art organizations) on this group of independents, who are believed to represent a model of independence different from that of either the former Soviet Union or the United States.

In chapter 6, "Trapped Freedom and Localized Globalism," Tonglin Lu problematizes the notions of unrestricted freedom and global modernity because, for her, Jia's film dramatizes the dilemmas of underprivileged inland youths left behind by China's overzealous drive to pursue transnational capitalism. In chapter 7, "Chinese Underground Films: Critical Views from China," Chen Mo and Zhiwei Xiao take us back to China in the 1990s, when scholars negotiated through cracks and fissures in the Chinese censorship system and managed to intervene in underground and independent filmmaking as it developed under extremely difficult circumstances. In chapter 8, "Film Clubs in Beijing: The Cultural Consumption of Chinese Independent Films," Seio Nakajima continues to emphasize the actual Chinese cultural scene by leading us through an ethnographic tour of the little-known operations of film clubs in Beijing, organizations that reveal much about the field of cultural consumption in urban China. Particularly noteworthy are Nakajima's extensive catalogues of Chinese underground films shown in four major Beijing film clubs. Finally, in an appendix entitled "The Chinese Underground Film Collection at the University of California, San Diego," Jim Cheng surveys the UCSD collection of underground Chinese films, perhaps the largest single holding of its kind in a university library system.

The editors wish to thank Jim Cheng for building and constantly expanding a unique collection of Chinese underground films at UCSD and for organizing a well-attended Chinese underground film festival in 2003. Acknowledgments are also due to other invited speakers who attended the festival: Nick Browne of UCLA, Cui Zi'en of the Beijing Film Academy, and Richard Madsen of UCSD. In addition, we appreciate the patience and cooperation of all contributors, people who have enriched our understanding of alternative film culture in contemporary China and whose pathbreaking research will certainly generate new interest and new scholarship in the years to come.

NOTES

1. See, for example, Bérénice Reynaud, "New Visions/New Chinas: Video-Art, Documentation, and the Chinese Modernity in Question," in *Resolutions: Contemporary Video Practices*, ed. Michael Renov and Erika Suderburg, 229–57 (Minneapolis: University of Minnesota Press, 1996).

2. For preliminary analyses of such recent works in English, see Jian Xu, "Representing Rural Migrants in the City: Experimentalism in Wang Xiaoshuai's *So Close to Paradise* and *Beijing Bicycle*," *Screen* 46, no. 4 (2005): 433–49; Lü Xinyu, "Ruins

of the Future: Class and History in Wang Bing's *Tiexi District*," *New Left Review* 31 (2005): 125–36; Ban Wang, "Documentary as Haunting of the Real: The Logic of Capital in *Blind Shaft*," *Asian Cinema* 16, no. 1 (2005): 4–15.

3. For a brief discussion of these terms, see Yingjin Zhang, "Rebel Without a Cause? China's New Urban Generation and Postsocialist Filmmaking," in *The Urban Generation*, ed. Zhen Zhang (Durham, N.C.: Duke University Press, 2006). For post-socialism, see Chris Berry, *Postsocialist Cinema in Post-Mao China: The Cultural Revolution after the Cultural Revolution* (London: Routledge, 2004); and Paul G. Pickowicz, "Huang Jianxin and the Notion of Postsocialism, in *New Chinese Cinema: Forms, Identities, Politics*, ed. Nick Browne, Paul G. Pickowicz, Vivian Sobchack, and Esther Yau, 57–87 (Cambridge, England: Cambridge University Press, 1994).

1

Social and Political Dynamics of Underground Filmmaking in China

Paul G. Pickowicz

In late fall 2004 a Hong Kong news daily breathlessly reported that "underground filmmaker" Jia Zhangke was "joining the mainstream, with official approval."[1] In the past, it was said, Jia had "secretly created" such outstanding works as *Artisan Pickpocket* (aka *Xiao Wu*, 1997), *Platform* (2000), and *Unknown Pleasures* (2002) in his "small two-room studio in a dark Beijing basement." These low-budget films were acclaimed internationally, but rejected by officialdom and denied standard distribution in China.[2] By contrast, the report stated, his new, "legitimate," and very expensive movie, *The World* (2004), filmed at the socialist state-run Shanghai Film Studio as a coproduction with United Star (Hong Kong), Office Kitano (Japan), and Celluloid Dreams (France), failed to win the Golden Lion award at Venice, though it will be screened in China. "It's the work that I've spent most time and energy on," Jia observed, "but so far it hasn't landed a prize."

According to Jia Zhangke, it was an overture from the state film bureaucracy in late 2003 that resulted in his movement from underground to aboveground creative activity. He added that Wang Xiaoshuai (*Beijing Bicycle*, 2000) and other leading underground filmmakers were successfully wooed by the state at about the same time. Jia said he agreed to work aboveground because he wanted his films to be viewed beyond the confines of international art-house venues. He wanted the Chinese people to see his work. "If you want to reach a wider audience, you have to go through the system," he conceded. "It's just the way it is."

The pesky Hong Kong reporter asked Jia if he now had to engage in "self-censorship." A bit defensive, Jia claimed that "I didn't change," the censorship system had changed in ways that supposedly allowed greater artistic freedom these days. When it was pointed out that Jia's earlier underground films are still

A distant view of the theme park in Jia Zhangke's The World *(2004)*

banned, Jia actually came to the defense of the censors. "It's an issue involved with previous [state] opinions on underground films," he stated. If the authorities permitted his blacklisted films to be shown, "it would mean they'd have to overturn the verdict on underground films that they've had for ten years."

Jia Zhangke's posture seems riddled with contradictions. He was flattered to be courted by the state and given access to its vast resources, but quickly recalled that not long ago "whenever I heard a police siren, I'd jump out of bed to check if the film rolls were hidden." Now he wants to make films for the vast Chinese audience, but he does not want to "cater to their commercial taste." Former underground filmmakers, he says, should guide the people "towards appreciating the sense of modernity in our movies." Underground artists who have not yet been seduced by state patrons are skeptical of Jia's sense of optimism. As one pointed out, "The government has appeased these directors in order to better control them. Now they can bring down the axe at any moment."[3]

With the appearance in the early 1990s of Zhang Yuan's *Beijing Bastards* (1993) and other feature and documentary works, underground filmmaking became an undeniable fact of Chinese cultural life. By 2003 there was a virtual explosion of underground filmmaking. Individual underground works have received some critical attention outside China, but there have been few attempts to evaluate the genre as it has taken shape over the entire ten-year period. Indeed, the Hong Kong article on Jia Zhangke's apparent transition to aboveground activity raises more questions than it answers. Conceptual problems abound. For example, what do we mean by "underground film" (*dixia dianying*)? Is it a useful term?

One advantage of the term "underground" is that many Chinese filmmakers (including Jia Zhangke) choose to use it themselves. It is part of their identity. People outside the underground camp, including both friends and foes of the movement, also use the term. "Underground film" seems better than "independent film" (*duli dianying*), a concept in the American art lexicon that suggests a small art-house movie privately financed by someone like Robert Redford. "Independent" in the American setting means independent from "Hollywood." This American distinction between "independent" and "Hollywood" has little to do with the role of the state, since almost all American filmmaking takes place in the private sector (see Chris Berry's chapter).

If scholars and critics decided to make exclusive use of the term "independent" to refer to the early films of Zhang Yuan, Wang Xiaoshuai, and Jia Zhangke, it would be necessary for them to point out that in the Chinese case the concept means independence from the Chinese state rather than independence from the sort of powerful private conglomerates that have dominated Hollywood. It is true that in the early decades of Chinese filmmaking (from the early twentieth century to 1937), Chinese filmmaking was in fact almost totally controlled by the private sector, including such legendary studios as Lianhua and Mingxing. Chinese government-controlled filmmaking began in fits and starts only in 1938 at the beginning of the Pacific War and picked up a measure of steam in the postwar period with the nationalization in 1945 of two studios in Shanghai and one in Beijing. But during the late 1930s and 1940s the industry was dominated by the private sector, including such stellar enterprises as the Wenhua and Kunlun studios.[4]

The Communist Party moved aggressively to strengthen the state filmmaking sector after it came to power in 1949.[5] By 1953 private filmmaking was completely eliminated and played no role whatever in the nearly forty years of exclusively state-controlled socialist film production that followed. During that period, all filmmakers worked for the state, and all production, censorship, and distribution was controlled by the Communist Party or its state organizations, as was nearly all film-related critical and scholarly publishing.

In the early 1990s younger filmmakers began very quietly to challenge what remained of the system of state control of Chinese filmmaking. The term "underground," though not without problems, does a better job of capturing the unofficial nature of the work and the clear intention of these young artists to resist state control.[6] To put it starkly, most of their work was (and still is) illegal. For reasons that will be explained later, the state was not inclined to enforce the law in a rigorous way, but the activity of almost all early underground filmmakers was illegal nonetheless.

What about the suitability of the term "private" filmmaking? It is true, of course, that all underground filmmaking since the early 1990s has been private in the sense that the state does not provide meaningful funding, including American-style National Endowment for the Arts–type production grants. As a rule, funding for underground projects must come from nongovernment sources, including both domestic and foreign. But in the Chinese case "private" is a misleading label because to many readers it might suggest "capitalist," "commercial," and "motivated by profit making." To those who have seen many of these works, it seems highly unlikely that typical Chinese underground films are motivated by "capitalist goals." The people who make them are clearly entrepreneurial, but they are artistic, cultural, and political entrepreneurs more than they are economic entrepreneurs. The filmmakers want greater freedom of expression, including freedom from oppressive and restrictive political and bureaucratic controls, more than they want vast sums of money. Clearly they are not the least bit opposed to money making, but, thinking realistically, they understand that there are unlikely to be many money-making opportunities for them in the near or even distant future. For every Jia Zhangke now courted by the state, there are a thousand underground filmmakers who will never be wooed. And even Jia, poised now to enter the mainstream, insists he is motivated by access to audience, not money.

In the end, it appears useful to acknowledge that unofficial, nonstate work is indeed "underground" in many respects. Most producers of this work submit neither their scripts nor their rough cuts to state film bureaucrats as required by the law. Others submit the scripts, but then complete production, and even screen their films for private audiences, before getting an official response from the state.

Still, the term "underground" poses difficulties, and some Chinese filmmakers and scholars prefer not to use it. One reason is that the films are not really made "underground." Underground suggests politically illicit, secret production that stands in subversive opposition not only to state domination of the film industry, but more importantly to the state's and the party's domination of political life. To some extent, underground filmmaking started out in a highly critical mode in China in the early and mid-1990s with fine works like Tian Zhuangzhuang's devastatingly oppositional *The Blue Kite* (1993) that treated unwelcome state intrusions in family life in Beijing in the 1950s and 1960s. But politically critical production is not a major characteristic of more recent underground filmmaking. For instance, there are oblique references in some films to the ghastly events of spring and summer 1989, but no works that deal explicitly with the bloodletting and persecutions that followed the popular demonstrations staged in Beijing and elsewhere.

In truth, there is no term in either Chinese or English that perfectly captures the Chinese filmmaking phenomena described in this volume. The character of the movement seems to change each year with the latest flood of works. Many analysts will persist in using "underground," even though most of the films in that category are in view well aboveground during production, even though the state is fully aware of the activities of unofficial filmmakers, and even though very little of the work is explicitly oppositional in political terms. Indeed, much of it is surprisingly apolitical. To avoid conceptual problems, some writers in China prefer to use the politically neutral term "post–sixth gen-

A Mao-style wedding in Tian Zhuangzhuang's The Blue Kite *(1993)*

eration" (*hou liudai*) when discussing this body of work. Others complain that the notion of a "post–sixth generation" is as conceptually sterile as the notions of a "fifth" and "sixth" generation (see Chen Mo and Zhiwei Xiao's chapter).

DANCING WITH THE STATE

If underground filmmakers have not been hiding out, toiling in secret, or trying to overthrow the state, what have they been doing? The answer is that

A boy beaten by Red Guards and left alone in Tian Zhuangzhuang's The Blue Kite *(1993)*

they have been constantly negotiating with the state. They have been involved in an elaborate dance with the state, a state that is itself evolving politically in various ways.[7] Few deny that the state, controlling the means of repression and knowing when and in most cases where underground films are being made, is in a position to snuff out any particular underground project. At present, the state clearly prefers not to repress on a grand scale. Later, we will discuss why that is the case.

The main problem in the delicate dance involving underground filmmakers and the state is the issue of content, not form. This may surprise those who have not yet seen Chinese underground productions. Film buffs and critics in the West are in the habit of thinking of "underground" or "independent" films as being artistically experimental by their very nature. But, in the Chinese case, with very few exceptions, underground filmmaking has had very little to do with artistic innovation. Whether one speaks of underground documentaries or underground features, there is little in China that departs in any meaningful way from the familiar conventions, including narrative conventions, of mainstream Chinese and international documentary and feature production. Indeed, when it comes to aesthetics, Chinese underground movies are quite disappointing. An exception that proves the rule is Ying Weiwei's fascinating film, *The Box* (2001), which employs both color as well as black-and-white cinematography. It "looks" like a documentary (and is usually classified as a documentary), but shows many signs of the involvement of people who are taking direction, that is, acting.[8]

In China, nuanced negotiations about content are both complicated and intriguing. The state clearly "allows" underground films to be made. But, with one important exception, the state refuses to spell out in any detail what is acceptable and unacceptable in terms of subject matter. The exception, of course, is that no direct criticism of the party or state is allowed. Those who engage in such criticism will be isolated, detained, even jailed. It is crystal clear that underground filmmakers generally accept this foundational ground rule. That is to say, despite Jia Zhangke's protestations to the contrary, they willingly engage in self-censorship as the price that must be paid to make underground, private, independent, unofficial films. Jia's denial of self-censorship is itself a transparent act of self-censorship.

In return, underground filmmakers get to explore subjects that are not treated in mainstream state productions. Needless to say, there is no guarantee that just because a topic is not taken up in the state sector, it automatically can be addressed in underground works. Each new probe is attempted on a shaky trial-and-error basis. Underground filmmakers, to their eternal credit, persistently try to push out the boundaries of what can be done. Sometimes they get slapped back, only to try again with success at a later date.

Gay sexuality is a subject that the monopolistic state sector has never been willing to treat seriously—even though gay sexuality is an important facet of Chinese life. Initial efforts by underground filmmakers to deal with this subject (for example, Zhang Yuan's *East Palace, West Palace*, 1996) were highly controversial.[9] Filmmakers moved ahead only at considerable risk. But, for reasons I will explain later, at a certain point the state no longer felt threatened by this topic—even though state studios still avoid it in their own work. Suffice it to say that the state now has little problem with underground filmmakers treating gay sexuality as a strictly personal matter that involves private behavior behind closed doors. As a consequence, a significant percentage of underground films that appeared just before and after 2000 explored gay and lesbian themes.

Filmmaking about gay sexuality sheds light on the issue of agency in contemporary Chinese cultural production. Where does the agency responsible for this notable change in the content of underground filmmaking reside? It clearly resides with "society," but it also resides with the "state." We must constantly remind ourselves that change in this and other cases could not have happened without the tacit approval and indirect participation of the state. The same forces are at play in underground films that take up the subjects of prostitution, incest, child abuse, drug addiction, decadent life styles, and extreme poverty, all of them themes that the state sector refuses to treat because it is believed that such phenomena reflect poorly on the Chinese "nation" and "people" and thus on the Chinese state and party.

It is important to ask why the state allows underground filmmakers to make movies about these unsettling topics when the state itself will not touch them. The answer has something to do with the fact that there are cultural liberals in the party and state who believe there are many advantages to allowing such artistic activity.[10] They are opposed by conservative Stalinist/Confucian-type state cultural bureaucrats who continue to insist on state control of all cultural production and who are highly suspicious of all individual, private, and entrepreneurial initiatives. The combatants are locked in a moral (and political) struggle among the ruling elite. The conflict does have economic implications with regard to who would gain income and who would lose if the state's near monopoly on cultural production is broken. But it is the moral dimension that concerns us here.

The liberals see underground filmmaking as a useful pressure release mechanism. They argue (mostly out of public view) that it is in the state's political interest to let these young people blow off steam in the unofficial sector. Moreover, since the liberals see themselves as more cosmopolitan and more global than the conservatives, they insist that allowing underground film production in China, along with turning a blind eye to the overseas screening of underground films made in China, makes China look good. As the 2008 Olympics approach, foreigners will be impressed, they think, by China's apparent flexibility. The goal is to project a softer image of China (considerably friendlier than the image of tanks in Tiananmen Square). This approach is a variation of the "velvet prison" paradigm tested in some Eastern European late-socialist states during the late 1960s.[11] In such an arrangement, artists are granted special privileges and a degree of freedom of expression so long as they police themselves in ways spelled out by the state.

Underground filmmakers, the liberal elites suggest, will accept the ground rules. They will refrain from criticizing the party/state and avoid making explicitly mobilizational films in exchange for the right to make films on many subjects the state usually ignores. Moreover, since there is an acute shortage of job opportunities in the state filmmaking sector (primarily because worn-out senior people with special access to state resources do not want to compete on a daily basis with the vast pool of young talent), the underground sector gives ambitious newcomers something to do. In fact, the state sector can recruit among the ranks of the best (and most willing to compromise) of the outsiders. Indeed, the underground film world, from this perspective, may be viewed as a training ground in which the cream of the crop will eventually rise to film in the state sector.

It is clear that this ongoing negotiation—this complex dance with the state—actually allows some underground filmmakers to move rather freely back and forth across underground and aboveground boundaries. Aboveground superstars like Tian Zhuangzhuang and Jiang Wen occasionally move underground to make certain works the state is unwilling to touch, then they move back aboveground for their next project. Tian's underground *The Blue Kite* was followed by his disappointing aboveground *Springtime in a Small Town* (2000). Jiang Wen, one of the most interesting state-sector actors and directors, went underground to make *Devils on the Doorstep* (2000), a stunning film that deals quite sympathetically with Shandong peasants who, from a doctrinaire party perspective that is openly questioned by Jiang, "collaborated" with Japanese forces during World War II. The openly gay Cui Zi'en, a well-known producer of underground films on the theme of gay sexuality (e.g., *Old Testament*, 2001), was also a faculty member at the prestigious Beijing Film Academy, and, as such, an employee of the state.

Zhang Yuan, a noted pioneer of the underground movement, is another important figure who moves with ease back and forth between underground and aboveground. In late 2003 Zhang cancelled on short notice a scheduled appearance at a film festival in the United States. This led to concerns that he might be in political trouble. No, he reported from his mobile phone, he could not attend because he had just received delivery of his new Porsche and needed to break it in on the open road. Younger underground filmmakers take

A peasant couple devastated by the scene of their village burned down by Japanese soldiers in Jiang Wen's Devils on the Doorstep *(2000)*

A surrealistic execution scene in Jiang Wen's Devils on the Doorstep *(2000)*

Beijing's gay filmmaker Cui Zi'en directing a scene in Old Testament *(2001)*

careful note of Zhang's career trajectory. Some frankly concede that their goal is to make a big splash in a foreign film festival by entering "controversial" underground works, thus forcing the state to pay attention to them and later provide them with opportunities to make expensive aboveground movies and earn substantial amounts of money (and buy a Porsche for themselves). In short, they need to make a large impact abroad, but without offending the party. This can be a delicate balancing act.

It will be interesting to see what happens to underground director Li Yang. His excellent film *Blind Shaft* (2002), a work that deals frankly with the rough-and-tumble coal mining industry in northwest China and the hustlers who circulate in the "floating" population of migrant mine workers, won the Silver Bear award at the Berlin Film Festival in 2003.[12] Will Li remain underground for a few more pictures? Will he be recruited for work in the state sector? Will he move back and forth between the two worlds? Only time will tell, but the main point is that a simple binary interpretive approach that pits heroic political dissidents against a ruthless police state does not work very well in the complicated Chinese case.

THE QUESTION OF IMPACT: WHO CARES?

What sort of impact do underground films have on the film audience in China? The short answer is that they have very little impact. So far, their influence

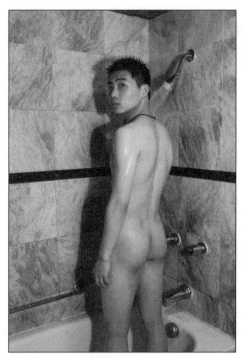

A challenging scene in Cui Zi'en's queer film,
Enter the Clowns *(2001)*

outside China has been far greater than their impact in China. In fact, this is a point that party cultural liberals no doubt make when they battle with cultural conservatives. They ask the conservatives what they are so worried about. Let the young people make underground films; few in China will ever see them.

The liberals are right for the simple reason that while underground filmmaking is allowed, the state socialist system still controls virtually all the important film distribution and film exhibition networks. Young artists can make underground films, but if they want to exhibit them in conventional ways and in meaningful venues, they will have to deal with the state. This sort of exhibition is, of course, not going to happen. It appears that even extremely high-quality and high-budget underground works like *The Blue Kite* and *Devils on the Doorstep* were not allowed to be screened domestically in state venues.

There are both political and economic forces at work here. It is true, of course, that the state has political reasons for blocking domestic screening of these films. It is also true that the directors (and their publicists at home and abroad) make much of "censorship" issues when these works are exhibited abroad. It is as if ambitious underground films actually require a "banned in Beijing" pedigree to get attention abroad. But in the cases of *The Blue Kite* and *Devils on the Doorstep*, "censorship" issues were largely a smoke screen. The political problems were not that serious. It is possible to argue that economic issues were as important, if not more important. Just as the stuffy veteran directors in the state-run film studios do not want artistic competition from young upstarts, state distributors do not want to compete with underground filmmakers for domestic and foreign market share. It is for this reason (economic monopoly of cultural production) that the state-controlled television industry is not a viable option for underground works at this point. Television programming is expanding rapidly in China, but still very much under the control of the state broadcast system.

But is it really the case that underground films, including both documentaries and features, have no domestic impact at all? No, it is not. But the domestic impact is limited to videotape and especially VCD and DVD sales, which are brisk in some sections of some major cities. The Geisel Library at the University of California, San Diego, contains a collection of more than three hundred underground titles, with many more on the way. A survey of many items in this archive is contained in Jim Cheng's contribution to this volume. Determined people in China can acquire these films almost as easily as foreign institutions. It is apparent that small groups gather in homes to view these works. Underground film festivals are sometimes scheduled on university campuses. Some of these events have been successfully staged, while others have been shut down by the police or school officials. It is possible, though, for couples or small groups to rent private rooms for film viewing. Seating capacity is limited and enterprises of this sort open and close on an irregular basis. But they do exist, even in small towns, and are frequented by students and urban youth. Jia Zhangke's *Unknown Pleasures* includes several scenes in which young people gather to view videotapes. As Seio Nakajima points out in his chapter in this volume, increasing numbers of "film clubs" provide additional venues for the viewing of independent titles. The Internet revolution in China, a dynamic and ever-changing phenomenon, also offers various ways for film fans to download and view underground Chinese titles available at home and abroad. Finally, it is also interesting to note, as Zhiwei Xiao and Chen Mo do so well in this volume, that there are lively discussions of and even debates in the Chinese media about underground filmmaking, especially in art-related and scholarly publications.[13] In short, there is in China a critical and scholarly literature on underground filmmaking that scholars outside China have not yet examined in a systematic way.

Nevertheless, it is still the case that Chinese underground films have a bigger impact abroad than at home. In most cases the state allows underground filmmakers to travel abroad to attend festivals and special events. It is no exaggeration to say that underground artists are deeply concerned about the foreign reception of their works. Many seem to adopt the following strategy: make a relatively low-budget underground film on a fresh and somewhat sensitive topic (prostitution, for example), call it a "censored" work, find an agent who will help "place" the film, try to enter the film in a foreign film festival, hope it gets attention, hope it gets picked up by art-house circuits abroad, if necessary bribe a critic to write about it as a "wonderful but controversial work banned in China," hope against all odds that it gets broadcast on foreign cable television, hope the attention it gets abroad permits funding for another (even more notable) underground work, hope that the Chinese state finally takes notice, hope the state makes friendly overtures by offering aboveground (mainstream and money-making) opportunities, and hope it will be possible to move back and forth aboveground and underground in order to address the different consumer needs and interests of both foreign and domestic viewers. Naturally, an indispensable element in this new formula for success is an understanding of and entry into foreign funding, production, and distribution networks. Without the foreigners, the sequence of events described above simply cannot unfold in the desired way.

FRACTURED IDENTITIES: THE NEW OCCIDENTALISM?

The need for underground artists to chase foreign funding, production, distribution, and discourse networks causes various difficulties, the most obvious of which is the need to make movies about China that one imagines foreign viewers, especially foreign art-house viewers and critics, would like to see. This phenomenon gets to the heart of the issue of "Occidentalism," that is, the domestic social, political, economic, and cultural considerations that shape the ways in which Chinese artists talk about the "Occident" and the "Occidental" viewer, meant here to include places like Japan, South Korea, and Taiwan that are part of the "Occident" in various economic, social, and cultural senses, but not part of the "Occident" in a strictly geographical sense. Just as "Orientalist" perspectives have been driven historically by domestic priorities in the Occident, Chinese Occidentalism has been shaped primarily by domestic agendas in China.[14] Indeed, Occidentalist and Orientalist views are said to be crude caricatures of the imagined "Other" that tell us more about the people who are doing the imagining that the people who are being imagined.

Underground filmmakers in China are probably close to the truth when they conclude that Western audiences would like to see politically dissident films (even politically suicidal films) that boldly confront the party and directly challenge party/state domination of Chinese life, films that deal with the massacres of 1989 or films that expose official corruption at the highest levels. But this sort of filmmaking is precisely what is not going to happen very often under current circumstances. Such work would violate the unofficial contract underground filmmakers have with the party.

But many underground filmmakers also imagine that films on another topic—films that scream out: "Look at me!"—can attract foreign audiences and perhaps even foreign investment without violating the filmmakers' contract with the party/state. These are films that explore the "self" and rapidly evolving notions of self-identity. The state, for its part, is clearly indicating that it is no longer necessary, as it was in the Mao era, for citizens to think solely in terms of a single national identity that characterizes all decent people in China. It is fine to engage in identity explorations. Thus, it comes as no surprise that a very high percentage of underground work deals with the topic of "Who am I?" As a consequence, many—perhaps most—underground films involve a marked, often irritating, self-centeredness. Many underground directors seem to think that people in the Occident like films about exploration of self because they resonate with "ego-centered" Western artistic agendas, and because the picture of China that emerges in them is a diverse one, the image of a society that looks more like a complicated "human" one and less like the artificial "inhuman," "lock-step" society of Mao-era propaganda.

Preoccupation with self-exploration and the liberation of the ego is by no means new in modern Chinese cultural production. Priorities of this sort may not have been sanctioned in the Mao era, but they were an extremely important part of the New Culture and May Fourth era of the 1910s, 1920s, and 1930s, a time when urban young people sought to break away as "individuals" from the Confucian, family-centered "group." Yu Dafu, Ding Ling, and many others produced a great deal of highly self-indulgent fiction of self-exploration early in this period.[15] Thanks to the pathbreaking scholarship of Leo Ou-fan Lee, we have a wonderfully rich portrait of the fascinating and profoundly decadent modernists who flourished in Shanghai in the 1930s.[16] In the aftermath of the Mao-era interlude, a related pattern of cultural output is clearly reemerging in both the realms of off-beat fiction and underground filmmaking, output that so far has had relatively little impact on society at large. But while urban young people seem once again to be asserting "self" and breaking away from "society," this time it is Mao-era norms that are being abandoned, a direction that gives the new movement a decidedly "postsocialist" coloring.[17] In both cases, though, the direction is from "group, group, group" to "me, me, me."

Current preoccupation with self underscores yet again the explanatory power of Ci Jiwei's thesis about the highly disturbing but remarkably logical shift from "utopianism" to "hedonism" in the post-Mao period.[18] Ci argues, quite convincingly, that the ascetic, self-denying, collective-oriented excesses of Chinese utopianism laid the groundwork and then generated the hedonistic and narcissistic excesses of the post-utopian or postsocialist era. The individualist excesses of the present, that is, presuppose the collectivist excesses of the past.

The picture of China that emerges in many underground films is thus not merely "diverse"; it is a view that reveals a China that is fractured into many parts and strikingly disconnected, a China in which people go about, without much guidance or knowledge, sorting out their own individual "identities." Earlier it was everyone as "patriot," "revolutionary," and "Chairman Mao's Little Red Soldier." Now it is specialized, individualized identities. I'm homeless. I'm a prostitute. I'm a club singer. I'm a homosexual. I'm confused. I'm a drug addict. I'm a lesbian. I'm a migrant. I'm really confused. I'm a bohemian. I'm a con artist. I have AIDS. I'm a criminal. I'm crazy. I'm confused beyond imagination. Interestingly, the state seems to have no fundamental objection to these identity explorations and the various (sometimes outrageous, sometimes immature) expressions of individuality that get articulated along the way. The state seems to be saying (and underground filmmakers are always listening very closely) that it no longer cares very much about what people do in their private life, especially behind closed doors. The state, or at least the cultural liberals in the bureaucracy, have apparently given up on the Maoist (and Confucian) desire to order family and private life.

This explains why underground cinema seems so obsessed with the search for individual identities and why so much of what has been produced to date seems so self-centered (and self-indulgent). Many of the characters who appear in documentaries and feature films seem superficial precisely because they are so self-absorbed. The portraits, coming after so many decades of "group-oriented" socialist filmmaking, are fascinating at first, but with repeated viewing the people who appear on screen seem quite shallow and unattractive — and remarkably humorless.

In various ways, the "contract" with the state ties the hands of underground filmmakers. That is, the problems faced by their protagonists are often interesting, but little or no effort is made to explain the origins or sources of their problems beyond the incredibly narrow confines of closed, private, residential spaces. The films often feel claustrophobic. Still less is there an inclination to assign blame for social problems or to hold the party or state accountable. Moving beyond private spaces and locating the problems of the individual in a larger social or political context rarely occurs because it would violate the informal contract. There are plenty of problems to see (problems avoided by the state studios), but only rarely are explanations offered as to exactly why there are so many problems. Mainly we see individuals trying to give meaning to their fractured lives by latching on to some specialized identity. Underground films, to their credit, are long on ethnographic descriptions, but frustratingly short on analysis.

In trying to resolve their personal problems, it never occurs to most protagonists to connect their problems to trends unfolding in the larger society. They seem utterly uninformed. They have few or no political or social ideas.

Their lives are not embedded in any social context, and we learn little or nothing about the society in which they live. With important exceptions, they seem like characters in an endless, asocial, ahistorical soap opera that might be called *As the Chinese (Postsocialist) World Turns*. Detached in this way, the protagonists seem rather hollow. And China seems to have no history. Today is center stage; there is no yesterday.

What factors are responsible for the shallowness and sadness we witness on screen? Are underground filmmakers, limited by self-censorship, unable to tell a more socially and historically grounded story? Or do the films reflect a postsocialist anomie that has in fact reduced people to such a state of shallowness? Perhaps is it an Occidentalist preoccupation with the imagined needs of foreign audiences that explains why the quest for individual identity has been represented in post-Mao China in this particular manner. In all likelihood, the fixation on self in underground Chinese films involves a convergence of all these forces. In any case, the phenomena described above necessarily give rise to characters like Coco, the central figure in Chen Miao's documentary entitled *The Snake Boy* (2001). These conditions produce floating characters who seem lost and without cultural bearings. Coco—a gay youth who sings in the "trendy" jazz clubs of Shanghai—obviously believes that he is a charming, hip, slick, cutting-edge, young, urban guy. But something very sad and melancholy comes through in the film. Coco seems superficial, shallow, incapable of self-reflection, and, worst, unable to see himself as a neocolonial invention and soulless plaything of the new and profoundly unattractive "expatriate" community in Shanghai, a group that wants to see more Chinese who look and act like "us." Coco's appeal to the expatriates is that he is a "Chinese" Billie Holiday or a "Chinese" Lena Horne. In their imagination Coco can never be "better" than Billie Holiday or Lena Horne. He is merely a Chinese Billie Holiday, that is, a patronized, amusing, lesser version of the original. Anyone familiar with the piano bar scene in Japan, Taiwan, and Hong Kong from the 1970s to the present recognizes at once that Coco is not that talented and will soon be replaced by someone just like him. An underground movie has been made about him only because he arose in the immediate aftermath of the wreckage of post-Mao China. His expatriate patrons like him because he is not "like" Mao. He is "like" a foreigner. Coco's friend Casper is even more pathetic. We are never even told the Chinese names of Coco and Casper.

The bohemian artists featured in Wu Wenguang's early underground documentary *Bumming in Beijing* (1990) are alienated, even lost, in postsocialist China. The viewer never gets any solid clues that explain why they are lost. They are just lost. At the outset, one is sympathetic with these "free spirits," but soon tires of their often incoherent whining. Each artist eventually leaves China, and Wu monitors their activities in places like Paris and Palo Alto in his sad, genuinely interesting, and ironically titled sequel, *At Home in the World*

(1995). Abroad, the artists are lost (again). Like Coco, who is back in Shanghai, they want, but cannot win, genuine acceptance in Europe and America. They are amusing curiosities. Ignored or patronized, they are forced to deal with Orientalist expectations. But unfortunately for the viewer, the artists rarely reflect on exactly why they are abroad and how their lives are related to patterns that have been unfolding in China over a twenty-five-year period.

GLOBALIZATION OR MAOISM WITH POST-MAO CHARACTERISTICS?

The problems of self-indulgence, shallowness, and excessive self-centeredness evident in underground filmmaking in China are hardly confined to this filmic realm of contemporary cultural production. It is also quite apparent in the world of popular fiction. Sensational and trashy novels such as Wei Hui's *Shanghai Baby* (Shanghai baobei, 2000), Chun Shu's *Beijing Doll* (Beijing wawa, 2002), and Mian Mian's *Candy* (Tang, 2000) are remarkably similar to many of the underground films discussed in this volume.[19] One suspects that this is because they are shaped by many of the same cultural forces. Self-indulgent to an extreme, *Shanghai Baby* is described by its foreign publisher as an "everybody-look-at me" story that explores "the outer limits of a woman's sexuality." Its dust jacket trumpets the claim that the book has been "banned and burned in China." Likewise, *Candy* is marketed abroad as an "underground best-seller" that has been banned in China.

This sort of new fiction resembles underground films in several obvious ways: it deals with "controversial" subject matter that mainstream publishers are disinclined to touch, it is highly conventional in stylistic terms, and it is preoccupied with post-Mao identity explorations. Indeed, the last line of *Shanghai Baby* is "Who am I?" These works are also similar to many underground films in that they show a fractured China that seems to have no history. Somehow, China's history, politics, and society have been erased. Social and cultural phenomena (including disturbing problems) are almost never located in the context of China's own history; instead they are seen in a larger and decidedly global context. Wei Hui's tiresome protagonist in *Shanghai Baby* is constantly dropping in-the-know global cultural references (Joni Mitchell, Erica Jong, Allen Ginsberg, Quentin Tarantino, Mother Teresa, Van Morrison, Bob Dylan, Marilyn Monroe, and Salvador Dali), but is totally ignorant of China's own recent and distant history. No connections are made between the problems that plague troubled young people and China's own history or contemporary society. It is as if China does not have a history. There are virtually no references to socialism, the party, Mao, the Cultural Revolution, and Tiananmen, nor is anything said about longer-term cultural legacies. The characters are certainly aware of being Chinese, but strangely, they know little or nothing about China. They do, however, know a great deal about the global "scene" and take great pride in their global identities.

What accounts for the preoccupation with "self" and "world" (especially the capitalist world) and disinterest in "nation" in recent Chinese underground artworks? One explanation is self-censorship. It is fine to talk about self and it is fine to talk about the world. But is not fine to talk about power and politics in China itself, past or present.

Another explanation centers on the dynamics of globalization and commercialization. The protagonist of *Shanghai Baby* proudly announces, "Every morning when I open my eyes I wonder what I can do to make myself famous."[20] In short, underground filmmakers and young writers are busy chasing global fame (and in some cases global money). The themes of hedonistic excess and self-indulgence are highlighted not only because post-Mao China produced postsocialist malaise and alienation (which it clearly did), but because young artists and writers have convinced themselves that this is what foreign audiences expect.

Critics of globalization lament the fact that young people in places like China twist, turn, and distort to adjust to the needs of the global market. If underground films or trashy novels reveal disturbing excesses in contemporary Chinese society, it is the fault of globalization in two respects: first, alien modes have indeed penetrated China and negatively influenced Chinese youth and, second, Chinese artists are all too eager to give the foreign market what it seems to want. There is some validity, of course, to the notion that the dynamics of the global market force marginalized Chinese artists to deliberately engage in self-Orientalization.

But a problem with the globalization explanation is that it is one-dimensional. It not only focuses all the attention on a single external factor, it ignores internal factors, fails to locate globalization in the context of recent domestic history, and in many ways denies agency to the Chinese people. Globalization is thus a convenient scapegoat for all that ails China, an excuse for neglecting research on the internal factors that have shaped the current cultural scene.

Following Ci Jiwei's lead, it is possible to argue that the hedonistic excesses of the present, detailed so graphically in underground films and trashy fiction, are best understood as the logical result of failed Maoist asceticism. After all, few would argue that the representations of global modernity and globally modern lifestyles contained in sensational underground films and literature have much in common with daily life in the global industrial world. They are more like Occidentalist caricatures of life and values in modern nations. But what is the source of the caricatures? It is hard to avoid the conclusion that images of the modern condition that dwell on gluttony, drug addiction, greed, social climbing, alcoholism, selfishness, and sexual excessiveness are derived in one way or another from the sort of Maoist propaganda stereotypes that dominated in China from the 1950s. Ironically, anti-Maoism in the 1990s and after sometimes embraced and celebrated precisely those excesses of modernity that Mao was believed to despise. Never mind that the representations of modernity were one-sided and distorted in the first place. Once the ascetic self-denial modes of the revolution were rejected, the hedonism of the modern global enemy imagined by Maoism was embraced with a passion. Thus, if anything is to blame for the soullessness, emptiness, and directionlessness of many of the urban youth on display in underground films, it is not globalization, it is the excesses of Maoism. In brief, one excess gives rise to another. In rejecting Maoism, many post-Mao youth consciously or unconsciously took Maoist caricatures of global modernity at face value and embraced the caricatures as their own modern values.

It is, of course, easy to be critical of underground filmmaking in China. But critics should not lose sight of the extremely difficult fiscal and political circumstances under which this new work has been produced in the last decade. As Yingjin Zhang reminds us in his chapter in this volume, China is much better off for having such an active unofficial filmmaking sector. But, he insists, it would be wrong for sympathetic scholars to adopt a patronizing attitude toward these films. It is hard to avoid the conclusion that most of the work is quite rough and much of it is quite forgettable. A good deal of it is numbingly depressing. That is why we need constantly to remind ourselves that the best underground work is far more interesting and vastly superior to anything that is being produced in the sterile state socialist sector.

Whither underground filmmaking in China? A central goal of underground work, of course, is to liberate the bottled-up creative genius of the Chinese

Maggie Cheung as a gorgeous swordswoman in Zhang Yimou's Hero *(2002)*

people from repressive state controls. It is hard to imagine this happening as the result of the activities of independent filmmakers working in isolation. It is also difficult to imagine it happening without an underground sector constantly pushing in new directions. But nonstate filmmakers will continue for the foreseeable future to need liberal allies in the state bureaucracy and even in the party. Pressures from below (an increasingly sophisticated film audience) and beyond (the global community) will also play a role. Underground filmmakers surely fantasize about what life would be like if the state continued to relax political controls and provide no-strings-attached grants for independent productions instead of wasting vast resources on such disappointing state-sponsored embarrassments as Zhang Yimou's *Hero* (2002) and *House of the Flying Daggers* (2004). But no matter what happens in the future, the underground film movement is here to stay and scholars of contemporary Chinese culture need to understand it much better than we do at present.

NOTES

1. Joey Liu, "Welcome to the Reel World," *South China Morning Post*, Nov. 2, 2004, C5.

2. *Artisan Pickpocket* won the Wolfgang Staudte Prize at the Berlin International Film Festival in 1998, among other prizes.

3. Liu, "Welcome to the Reel World."

4. For a recent study that discusses the prewar private-sector film industry, see Yingjin Zhang, *Chinese National Cinema* (London: Routledge, 2004), 58–83.

5. For general histories of state-sector filmmaking in post-1949 China, see Jay Leyda, *Dianying: An Account of Films and the Film Audience in China* (Cambridge, Mass.: MIT Press, 1972), 181–344; Paul Clark, *Chinese Cinema: Culture and Politics since 1949* (Cambridge, England: Cambridge University Press, 1987), 25–184.

6. For a discussion of the term "unofficial," see Perry Link, Richard P. Madsen, and Paul G. Pickowicz, eds., *Unofficial China: Popular Culture and Thought in the People's Republic* (Boulder, Colo.: Westview Press, 1989), 1–12.

7. For a stimulating discussion of interactions between artists and the state, see Richard Kraus, *The Party and the Arty: How Money Relaxes Political Control over China's Arts* (Lanham, Md.: Rowman & Littlefield, 2003).

8. I want to thank Nick Browne for sharing this observation with me.

9. For a discussion of *East Palace, West Palace*, see Paul G. Pickowicz, "Filme und die Legitimation des Staates im Heutigen China," in *Peking, Shanghai, Shenzhen: Stadte des 21. Jahrhunderts*, ed. Kai Vockler and Dirk Luckow, 402–11 (German), 566–570 (English) (Frankfurt: Campus Verlag GmbH, 2000).

10. For an example of how cultural liberals in the party approach and cultivate young artists, see Zhao Shi, "He qingnian pengyou tanxin" [A Heart-to-Heart Talk with Young Friends], *Dianying yishu*, 2000, no. 1: 4–7.

11. For a discussion of the "velvet prison" cultural model, see Paul G. Pickowicz, "Velvet Prisons and the Political Economy of Chinese Filmmaking," in *Urban Spaces: Autonomy and Community in Contemporary China*, ed. Deborah Davis, Richard Kraus, Barry Naughton, and Elizabeth Perry, 193–220 (Cambridge, England: Cambridge University Press, 1995).

12. For an analysis of *Blind Shaft*, see Ban Wang, "Documentary as Haunting of the Real": The Logic of Capital in *Blind Shaft*," *Asian Cinema* 16, no. 1 (2005): 4–15.

13. For an example of one such publication in 2003, see Cui Zi'en, *Diyi guanzhong* [The First Audience] (Beijing: Xiandai chubanshe, 2003).

14. For a stimulating discussion, see Xiaomei Chen, *Occidentalism: A Theory of Counter-Discourse in Post-Mao China* (New York: Oxford University Press, 1995).

15. Celebrated works of this sort include Yu Dafu's famous short story entitled "Sinking" (Chenlun, 1921) and Ding Ling's provocative work entitled "The Diary of Miss Sophia" (Shafei nüshi de riji, 1927).

16. Leo Ou-fan Lee, *Shanghai Modern: The Flowering of a New Urban Culture in China, 1930–1945* (Cambridge, Mass.: Harvard University Press, 1999).

17. Chris Berry, *Postsocialist Cinema in Post-Mao China: The Cultural Revolution after the Cultural Revolution* (London: Routledge, 2004).

18. Ci Jiwei, *Dialectic of the Chinese Revolution: From Utopianism to Hedonism* (Stanford, Calif.: Stanford University Press, 1994).

19. See Chun Sue, *Beijing Doll: A Novel*, trans. Howard Goldblatt (New York: Riverhead Books, 2004), and Chun Shu, *Beijing wawa: shiqisui shaonü de canku qingchun zibai* [Beijing Doll: Confession of Cruel Youth by a Seventeen-Year-Old Girl] (Hohhot: Yuanfang chubanshe, 2002); Mian Mian, *Candy*, trans. Andrea Lingenfelter (Boston: Back Bay Books, 2003) and *Tang* (Taipei: Shengzhi chubanshe, 2000); Wei Hui, *Shanghai Baby*, trans. Bruce Humes (London: Robinson, 2001) and *Shanghai baobei* (Taipei: Shengzhi chubanshe, 2000).

20. Wei Hui, *Shanghai Baby*, 1.

2

My Camera Doesn't Lie?
Truth, Subjectivity, and Audience
in Chinese Independent Film and Video

Yingjin Zhang

[The film] can express my true impression of Suzhou River. My camera doesn't lie.

—Lou Ye, 2002

You scrutinized yourself and discovered that you no longer belonged to any group, not to the stage nor to the audience—you belong to yourself.

—Wu Wenguang, 1999

Truth itself never exists in a work of art. What we have are the author's vivid imagination, his [*sic*] attitude, taste, sensibility, and personality, as well as the extent to which you as an audience member identify with all these items.

—Zhang Ming, 1996

Since the early 1990s, independent film and video making has developed as a new player in Chinese cultural production—a player who is enthusiastically welcomed at international film festivals overseas but who has been ignored and occasionally banned by Chinese state censorship.[1] In sharp contrast to mainstream press coverage over the past decade, relatively little scholarship has focused on Chinese independent filmmakers so far, and much less on their persistent claims to truth.[2] Two points deserve our attention right away. First, we should not blindly follow contemporary Western media reports, which tend to emphasize politics and ideology and accept independent directors' truth claims at face value. Second, we must distinguish our position as media critics, whose mission is to scrutinize the objects of our investigation, from

that of the promoters of alternative media practices, whose moral responsibility might make them rather reluctant to criticize even obvious weaknesses in
independent productions. It is in the spirit of constructive criticism that I start
this investigation of truth claims in Chinese independent film and video.

In May 2002, *My Camera Doesn't Lie* (Wode sheyingji bu sahuang), a book
bearing a manifesto-like title, appeared in China. Designed as the "document
of the avant-garde [*xianfeng*] filmmakers born in 1961–1970" (used as the
book's subtitle), this publication offers biographic information on, interviews
with, and directorial notes from eight male representatives—Zhang Ming,
Jiang Wen, Zhang Yuan, Wang Chao, Lu Xuechang, Lou Ye, Wang Xiaoshuai,
and Jia Zhangke.[3] Around the same time, Solveig Klassen and Katharina
Schneidere-Roos, two female European scholars based in Beijing, were busy
completing their independent documentary video, which includes discussions
of and film clips from the above-mentioned representatives as well as numerous other Chinese independents, such as women directors Li Yu (*Fish and
Elephant*, 2000) and Emmy Tang (Tang Xiaobai, *Conjugation*, 2001).[4] During
2003, the documentary, also entitled *My Camera Doesn't Lie*, toured international film festivals in Berlin, Hong Kong, Singapore, and Los Angeles.

I begin with the book and the documentary because their shared title provides an ideal entry point for my investigation. By critically analyzing the
statement "My camera doesn't lie," I want to explore not merely truth claims
but also the dilemma of self-positioning and audience interaction in Chinese
independent film and video making. If my (i.e., the avant-garde generation's)
camera does not lie, whose cameras do? On what basis can one claim that the
camera never lies? What constitutes the validity in the persistent truth claims
from this generation for over a decade? For whom (e.g., auteur, audience,
or authority) does a film appear true or real? What modalities of truth are
documented or developed? And how does the director's subjectivity infiltrate,
negotiate, or enhance the perception and representation of the real? Indeed,
where do we situate the audience (domestic as well as international) in such
a reproduction of truth or reality? To what extent do independent production and overseas investment and distribution impact the reception of these
"independent" films and videos as "documents" of truth? And what are the
channels and platforms of their receptions? Finally, how do we reconcile the
politics of such unusual circulations of "truths" and the poetics of independent film and video making in contemporary China? These are among a host
of pressing questions I plan to investigate. However, as indicated in the three
opening quotations above, I will concentrate on three key questions—truth,
subjectivity, and audience—by attending not so much to the visual as to the
discursive materials, in particular what I see as ambivalences and contradictions in recent directorial announcements.

THE POLITICS OF DIFFERENTIATION: WHOSE CAMERAS LIE?

After the appearance of the book and the documentary bearing the same title, "My camera doesn't lie" may be taken more than ever before as a statement of truth behind which the avant-garde or the sixth generation would like to rally. To be sure, independent directors had already made similar claims to truth, reality, and objectivity years before. Zhang Yuan, for one, thus differentiated himself from fifth-generation auteurs like Chen Kaige and Zhang Yimou:

> Our thinking is completely different. . . . They are intellectual youths who've spent time in the country, while we're urbanites. . . . They all went through the Cultural Revolution and they remained kind of romantic. We don't. . . . I make films because I am concerned about social issues and social realities. . . . I don't like being subjective, and I want my films to be objective. It's objectivity that'll empower me.[5]

Like Zhang Yuan, many independent directors perceived the fifth generation and its imitators, who had been busy reconstructing national myths and legends since the late 1980s, as their first target—artists whose cameras presumably lie.[6] Before shooting his debut feature *Rainclouds over Wushan*, aka *In Expectation* (1996), Zhang Ming was fed up with the yellow earth, sorghum fields, waist drums, red cloth, bandits, landlords, and the like on the Chinese screen, and he lamented the lack of a "sense of reality" (*xianshi gan*) in Chinese filmmaking.[7] Similarly, Jia Zhangke, who had quickly replaced Zhang Yuan as the icon of defiant independents in the late 1990s, was indignant at all those "lies" (*huanghua*) he found on screen that obscured the contemporary condition of a great many people. Jia's indignation points to the second—and more politically sensitive—target for independent directors: "Remembering history is no longer the exclusive right (*tequan*) of the government. As an ordinary (*putong*) intellectual, I firmly believe that our culture should be teeming with unofficial memories (*minjian de jiyi*)."[8]

Jia's notion of *minjian*, which at once means "unofficial" (i.e., nongovernmental), "popular," and "folk" (as in "folk art" or *minjian yishu*), reveals inherent differences among the so-called "avant-garde" generation. Apart from their reputation as "unofficial" (working outside the state system) and "subversive" (challenging conventional wisdom), independent directors themselves differ considerably in artistic visions and social orientations. On the one hand, Jia's implicit argument is that, as "ordinary intellectuals" (to be differentiated from their official and semiofficial counterparts), independent directors must accept the social obligation of representing unofficial memories in addition to, if not in lieu of, projecting their artistic visions; consequently, he intended his second feature, *Platform* (2000), to be such a cinematic rendition of unofficial history through "personal memories" (*geren de jiyi*).[9] On the other hand, when the term "the sixth generation" was first coined in the early 1990s to designate "underground" or "outlawed" feature productions from Zhang Yuan, Wang Xiaoshuai, and He Jianjun (aka He Yi),[10] the emphasis was placed on their rebellious, almost antisocial spirit and their decisive break—in terms of styles and subject matter—from the much-celebrated tradition of the fifth generation. By renouncing cultural myths and national identity, these young directors announced the arrival of "personal filmmaking" (*geren dianying*) and were sometimes designated as the "newborn generation" (*xinsheng dai*).[11]

Ostensibly, the naming of this new generation has been problematic both in China and overseas (see Chen Mo and Zhiwei Xiao's chapter). Whereas the "newborn generation" and the "sixth generation" refer to the directors' ages and the period of their emergence in Chinese film history, the "avant-garde" and the "personal" denote their artistic or stylistic character. For political reasons, most young directors refuse the term "underground" and prefer "independent," which is my choice in this chapter because it best describes the *alternative* modes of production and circulation of their works: if not entirely independent of state institutions (for nominal affiliation was required in some cases), at least *independent of official ideology*. Their "independent" status, accordingly, is defined not in relation to the private sources of their funding (increasingly from overseas, which means they are not financially independent) but with reference to their lack of approval by the government.[12]

As a result of their preferred "personal" standing, critics have discerned a kind of "zero degree writing" or a "nonpolitical" type of "automatic writing" (*zidong shuxie*) by means of which independent directors resolutely refuse to be a messenger of the dominant ideology.[13] Nonetheless, since their apparently "nonpolitical" stance was initially defined in counterpoint to official ideology and the mainstream discourses of nationalism and heroism, Chinese independent film and video cannot but become *political* once they enter the realms of production and circulation (as illustrated by Zhang Yuan's films of the early 1990s). Furthermore, the technology of the camera itself does not permit "zero degree writing" because, once produced, all moving images are loaded with textual, intertextual, subtextual, and contextual meanings that may or may not fit the intentions of the producers themselves.

THE PERCEPTION OF TRUTH: CAMERA, REALITY, AND SUBJECTIVITY

We should take a moment to consider the question of whether the camera lies and, if it does, what motivates Chinese independent directors to hold on to an apparently unsustainable (or even self-defeating) claim to truth. Theoretically speaking, the sheer possibility—indeed, an impassioned accusation—that official and fifth-generation filmmaking have produced "lies" on screen already proves that the camera, as a technological device, can and does lie. What invites further scrutiny, then, is not that a certain ontological nature of the camera precludes it from being used as an instrument of lies, but that independent directors claim to have directed their camera at what they *perceive* as truth or reality—subjectively, I must add.

Contrary to Zhang Yuan's claim cited above, I contend that "objectivity" is rarely a concern for most independent directors; rather, the desire to reclaim the artist's *subjectivity* is that which has motivated their disassociation from or competition with official and commercial filmmakers in the representation of the real. This is why Jiang Wen, the director of the acclaimed features *In the Heat of the Sun* (1994) and *Devils on the Doorstep* (2000), declares that the more a director is subjective the better the film becomes, because "everything is subjective, and objectivity resides in subjectivity."[14] Zhang Ming's preference for subjectivity is equally strong when he asserts that, although "truth" (*zhenshi*) is the weapon each new generation of directors uses to break new ground for themselves, he does not want the kind of truth that is as authentic as life itself. So he continues,

> Who has ever obtained truth? Truth itself never exists in a work of art. What we have are the author's vivid imagination, his [*sic*] attitude, taste, sensibility, and personality, as well as the extent to which you as an audience member identify with all these items.[15]

Zhang Ming's perception of truth is significant because he acknowledges not only the importance of the artist's subjectivity but also the necessity of the audience's identification with—or at least appreciation of—the author's perception (a point to be elaborated later).

It is worth observing that independent directors, for all their claims to truth and reality, have always avoided the term "realism" (either *xianshi zhuyi* or *xieshi zhuyi*), although "documentary" (*jishi*) is used from time to time, especially in connection with the much-acclaimed "documentary style" (*jishi fengge*). The absence of references to realism is understandable in China of the 1990s because, in its variant forms (e.g., "socialist realism" and "revolutionary realism"), realism has been endorsed officially for decades as the primary, politically correct method of producing literature and art in China. As an overloaded concept, realism has become formulaic and prescriptive, and symbolizes an authoritarian tradition that has alienated and infuriated many independent directors.

Although the majority of independent directors almost never shows serious interest in theoretical issues, one can still draw parallels between their productions and cinematic realism in film history. André Bazin's discussion of Italian neorealism, for instance, is quite illuminating. According to Bazin, neorealism calls upon actors "to be" rather than "to act" (hence, nonprofessional or at least nontheatrical acting); it prefers an open, natural setting (hence, nonspectacular images) and respects the actual qualities and duration of the event (hence, fixed-frame long takes); and it leaves fragments and gaps in a narrative (hence, not plot-driven) on the conviction that "the film must never add anything to the existing reality . . . [and that] we do not know everything that happens to others."[16]

In comparison, what Jia Zhangke sought to achieve in his debut feature *Artisan Pickpocket* (aka *Xiao Wu*, 1997) corresponds to much of what Bazin theorizes about neorealism. In Jia's case, an objective rendition of external reality is merely part of the picture; what really counts is his subjective perception of the real "condition of life" (*shenghuo zhuangkuang*) in his hometown of Fenyang in Shanxi province.[17] Subjective perceptions such as Jia's have produced what Zhang Ming calls a special "point of view" (*shidian*), something that distinguishes the "new films" of his generation from the "old films" of the previous generations:

> We no longer value Balzac's type of omniscient point of view. We cannot see nor can we know everything. We are not the spokespersons of the nation. The age of the grand panoramic film is over. As ordinary people, we see from the inside of human hearts, adopt a concrete human point of view, and accept individual personality (good or bad) and all its limitations—this kind of truthfulness (*zhenshixing*) is hard to conceal.[18]

This personal—which is necessarily subjective—point of view has empowered Zhang Ming to capture, in *Rainclouds over Wushan* at least, the "mode of life" (*shengming zhuangtai*) characteristic of Wushan, his riverside hometown in Sichuan province, perceived as "a kind of truthful existence (*zhenshi cunzai*) that escapes the naked eye but can be sensed spiritually."[19] Not surprisingly, a sympathetic critic maintains that a similar point of view has enabled "truth" to appear in a new light in He Jianjun's feature *Postman* (1995), reputedly a "genuine, excellent 'personal film' (*geren dianying*)" that offers us "a naked soul" through an inquisitive camera's slow movements.[20]

I repeatedly refer to some independent directors' emphasis on their points of view on certain conditions or modes of life because, deep in their minds, truth pertains not so much to external reality (e.g., physical landscape) as it does to their subjective perceptions of some transcendent entity (e.g., the soul or the spirit, as hinted above) beyond or behind the visual or visible realm. The question that obsesses them most, therefore, is not "Does my camera lie?" but "How can my camera capture what I perceive as truthful?" In this sense, styles, subjects, and subject matter become instrumental in their works as modalities of truth, as vehicles that facilitate a two-way communication between their subjective perceptions and external realities.

MODALITIES OF TRUTH: STYLES, SUBJECTS, AND SUBJECT MATTER

In his preface to the book *My Camera Doesn't Lie*, Tony Rayns enumerates independent directors' stylistic innovations in an exaggerated manner. First, in the category of documentary, he claims that China did not have this genre in the strict sense until people like Wu Wenguang and Duan Jinchuan took up documentary methods (see chapters by Matthew Johnson, Valerie Jaffee, and Chris Berry),[21] and that Zhang Yuan and Wang Xiaoshuai "might be the first" Chinese filmmakers to interweave fictional and documentary episodes together. Second, in pursuit of "street realism," independent directors are said to have succeeded in straightforwardly presenting reality without dramatic, stylistic, or manipulative filtering, and Jia Zhangke is credited for his "groundbreaking" use of the fixed-frame long take that minimizes the director's influence on the cast and environments. Third, thanks to improvisation, Chinese film is believed to have finally broken away from the category of "literary art" because a film like Lü Yue's debut feature *Mr. Zhao* (1998) might proceed without a written screenplay, and the structure of a feature film like Zhang Yuan's *Beijing Bastards* (1993) did not come into place until the postproduction stage. Fourth, formal fractures have become integral to the works of Wang Xiaoshuai, Lou Ye, and He Jianjun, all of whom have resorted to fragmented narrative, disproportional composition, and discontinued sound effects to subvert conventional film forms. Finally, the ontology of the image has been established in the Chinese screen because independent directors prefer their images to be signifiers (i.e., pure visual images) rather than signs for the signified (i.e., coded meaning deducted from a pregiven framework).[22]

Regrettably, Rayns's enumeration does little to confirm the validity of independent directors' truth claims because many of the "innovations" he lists were implemented long before the 1990s. For instance, documentary footage was integrated into leftist films in the early 1930s—an era Zhang Yuan appreciates for its dynamic energy, innovative styles, and emotional impact.[23] The so-called "long-take aesthetics" existed in Fei Mu's work of the late 1940s and has been the trademark of Hou Hsiao-hsien, a leading contemporary auteur from Taiwan admired by Jia Zhangke and other independent directors.[24]

If we disregard Rayns's exaggeration of the "firsts" and "breakthroughs," we may realize that improvisation, nondramatic plot, fragmented narrative

Director Lü Yue with actor Shi Jingming while shooting Mr. Zhao
(1998)

and images have indeed offered *alternative stylistic choices* for independent
directors in their pursuit of truthfulness. Other options, such as natural setting and nonprofessional acting, have also been fruitfully explored. For Zhang
Yuan, the first step toward truthfulness is to draw inspirations directly from
"real people and real events" (*zhenren zhenshi*), as he did with his debut feature, *Mama* (1991), and the second step is to let real people (nonprofessionals)
play themselves, as an alcoholic family did in his feature *Sons* (1996). As a
schoolmate who had started working on *Mama* before Zhang Yuan took over
the project, Wang Xiaoshuai cast a real-life artist couple (Yu Hong and Liu
Xiaodong) in his debut feature *The Days* (1993) and shot *Frozen* (1997), a
fictional re-creation of the shocking suicide of Qi Lei, a Beijing performance
artist, as if it were a documentary.[25] Zhang's and Wang's international successes soon spawned imitations. Just as Wang Guangli went further by adding
Shanghainese dialect to the formula of real people playing themselves in his
feature *Go for Broke* (2000), Zhang Yang asked Jia Hongsheng to play himself
as a drug addict struggling to rehabilitate himself with his parents' help in the
feature *Quitting* (2001). But significantly, such early pursuits of "documentary styles" (*jilu de fengge*) did not prevent Zhang Yuan from experimenting
with film's "theatricality" (*xijuhua*) in his feature *East Palace, West Palace*
(1996).[26] This case reveals that what sustains independent directors' truth
claims may have as much to do with alternative film styles, marginal subjects,
and sensitive subject matter as with their subjective perceptions.[27]

A common characteristic of independent directors in the 1990s is their ded-
ication to exploring marginal people and their marginalized life. Just as Zhang

Yuan focuses his camera on the handicapped, rock musicians, alcoholics, gays, and prisoners in his features, Wu Wenguang documents the despondent life of a group of provincial artists who pursue their elusive dreams in *Bumming in Beijing: The Last Dreamers* (1990) and a group of traveling performers who struggle to make a living in *Jiang Hu: Life on the Road* (1999), both full-length documentaries. Other marginal subjects quickly followed, in particular prostitutes, lesbians, and bisexuals, as well as the newly unemployed and migrant rural workers in the city.[28]

Admittedly, lives of these marginal subjects, who have otherwise remained voiceless and powerless, constitute some of the politically sensitive subject matter in contemporary Chinese media. Such subject matter is sensitive not because it cannot be addressed (for the official and semiofficial media have covered them regularly) but because its coverage requires an unwavering alignment with the official line of interpretation. Since official interpretations of such subject matter are judged to be nothing but "lies," independent directors therefore present their reinterpretations as real and truthful. Interestingly, precisely due to censorship issues in China, Chinese independent productions are treated favorably at international film festivals as daring revelations of the otherwise "hidden" truths and realities.

However, just as the ontology of the camera does not verify any claim to reality, the mere treatment of sensitive subject matter and real subjects does not validate truth in a given independent work. Apart from styles, subjects, and subject matter, what further sustains the claim "My camera doesn't lie" is the decision of most independent directors to "see" from the otherwise alien point of view of "ordinary" people (the adjective emphasized by Jia Zhangke and Zhang Ming) and to resist the feeling that they are intellectually superior to their subjects. This is why Wang Chao intended his debut feature *The Orphan of Anyang* (2001) to be a testimony to "certain modes of life" of the underprivileged (e.g., unemployed workers, prostitutes, gangsters). Wang's justification of his documentary-like, minimalist presentation of his miserable subjects is worth quoting: "What right do you have to arrange plots for them? What right do you have to script dialogue for them? What right do you have to declare their salvation as your theme? . . . And what right do you have to assert your moralist stance?"[29]

THE DILEMMA OF SELF-POSITIONING: AUTEUR, AUTHORITY, AND AMATEUR

Wang Chao's emotionally charged questions bring us to the dilemma of self-positioning among independent directors. After renouncing their preassigned role as the "spokespersons" of the nation and the party (as articulated by Zhang

A picture of a makeshift "happy family" in Wang Chao's The Orphan of Anyang *(2001)*

A laid-off worker struggling to raise a prostitute's baby in Wang Chao's The Orphan of Anyang *(2001)*

Ming), they inevitably confront the question of whether they, as "auteurs," are speaking for "ordinary people"—a new term to be distinguished from "people" (*renmin*), an official ideological construct as in "serve the people." Wang Chao seems to suggest that they do not have the right to speak for the underprivileged, but the way he voices their concerns about daily survival—albeit in a fictional film—squarely places him in a position to speak, if not *for*, at least *on behalf of*, them. Wang's dilemma is unavoidable in that, even though he tries to script his characters in so many "speechless" or silent scenes, as a whole *The Orphan of Anyang* gives voice to the otherwise voiceless.

Wang Chao's case is not unique. In the second half of the 1990s, Wu Wenguang also experienced the dilemma of repositioning himself and went so far as to dismiss as "trash" his earlier documentaries about marginal artists who now appeared to him to be a group of "weaklings" engaged in "collective masturbation."[30] While working on *Jiang Hu*, Wu lived with performers in a song-and-dance troupe traveling among rural towns and small cities, and arrived at this vision of self-positionality: "You scrutinized yourself and discovered that you no longer belonged to any group, not to the stage nor to the audience—you belong to yourself."[31] Wu thus clarifies the positionality that authorizes his call for "returning to yourself" (*huidao zishen*): his new position is not an official position (government), not a popular or folk position (*minjian*), not a people's position (*renmin*), not an intellectual's position (enlightenment), not an underground position (marginality), nor even an oppositional position (rebellion), but simply an individual's position—"I would speak of myself rather than my position."[32]

Here, Wu represents one extreme position for independent directors: as if tired of all responsibilities, an auteur chooses to retreat into the safe haven of subjectivity and remove oneself from all social obligations. This new position of speaking simply of oneself is definitely not identical to Wang Chao's position of not speaking for the underprivileged subjects and their salvation. But like Wang, Wu faces a similar dilemma in that his *Jiang Hu* cannot but speak for the migrant performers, even though his way of speaking is to provide a documentary context in which they speak to and for themselves on screen.[33]

Contrary to Wu, who has settled for the individual in his new self-positioning (with which Zhang Ming would most likely concur), Jia Zhangke suspects that the current slogan of the "personal film" (*geren dianying*) is misleading in spite of its manifesto-like rebellion against the state system. After all, Jia reasons, film requires collective work. In order to get rid of any lingering sense of superiority many directors have acquired through their formal training in China, Jia has chosen to advocate the notion of "amateur filmmaking" (*yeyu dianying*).[34] In an attempt to reclaim the right of filmmaking to a majority, Jia promotes "amateurism" (*yeyuxing*) as a kind of avant-gardism supportive of the freedom of expression and the democratization of filmmaking in contemporary China (see Valerie Jaffee's chapter).[35]

But what does such amateurism entail? Other than anticipating a more egalitarian field of film and video making, which is now feasible in the age of the personal DV (digital video), does amateurism mean an endless proliferation of the by now formulaic "documentary methods" (e.g., extreme long takes and shaky handheld camera) or of the equally formulaic construction of symbolic rebellion by way of staging subcultural rock music?[36] Or does amateurism, instead, look forward to a new stage of diverse artistic styles? With respect to the second possibility, Duan Jinchuan warns us against a facile celebration of an age of insubstantial amateurism and diagnoses a persistent problem in China—"film lacks artistic power as it has become more and more amateur, more and more nonprofessional, and therefore more and more insignificant."[37]

Again, the discrepancies between Duan Jinchuan and Jia Zhangke as well as Wu Wenguang and Wang Chao further highlight the dilemma of self-positioning among independent directors. Nonetheless, most of them would probably agree with Jia that Chinese independent film and video making must move past the current "stage of slogans" and strive to produce high-quality works of art that stand the test of time.[38]

THE QUESTION OF AUDIENCE: DISMISSED, DESIRED, AND DISPERSED

The dilemma, in which Wang Chao and Wu Wenguang found themselves simultaneously distanced from a moralist stance and engaged in speaking for the marginal people, is compounded by a number of related questions. Do their works speak to their subjects? If so, in what condition do they reach their intended audience? And what effect does their communication generate? If not, how do they convey their perceptions of reality to others? Indeed, how can they convince their audience that their works are truthful representations of the real? Like it or not, the question of audience pops up on these directors' radar screen, but its flickering image points to an uneasy relationship between artist and audience.

Understandably, independent directors position themselves differently toward the audience. In an idealistic way, Cui Zi'en thus speculates on "the first audience" (a phrase used as the title of his 2003 book): in a society where audience has been worshipped as "god," his resistance against binary oppositions has motivated him to place the author in the audience's position—an author cannot but watch his or her own work in the audience's place.[39] But if audience is understood as a "fictive construct" in the market, Cui declares that he "despises" this audience because he does not want his creative freedom to be restricted by commercial considerations.[40] However, in spite of Cui's creative reimagining of audience, as a concept and in reality the audience undeniably exists vis-à-vis the author and the text.

In contrast to Cui's position, several independent directors do not hide their desire for audience. Zhang Ming acknowledged in 1996 that subconsciously the goal most new directors desperately wanted to achieve was to get an audience—at least a "respectable audience"—to see and discuss their films; as he puts it succinctly, "You are successful as long as you find your own audience."[41] To tone down Zhang's implicit elitist stance, Lu Xuechang states in a more defensive manner that he has not forgotten the "ordinary audience" and that he felt terribly dejected when a viewer who looked like a worker expressed his confusion after watching Lu's feature *The Making of Steel* (1995, released in 1997) in a theater.[42] Among independent documentarians, Jiang Yue argues that since they are making videos now, they necessarily hope to have audiences right away rather than wait for the future.[43] Surprisingly, even Zhang Yuan, a figure of absolute defiance in the early 1990s, later admitted that he had struggled for years to communicate with more audiences (in particular, domestic audiences) and that he had succeeded in this goal after directing *Seventeen Years* (1998), his first feature produced inside the state system and released commercially in China.[44]

But where are their audiences, and who are they? Historically, the audience for independent Chinese film and video has been dispersed all over, especially outside China in Europe and North America. Dai Jinhua, who had denied the existence of a sixth generation back in 1994, made this telling observation: "News about 'China's underground films' . . . was communicated to me only through overseas publications and friends. They were seen only at Western film festivals and foreign embassies in Beijing, and in the cramped, small rooms of friends."[45]

It is safe to estimate that the majority of theater audiences for Chinese independent works are film festival goers, who, as Bill Nichols observes, are mostly "white, Western, and middle-class" (except in Asian cities like Hong Kong and Tokyo) and who travel along with screen images in search of audacious political ideas, distinctive artistic visions, and authentic (i.e., exotic) national cultures.[46] The categories of new artists or debut works in many film festivals encourage the entry of independent works, and remnant cold-war ideology compels the Western media to play up potentially subversive elements in Chinese independent works. In many cases, Chinese directors are fully complicit: they want their films played up in just this sense.

In turn, the awards from international film festivals and the "underground" or "banned" status of most independent works in China generated a certain curiosity among the Chinese urban intellectual sector. To reach this audience (and beyond circulating works among their friends), independent directors often make their works available to local art galleries, film clubs, and cafés, where a duplicated, low-quality video version is screened (see Seio Nakajima's chapter).[47] Du Haibin's *Along the Railroad* (2000), for instance, was shown in 2000 at the "Huangtingzi 50 Bar" (near the Beijing Film Academy, now demolished) and the Cuigong Hotel bar in Beijing as well as the 101 Film Club in Shanghai.[48] A one-day DV film program offered by "Loft Bar" (Zangku) in Beijing's Sanlitun area screened DV shorts from artists like Cui Zi'en. Other noted Beijing film-related bars include "Box Café" (Hezi) and "Sculpting in Time" (Diaoke shiguang) near Qinghua University, Chaihuoche, and "Swallowtail Butterfly" (Yanwei die).[49]

In addition to these small-size audiences, independent works may reach substantially more viewers in two other ways: first, unofficial film festivals on college campuses or special exhibits at art galleries; second, the Internet and the unauthorized or semiauthorized home video format. During September 22–27, 2001, Beijing University Online and the popular publication *Southern Weekend* (Nanfang zhoumo) cosponsored "The First Unrestricted Image Festival" on the campus of the Beijing Film Academy. The event was complete with a group of select jurors and open competitions in several categories, and *Along the Railroad* (voted as the best picture) and Ying Weiwei's *The Box* (2001) were outstanding among over fifty documentary titles exhibited.[50] Focusing on a lesbian couple, *The Box* was also included in "The Shanghai Exhibit of Unofficial Films." Similar events took place in bars and video rooms in large cities like Chengdu, Guangzhou, and Wuhan, and the exhibited works included *Jiang Hu* and Zhu Wen's feature *Seafood* (2001).[51] During December 26–29, 2001, an unofficial film festival in Kunming showed independent documentaries and features in two local bars, "Blue Velvet" (Lan sirong) and "Upriver Creative Workshop" (Shanghe chuangku). Leading independents like Wu Wenguang, Du Haibin, and Jia Zhangke met with the audiences. Among the lesser-known documentary titles screened there were Li Hong's *Out of Phoenix Bridge* (1997), Yang Tianyi's *Old Men* (1999), Ju Anqi's *There's a Strong Wind in Beijing* (2000), and Hu Shu's *Leave Me Alone* (2001).[52] More recently, Wu and Jia were featured in a series of monthly forums on independent directors sponsored by Shanghai's Dongdaming Art Center in its DDM Warehouse. Also included in the series, thirteen pictures by Cui Zi'en were screened to Chinese and foreign audiences on five different days during January 2–20, 2004, and a dozen media venues covered the event.[53]

Compared with the publicity and excitement of unofficial exhibitions generated by actual or potential bans implemented by the government, Internet access may be less problematic or confrontational, but it definitely involves a silent majority of domestic audiences. My discussions with recent Chinese undergraduate and graduate students at Beijing University and Nanjing

University typically confirm a relatively easy access to campus broadband systems, through which they frequently manage to upload and download available independent film works, although these titles might not stay in these systems for long. Their familiarity with the names of leading Chinese independents such as Zhang Yuan and Jia Zhangke testifies to the largely efficient circulation of their works through unofficial channels, and knowledge of current independent titles among a core group of film fans is also evident in some online film forums and Internet BBS chat rooms.[54] Directors like Cui Zi'en and Wu Wenguang, as well as film critics like Zhang Xianmin and Cheng Qingsong, have contributed film reviews and film columns to periodicals, a practice that further facilitates circulation of knowledge about independent works inside China and thereby heightens the curiosity of potential audiences (see Chen Mo and Zhiwei Xiao's chapter).[55]

A FILM OF DIVIDED RECEPTIONS:
ARTISAN PICKPOCKET IN CHINA AND ABROAD

The dispersed audience phenomenon complicates domestic and international reception. Using *Artisan Pickpocket* (produced by Hutong Film of Hong Kong on a slim budget of RMB280,000) as an example, we can discern a pattern of drastic difference in the reception of "truth" inside and outside China. After winning a top prize at the 1997 Berlin film festival, *Artisan Pickpocket* picked up distributors in France, Germany, Belgium, Switzerland, Austria, Australia,

Ju Anqi riding a tricycle on route to shoot the documentary There's a Strong Wind in Beijing *(2000)*

Japan, South Korea, and Hong Kong. In January 1999, the film showed in four French theaters and reportedly topped the French box office for four weeks. Additionally, Arta Television paid 400,000 francs for the exhibition rights, the French press had positive reviews, and a French foundation granted Jia Zhangke 700,000 francs for the postproduction work on his next project to be done in France.

In sharp contrast, a few film screenings in Beijing in 1998 generated mixed but mostly negative responses, at least to the best of Jia Zhangke's knowledge. The first one at Beijing University was hosted by the poet Xie Mian and attended by thirty or so faculty members, but one of them criticized the film for describing China as a poverty-stricken third-world country. Xie Fei, a professor and film director at the Beijing Film Academy (from whose Department of Literature Jia graduated in 1997), arranged a clandestine screening on the academy's campus, after which the film went on to be ridiculed as a negative example in some class lectures. The largest screening in Beijing, organized by the poet Ouyang Jianghe, took place in an art center and housed one hundred viewers, including Zhang Yimou. Although Zhang did not say anything, Jia heard that one of Zhang's close associates ruthlessly trashed the film. What distressed Jia the most during these unofficial Chinese screenings were the common accusations from his schoolmates and fellow filmmakers that his film was shot to please foreigners and that he was an opportunist whose "crude" style was nothing but a fixed camera taking random street scenes.[56]

On the other hand, Jia may take comfort in the fact that most critics and scholars appreciate his films, and a long list of illustrious awards from international film festivals testifies to the significance of his artistic vision.[57] Nonetheless, the sharply divided receptions of *Artisan Pickpocket* in China and abroad reveal not so much the politics of censorship in China (an old story repeated over and over by the Western media) as the seemingly unbridgeable gap between the artist's vision and its acceptability by the domestic audience. Given such a conspicuous gap, independent directors may find their claims to truth ultimately problematic. If what they perceive as truth is routinely dismissed in China—significantly not only by the authorities—as something that merely caters to international film festivals overseas, independent directors have a long way to go to reach their domestic audiences, especially those "ordinary people" as encountered in Lu Xuechang's case.

Collin MacCabe's comment on cinematic realism seems relevant here: "What is at issue is not simply the reality external to the text but the reality of the text itself. We must understand the text's effectivity within the social process, which is to say we have to consider the relation between reader and text in its historical specificity."[58] The historical specificity, in our case, stretches across cultural, linguistic, and national borders, and the apparent effectivity of *Artisan Pickpocket* in the foreign context and the lack thereof in the native one raise further questions. To what extent do overseas investment and distribution impact the production and reception of Chinese independent works as "documents" of truth? And how can one reconcile the sheer incompatibility between the politics of circulating these "truths" overseas and the poetics of representing the underrepresented (or voicing for the voiceless) in Chinese independent film and video? Obviously, more research, especially firsthand ethnographic work on audience and comparative study of diverse receptions, is needed to address questions like these.

MY VISION, MY CAMERA, AND MY TRUTH

We should return to the context in which the statement "My camera doesn't lie" first emerged. As Lou Ye explains in an interview, his feature *Suzhou River* (1997, 2000) was started as a documentary project because he wanted to capture the "real look" (*zhenshi mianmao*) of life along this polluted river in Shanghai.[59] We are reminded of Meimei's exchanges with the off-screen photographer, which echo like a haunting presence at the beginning and end of the film:

"If I left you, would you look for me? Like Mada?"

"Yes."

"Forever?"

"Yes."

"Your whole life?"

"Yes."

"You're lying (*sahuang*)."

Although *Suzhou River* is as much about lies and betrayals as about unreliable memory and disappearing idealism—themes similarly explored in Wang Quan'an's *Lunar Eclipse* (1999)—Lou Ye is nonetheless convinced that, in spite of all his tricks of cinematic doubling, narrative suspense, and optical illusions, as a filmmaker he himself does not lie. In his words, the film "can express my true impression (*zhenshi yinxiang*) of Suzhou River. My camera doesn't lie (*sahuang*)."[60] Although he immediately qualifies the statement— "my camera doesn't lie"—as a mere philosophical "thesis" (*mingti*) open to rebuttal, it is all the more noteworthy when we establish Lou's key words in the logical sequence of his two sentences—my impression (or vision), my camera (or style), and my truth (or text).

To conclude this investigation, I suggest that we take "My camera doesn't lie" as a statement not so much about certain inherent truth content in Chinese

Zhou Xun as mermaid-like Meimei in Lou Ye's Suzhou River
(2000)

independent film and video as about the new *strategic positions* independent
directors have claimed for themselves with regard to truth, subjectivity, and
audience. By declaring, "My camera doesn't lie," they intervened in Chinese
media and have succeeded in reestablishing the artist's subjectivity, which
authorizes them to proceed in a self-confident manner: my vision, my camera,
and my truth. Although at present it is still too early to celebrate the accom-
plishments of these independents, we must recognize that their intervention
since the early 1990s has altered the balance of power—however symboli-

A fashionable woman in a hip car in Wang Quan'an's Lunar Eclipse *(1999)*

cally—in Chinese cultural production and has remained an unrelenting challenge to the hegemony of official filmmaking and media representation in China. It is in posing this challenge that the statement "My camera doesn't lie" makes the most profound sense at home and abroad.

NOTES

A shorter version of this chapter was delivered at the lecturer series sponsored by the School of Cinema, Television, and Digital Media, the University of California, Los Angeles, March 9, 2004; my thanks to Nick Browne and his doctoral students.

1. An early example is the Chinese government's ban on Wu Wenguang, Zhang Yuan, and other independents in 1994; see Linda Jaivin, "Defying a Ban, Chinese Cameras Roll," *The Wall Street Journal*, Jan. 18, 1995, A12. State censorship activities like this could be seen as an official protest against a string of top awards and recognitions given to Chinese independent film and video since the early 1990s by international film festivals such as Berlin, Cannes, Chicago, Edinburgh, Hawaii, Locarno, Montreal, Nantes, Pusan, Rotterdam, Singapore, Tokyo, Vancouver, Venice, and Yamagata. For details, see relevant pages in Cheng Qingsong and Huang Ou, *Wode sheyingji bu sahuang: xianfeng dianying ren dang'an—shengyu 1961–1970* [My Camera Doesn't Lie: Documents on Avant-garde Filmmakers Born between 1961 and 1970] (Beijing: Zhongguo youyi chuban gongsi, 2002). A lower-level disciplinary mechanism is at work in the case of Cui Zi'en, a high-profile and openly gay video maker in China. After teaching homosexual films years ago, Cui has been banned from classroom instruction at the Beijing Film Academy. Although he offers lectures at some university campuses in Beijing from time to time, he has been discouraged from going a second time once the authorities find out about his "unofficial" activities.

2. Among a few early English studies are Bérénice Reynaud, "New Visions/New Chinas: Video-Art, Documentation, and the Chinese Modernity in Question," in *Resolutions: Contemporary Video Practices*, ed. Michael Renov and Erika Suderburg, 229–57 (Minneapolis: University of Minnesota Press, 1996); Xiaoping Lin, "New Chinese Cinema of the 'Sixth Generation': A Distant Cry of Forsaken Children," *Third Text* 16, no. 3 (2000): 261–84; Shuqin Cui, "Working from the Margins: Urban Cinema and Independent Directors in Contemporary China," *Post Script* 20, nos. 2–3 (2001): 77–93. But the scholarship situation will get better with the publication of Zhen Zhang, ed., *The Urban Generation: Chinese Cinema and Society at the Turn of the Twenty-first Century* (Durham, N.C.: Duke University Press, 2006).

3. The book also contains brief information regarding other "equally important directors" (again, all of them male): Li Jixian, Hu Xueyang, Liu Bingjian, Meng Jinghui, Wang Quan'an, Yu Liwei, Wang Guangli, Zhang Yang, Guan Hu, Zhu Wen, Tang Danian, Li Xin, and Shi Runjiu (see Cheng and Huang, *Wode sheyingji*, 398–429). For a more comprehensive discussion of "underground" productions (i.e., films banned from theatrical releases in China), see Zhang Xianmin, *Kanbujian de yingxiang* [Films Banned from Watching] (Shanghai: Sanlian shudian, 2004).

4. Solveig studied at the Beijing Film Academy, and Katharina taught German literature at Beijing University. Including postproduction, the two of them spent US$10,000 out of their own pockets on the documentary. Interview with Katharina, Friendship Hotel, Beijing, Dec. 27, 2003.

5. See Reynaud, "New Visions/New Chinas," 236.

6. For a discussion of fifth-generation films as a mode of "ethnographic cinema," see Yingjin Zhang, *Screening China: Critical Interventions, Cinematic Reconfigurations, and the Transnational Imaginary in Contemporary Chinese Cinema* (Ann Arbor: Center for Chinese Studies, University of Michigan, 2002), 208–220.

7. Cheng Qingsong and Huang Ou, *Wode sheyingji*, 31.

8. Cheng Qingsong and Huang Ou, *Wode sheyingji*, 362, 370.

9. Cheng Qingsong and Huang Ou, *Wode sheyingji*, 370.

10. See David Chute, "Beyond the Law," *Film Comment* 30, no. 1 (1994): 60–62.

11. Han Xiaolei, "Dui diwudai de wenhua tuwei: houwudai de geren dianying xianxiang" [A Cultural Breakaway from the Fifth Generation: The Phenomenon of Personal Film in the Post–Fifth Generation], *Dianying yishu*, 1995, no. 2:58–63; Yin Hong, "Zai jiafeng zhong zhangda: Zhongguo dalu xinsheng dai de dianying shijie" [Growing Up between the Fissures: The Film World of the Newborn Generation], *Ershiyi shiji* 49 (Oct. 1998): 88–93.

12. The "urban generation," another way of describing this group, derives from many directors' insistence on their unique urban sensitivities and the predominance of urban settings in their early films (see Yingjin Zhang, "Rebel Without a Cause? China's New Urban Generation and Postsocialist Filmmaking," in *The Urban Generation: Chinese Cinema and Society at the Turn of the Twenty-first Century*, ed. Zhen Zhang [Durham, N.C.: Duke University Press, 2006]).

13. Cui Zi'en, *Diyi guanzhong* [The First Audience] (Beijing: Xiandai chubanshe, 2003), 128–31.

14. Cheng Qingsong and Huang Ou, *Wode sheyingji*, 77.

15. Zhang Ming, *Zhaodao yizhong dianying fangfa* [Discovering a Film Method] (Beijing: Zhonggguo guangbo dianshi chubanshe, 2003), 27–28.

16. See Gerald Mast, Marshall Cohen, and Leo Braudy, eds., *Film Theory and Criticism: Introductory Readings*, fourth edition (New York: Oxford University Press, 1992), 39.

17. Cheng Qingsong and Huang Ou, *Wode sheyingji*, 362.

18. Zhang Ming, *Zhaodao yizhong*, 9. Jia Zhangke echoes Zhang's view by saying that no one has the right to represent the majority and one has the right only to represent oneself (see Cheng Qingsong and Huang Ou, *Wode sheyingji*, 367). Nonetheless, "For whom do you serve as a spokesperson?" still remains a thorny question, which Zhu Wen, the scriptwriter of *Rainclouds over Wushan*, refused to answer in an interview (see Zhang Xianmin and Zhang Yaxuan, *Yige ren de yingxiang: DV wanquan shouce* [All About DV: Works, Making, Creation, Comments] [Beijing: Zhongguo qingnian chubanshe, 2003], 83).

19. Cheng Qingsong and Huang Ou, *Wode sheyingji*, 25, 34.

20. Cui Zi'en, *Diyi guanzhong*, 22.

21. For further studies of Chinese documentary filmmaking, see Wang Weici, *Jilu yu tansuo: 1990–2000 dalu jilupian de fazhan yu koushu jilu* [Documentation and

Exploration: The Growth of Documentary in Mainland China and Its Related Oral Histories, 1990–2000] (Taipei: Guojia dianying ziliao guan, 2001); and Paola Voci, "From the Center to the Periphery: Chinese Documentary's Visual Conjectures," *Modern Chinese Literature and Culture* 16, no. 1 (2004): 65–113.

22. See Cheng Qingsong and Huang Ou, *Wode sheyingji*, vi–vii.

23. Cheng Qingsong and Huang Ou, *Wode sheyingji*, 126.

24. See Wu Wenguang, ed., *Xianchang (di yi juan)* [Document: The Present Scene, Vol. 1] (Tianjin: Tianjin shehui kexue chubanshe, 2000), 204. Likewise, Du Haibin, a documentarian himself, admires Hou Hsiao-hsien's films for their magical unraveling of familiar life experience (see Zhang Xianmin and Zhang Yaxuan, *Yige ren de yingxiang*, 117).

25. Cheng Qingsong and Huang Ou, *Wode sheyingji*, 283–328.

26. Cheng Qingsong and Huang Ou, *Wode sheyingji*, 113–17.

27. For a discussion along this line, see Yingjin Zhang, "Styles, Subjects, and Special Points of View: A Study of Contemporary Chinese Independent Documentary," *New Cinemas* 2, no. 2 (2004): 119–35.

28. In this area Cui Zi'en's recent DV features are most representative, such as *Enter the Clowns* (2001) and *Old Testament* (2001). For further information, see Chris Berry, "The Sacred, the Profane, and the Domestic in Cui Zi'en's Cinema," *Positions* 12, no. 1 (2004): 195–201; Qi Wang, "The Ruin Is Already a New Outcome: An Interview with Cui Zi'en," *Positions* 12, no. 1 (2004): 181–94.

29. Cheng Qingsong and Huang Ou, *Wode sheyingji*, 165, 173.

30. Lü Xinyu, *Jilu Zhongguo: dangdai Zhongguo xin jilu yundong* [Documenting China: The New Documentary Movement in Contemporary China] (Beijing: Sanlian shudian, 2003), 8–9.

31. Lü, *Jilu Zhongguo*, 9.

32. Lü, *Jilu Zhongguo*, 11, 31.

33. In addition to the audio-visual "documents" in *Jiang Hu*, Wu further develops a print space for his subjects to speak; see Wu Wenguang, *Xianchang (di yi juan)*, 242–73; Wu Wenguang, ed., *Xianchang (di er juan)* [Document: The Present Scene, Vol. 2] (Tianjin: Tianjin shehui kexue chubanshe, 2001), 276–93.

34. Wu Wenguang, *Xianchang (di yi juan)*, 190–91, 212.

35. Cheng Qingsong and Huang Ou, *Wode sheyingji*, 358–59. Jia Zhangke identifies three new forces that challenge the exclusive right of film institutions: independent productions, VCD (video compact disc, the affordability of which has disrupted the monopoly of film texts and enabled ordinary people to watch film classics), and DV (which democratizes the means of filmmaking by making it closer to individuals rather than the industry). See Fenghuang weishi (Phoenix Satellite TV), ed., *DV xin shidai 1* [DV New Generation 1] (Beijing: Zhongguo qingnian chubanshe, 2003), 10–17; Wu Wenguang, *Xianchang (di yi juan)*, 211; Zhang Xianmin and Zhang Yaxuan, *Yige ren de yingxiang*, 306–11.

36. This is what happened initially to the Hong Kong–based Phoenix Satellite TV (Fenghuang weishi) when it sponsored the "New DV Age," an exhibit of Chinese youth video works in which college students from China, Hong Kong, and Taiwan participated (see Fenghuang weishi, *DV xin shidai 1*, ii–iv). For further discussion,

see Yiman Wang, "The Amateur's Lightning Rod: DV Documentary in Postsocialist China," *Film Quarterly* 58, no. 4 (2005): 16–26.

37. See Lü, *Jilu Zhongguo*, 99.

38. Cheng Qingsong and Huang Ou, *Wode sheyingji*, 358–59.

39. Cui Zi'en, *Diyi guanzhong*, ii–iii.

40. Cui Zi'en, *Diyi guanzhong*, 7.

41. Zhang Ming, *Zhaodao yizhong*, 27, 35.

42. The confusion might in part have derived from the fact that *The Making of Steel* was forced to undergo eleven revisions from its completion in 1995 to its approval for release near the end of 1997 (Cheng Qingsong and Huang Ou, *Wode sheyingji*, 209).

43. Lü, *Jilu Zhongguo*, 138.

44. Still, it took seven months for *Seventeen Years* to clear censorship in China (see Cheng Qingsong and Huang Ou, *Wode sheyingji*, 110, 125). Zhang Yuan's subsequent films, such as *I Love You* (2002) and *Green Tea* (2003), are all officially approved projects, funded in part by his own Beijing-based company, "Shiji xixun" (Century Good Tidings). That is perhaps why, in the documentary *My Camera Doesn't Lie*, one critic labels Zhang as "corrupted" because he has joined the state system. As a matter of fact, Zhang's earlier rebellious work had already been diagnosed as "bankable dissent" because his political controversy at home frequently translated into overseas financial backing; see Geremie R. Barmé, *In the Red: On Contemporary Chinese Culture* (New York: Columbia University Press, 1999).

45. Dai Jinhua, "A Scene in the Fog: Reading Sixth Generation Films," in *Cinema and Desire: Feminist Marxism and Cultural Politics in the Work of Dai Jinhua*, ed. Jing Wang and Tani Barlow, 77, 91 (London: Verso, 2002).

46. Bill Nichols, "Discovering Form, Inferring Meaning: New Cinemas and the Film Festival Circuit," *Film Quarterly* 47, no. 3 (1994): 16–30.

47. In addition to cafés and other venues mentioned in the text, noted film clubs include the Practice Society (Shijian she) in Beijing, the Film Fan Club (Yuanying hui) in Guangzhou, the Free Cinema (Ziyou dianying) in Shenyang, the Marginal Society (Bianyuan she) in Zhengzhou, the M Commune (M gongshe) in Chongqing, and the Approximating Line (Jianjinxian) in Shanxi. See Yu Aiyuan, "Guanyu Zhongguo 'dixia dianying' de wenhua jiexi [Cultural Analysis of "Underground Film" in China], *Shiji Zhongguo*, Aug. 9, 2000, www.cc.org.cn/zhoukan/shidaizhuanti/0208/0208091002 .htm (accessed Feb. 20, 2004).

48. See Wu Wenguang, *Xianchang (di er juan)*, 132.

49. For a report on the Box Café's screenings of independent documentaries, see Zheng Wei, "'He' zhong de rizi" [Days Spent in the "Box"], *Dushu*, 2003, no. 6:105–9.

50. For detailed descriptions of these exciting days of screenings, see Cheng Qingsong, *Kandejian de yingxiang* [Films Permitted for Watching] (Shanghai: Sanlian shudian, 2004), 235–46; Zhang Xianmin and Zhang Yaxuan, *Yige ren de yingxiang*, 272–74.

51. See Zheng Wei, "Jilu yu biaoshu: Zhongguo dalu 1990 niandai yilai de duli jilupian" [Documentation and Expression: Mainland Chinese Independent Documentary since 1990], *Dushu*, 2003, no. 10:86; Zhang and Zhang, *Yige ren de yingxiang*, 265–92.

52. See Yan Jun, "Kan dianying, ting yinyue, guang gongyuan" [Watching Films, Listening to Music, and Visiting Parks], *Xin qingnian*, April 15, 2002, http://xueshu .newyouth.beida-online.com/data/data.php3?db=xueshu&id=kandianying (accessed Feb. 20, 2004). *Out of Phoenix Bridge* was reportedly collected by the Museum of Modern Art in New York City and was the first mainland Chinese independent documentary to air overseas (by Taiwan Public TV, March 2000), while *Old Men* was the first Chinese documentary DV work to be sold commercially (to a French television station for 12,000 francs). See Cui Weiping, "Zhongguo dalu duli zhizuo jilupian de shengzhang kongjian" [Space for the Growth of the Independent Documentary in Mainland China], *Ershiyi shiji* 77 (June 2003): 84–94. For an overview in English, see Bérénice Reynaud, "Dancing with Myself, Drifting with My Camera: The Emotional Vagabonds of China's New Documentary," *Senses of Cinema* 28 (Sept.–Oct. 2003).

53. See Michelle Qiao, "The Metaphysics of Film," *China Daily*, Jan. 14, 2004, www1.chinadaily.com.cn/en/doc/2004-01/14/content_298716.htm (accessed Feb. 25, 2004).

54. For example, Wei Xidi (a pseudonym based on the homophone of VCD) set up an Internet forum called "Rear Window" (Houchuan) in Nanjing in December 1998 (see Zhang Xianmin and Zhang Yaxuan, *Yige ren de yingxiang*, 293–98). A currently active online company in Beijing is Zhu Rikun's Fanhall (Xianxiang), which runs a comprehensive website, www.fanhall.com; operates campus screenings (e.g., at the Beijing Film Academy, the Beijing Broadcast Institute, and Beijing Normal University); and occasionally distributes printed magazines to thousands of registered members. More recently, Fanhall invested 120,000 RMB in He Jianjun's *Pirated Copy* (2004), an independent film that toured international film festivals overseas.

55. For instance, Cui Zi'en contributed articles on independent films to *Yinyue yu biaoyan* (Music and Performance), a research journal run by the Nanjing Art Academy, in 2000 as well as the literary magazine *Furong* (Hibiscus) in 2001.

56. Wu Wenguang, *Xianchang (di yi juan)*, 202–7. Jia Zhangke brought *Along the Railroad* to the Yamagata documentary festival in 2001. When he told Du Haibin that the documentary won a top prize, Du did not believe right away that his "crude" video could have won such an honor. See Wu Wenguang, *Xianchang (di er juan)*, 212.

57. For Jia's sample awards, see Cheng Qingsong and Huang Ou, *Wode sheyingji*, 339–40. For sample appreciative scholarship, see Lin Xiaoping, "New Chinese Cinema of the 'Sixth Generation'"; Tonglin Lu, "Music and Noise: Independent Film and Globalization," *China Review* 3, no. 1 (2003): 57–76.

58. See Mast et al., *Film Theory and Criticism*, 91.

59. Cheng Qingsong and Huang Ou, *Wode sheyingji*, 258, 265. *Suzhou River* was originally shot in 16mm in 1997 as part of *The Super City* (Chaoji chengshi), a projected ten-title series of made-for-TV drama shorts from young directors. The series was aborted due to a subsequent funding shortage, but Lou Ye was able to secure overseas investment for his own title, *The Rushing City* (Benpao de chengshi), converted it from 16mm to 35mm, renamed the full-length film *Suzhou River*, and had it released by a German company in 2000 to international acclaim. See Yingjin Zhang, *Screening China*, 329–30.

60. Cheng Qingsong and Huang Ou, *Wode sheyingji*, 265.

3

"A Scene beyond Our Line of Sight": Wu Wenguang and New Documentary Cinema's Politics of Independence

Matthew David Johnson

Among observers of mainland Chinese cinema, interpreting Wu Wenguang's films has elicited considerable debate, if not difficulty. This trend no doubt arises from the paradoxes particular to Wu's career. A former television cameraman and producer, his work is noted for its rejection of mainstream documentary norms in favor of a stripped-down, *vérité* approach. A prominent figure within the pantheon of independent Chinese directors, most public exhibitions of his films have taken place outside of China. A direct influence on mainland art cinema, most notably the directors of the so-called sixth or urban generation (Zhang Yuan, Wang Xiaoshuai, Jia Zhangke), he has written against the precepts of not only art, but filmmaking as a whole. Indeed, Wu's diverse oeuvre—one beginning with the quasi-documentary experiment *Bumming in Beijing: The Last Dreamers* (1990) and continuing on through more recent digital video (DV) works like *Jiang Hu: Life on the Road* (1999) and *What Is Film?* (2002)—seems to defy categorization. Yet Wu's work is categorized, insofar as it is often understood to exemplify unofficial, or independent, film within the context of 1990s mainland China. To ask how these designations apply to such an obviously "difficult" director is to inquire into the politics of reading Chinese film at the end of the twentieth century. It is, moreover, to inquire into the politics of mainland filmmakers' engagement with, and often courting of, the kind of critical attention from which such designations arise.

As implied by the term "unofficial," one of the most consistent themes raised in connection with Wu Wenguang's work is its perceived distance from, and opposition to, the state media system. This view is not without some basis in fact. During the early 1990s, aspiring mainland filmmakers such as Wu did

*An itinerant actress singing in Wu Wenguang's
documentary* Jiang Hu *(1999)*

begin to produce and circulate images of contemporary Chinese society, often illegally. Such practices made a visible break with state-sanctioned documentary filmmaking by circumventing the institutional procedures required to gain official support and approval for one's work. For this reason, contraband films such as *Bumming in Beijing*, a bleak exploration of the lives of five migrant artists, soon earned the eye-catching (although occasionally misleading) "underground" label, which referred to the secretive atmosphere within which they were produced and exhibited. Moreover, the increasing popularity of such methods meant that new documentary cinema's growth was paralleled by similar developments in the world of feature filmmaking, as Zhang Yuan's "underground" classic *Beijing Bastards* (1993) attests. For these reasons the early 1990s can be seen as marking a new era in mainland cinema, insofar as directors of diverse backgrounds began to seek professional opportunities beyond the official status quo.

Of course, what served to separate new documentary cinema from contemporaneous trends in Chinese cinema were its practitioners' claims to depict reality as it was. According to most observers, such "realist" rhetoric is what connects Wu's work to that of other new documentary figures such as Shi Jian (*Tiananmen*, 1991; *I've Graduated*, 1992), Duan Jinchuan (*The Square*, 1994; *No. 16 South Barkhor Street*, 1997), and Jiang Yue (*The Other Bank*, 1995). Mainland film scholar Lü Xinyu has even posited the existence of a new documentary "movement," depicting Wu Wenguang as the movement's founder and his *Bumming in Beijing* as the source of its artistic "bloodline" (*xueyuan*).[1] Endorsements of Wu's work by renowned documentary directors such as Frederick Wiseman and Shinsuke Ogawa also established a link between new documentary cinema and other traditions bearing the aura of social responsibility such as direct cinema, *cinéma vérité*, and *cinema du real*.[2] Yet while the notion that new documentary cinema is best understood as a "movement" remains debated (often by the filmmakers themselves), the term, along with labels like "underground" or "unofficial," clearly serves to heighten the attention paid to such realism's dissident potential. Indeed, among contemporary interpreters of 1990s Chinese film—nonmainland audiences and scholars in particular—this aspect of Wu Wenguang's oeuvre has received the most coverage by far, with the result that works like *Bumming in Beijing* are frequently praised not only in terms of their aesthetic qualities, but also as evidence of social iconoclasm and resistance to middle-class passivity. Production and distribution away from the purview of the state has, it appears, made such films into flashpoints for diverse political sympathies. Moreover, their realist or documentary aura has invited interpretations that are often extended to Chinese society as a whole.

Such "ethnographic" readings are, for the most part, organized around the idea that Wu Wenguang's works, and new documentary films in general, symbolize a kind of independence from the dominant structures and ideologies that shape mainland Chinese life. In a recent issue of *Senses of Cinema*, for example, Wu and other new documentary filmmakers are glowingly described by Bérénice Reynaud as "emotional vagabonds . . . unattached to any work unit and working underground."[3] This emphasis on Wu's peripatetic auteur status is amplified by yet another article locating him within a community of "experimental" or "nomadic" Chinese directors, whose recent work in film and

Amateur students performing an experimental play in Jiang Yue's
The Other Bank *(1995)*

video is characterized by "*vérité* form . . . [and] ethnographic responsibility and research, often involving the filmmakers living with their poor, marginalized subjects for an extended period of time."[4] Political interpretations abound as well. According to Ernest Larsen, *Bumming in Beijing* "portrays the lives of [China's] ordinary people" and "pursue[s], through video, the democratizing intentions that Tiananmen Square appeared to represent in 1989."[5] Similarly, Lü Xinyu's conception of a new documentary "movement" draws attention to ways in which these directors, and their works, might serve as catalysts of sociocultural transformation. There is, in other words, a demonstrated tendency to read such films as documents of disillusionment or potential resistance concerning the status quo.

This interpretive trend tends to dominate connotations of the more recent and generic term "independent film," particularly among those for whom the notion of artistic authenticity resides in its association with outsider qualities (see Chris Berry's chapter). The purpose of this chapter is not to dismiss a reading, but rather to offer an alternative by reversing a familiar metonym whereby films are understood to reflect larger categories of individual and social experience, and looking instead to the historical context of 1990s documentary practice itself. Indeed, one of my central claims is that, in the case of Wu Wenguang and other directors, it is impossible to understand the vicissitudes of artistic production apart from changes in the regulation—whether in terms of law, taste, or technology—of the "cultural marketplace," a prosaic term whose implication is nonetheless that even the most marginal cinema owes its visibility to conscious position-taking on the part of both audience and artist. To put it another way, new documentary filmmaking, and its consumption both within China and abroad, is more comprehensible in terms of changes in the politics and structure of mainland mass media. Given that these changes have generally accompanied state encouragement of market-based, profitable entertainment industries (and a corresponding decrease in emphasis on film's propaganda function, for example), to refer to contemporary Chinese film as "postsocialist" is hardly a misnomer, although the question of what images best represent this condition remains open-ended.[6]

Likewise, another question which has received little by way of an answer concerns how it is that new documentary cinema, as a "marginal" phenomenon, has received such a wide breadth of critical attention in the first place. Taking a closer look at the ways in which celebrated subversives like Wu have actually gone about producing, and exhibiting, their films may thus prove helpful in understanding yet another paradoxical condition—namely, that in which unofficial or independent documentaries have become authoritative as evidence of mainland Chinese realities and their potential for change. What follows is an examination of this process from a historical perspective, taking Wu's films and career as the primary lens.

THE AMBIGUOUS INDEPENDENT:
NEW DOCUMENTARY CINEMA IN PRACTICE

By his own admission, Wu had little understanding of nonmainland documentary standards when he began filming *Bumming in Beijing* during the late 1980s. Arriving in Beijing in 1988, he and several colleagues worked together on a series of "special theme" (*zhuanti*) television projects depicting official institutions and individuals before discussing the possibility of filming a "television essay" (*dianshi sanwen*) that would depart from such familiar conventions.[7] After one colleague, Chen Zhen, returned from a brief trip to Japan, the conversation quickly turned to "documenting" (*jilu*) in the style of an NHK television special, *Where Is My Home?* which followed the experiences of a Japanese orphan who had grown up in China. What struck Wu as important about Chen's description of the program was that the camera's "actual presence" and "uninterrupted [filming] process" during important events (such as the protagonist filling out a job application) seemed to convey more about those experiences than any amount of narration or interviewing ever could.[8] Wu's decision to film *Bumming in Beijing* arose out of a desire to apply this insight in practice, taking his friends as subjects while he himself acted out the part of the "detached" observer. Only later, he claimed, did he realize that he was making an actual "documentary" (*jilu pian*).

This story raises several important details relevant to the new documentary phenomenon insofar as its origins are concerned. The first is that Wu, along with Shi Jian (with whom Wu worked at the time), was involved in producing features for Chinese Central Television (CCTV) prior to his career as a celebrated independent. In fact, during 1988 both were working on projects related to the upcoming fiftieth anniversary of the PRC's founding, Wu for the multipart *Chinese People* (*Zhongguo ren*) and Shi for *Tiananmen*, which he would later release through unofficial channels.[9] As Wu himself has described this early period in his career, both during and after *Bumming in Beijing*'s production he relied on filming commercials, stock footage, and official propaganda (*xuanchuan*) films for income.[10] Another illustrative anecdote concerns Shi Jian's *Tiananmen* (1991), which was written and produced for CCTV, and had the sponsorship of an official work unit throughout most of its production. Unfortunately for Shi and his investors, *Tiananmen* failed to pass inspection on the grounds that it was not "infused with revolutionary thought, or [images of] happy lives," and thus "bleak" and "negative."[11] What seems most significantly "independent" about films like *Tiananmen* and *Bumming in Beijing* is the fact that both were circulated outside of state media channels after their completion. Yet it was never the case that the directors themselves abandoned the official system, especially when no guarantee of overseas success (and financial support) existed at the time.

Likewise, Wu Wenguang's admiration for long, continuous camera shots and focus on an unfolding "present scene" (*xianchang*) in *Where Is My Home?* indicates that formal innovation played a crucial role in distinguishing new documentary filmmakers from their immediate milieu. In Wu's case—and this is especially relevant given his claims of ignorance concerning documentaries in general—the major impetus behind his approach to *Bumming in Beijing* was a desire to avoid repeating mainstream (*zhuliu*) conventions while depicting contemporary Chinese life. What was required was a shift in perspective, or in techniques denoting perspective. Thus, in one of his essays Wu recalls that

> while I was filming . . . I really strove to take hold of a style resembling that of an onlooker, waiting nearby and soberly recording what those in the scene did and said. In order to maintain a "pure angle on the present scene," during the period of editing that followed I didn't add any explanation or music throughout the entire 150 minutes of film. At first, I ignorantly regarded this as a big revolution.[12]

With respect to officially produced television features of the day, the complete absence of voice-overs, instrumental accompaniment, and overdubbing did constitute something of a revolution, as did *Bumming in Beijing*'s lack of scripted dialogue (excepting the scenes in which Wu films his friend, Mou Sen, directing a Eugene O'Neill play). In fact, rejection of these familiar auditory methods for denoting mood or "official voice" was one of the most obvious similarities between Wu's film and Shi Jian's *Tiananmen*, and would become one of the distinguishing features of new documentary filmmaking as a whole.[13]

As for the choice of marginal subject matter, Wu's decision to record and interview five "drifter" (*mangliu*) artist friends living near Beijing University's west gate was influenced by similar concerns for originality, insofar as such individuals were typically excluded from official representations of the time. While practical considerations were surely a factor—independent filmmaking being illegal, and thus nearly impossible within state-dominated public spaces—*Bumming in Beijing*'s dual emphasis on cramped apartments and discussions of artistic freedom generates a tense atmosphere that no doubt cut against an official rhetoric of economic development and state triumphalism. More recently, Wu has renounced *Bumming in Beijing* for its unavoidable similarities to made-for-television documentary programming, claiming that he still possessed a director's "disgusting habits" when the film was made.[14] Yet by pointing also to the "filming of friends" as a key element in his early style, Wu suggests that what distinguishes *Bumming in Beijing* from the mainstream media is most of all its content, especially where attention to his subjects' illegal residential status and precarious economic existence is concerned. Regardless of the methods employed, there can be no doubt that *Bumming in Beijing*'s purpose was to re-create realities specific to these individuals' "actual lives" (*zhenshi shenghuo*), with particular emphasis on both the hardships and "rich experience" that downward mobility paradoxically provided.[15]

To put it simply, the term "new documentary cinema" can be understood as denoting films whose realist depictions exceeded those of official productions, and which attempted to make obvious their lack of a state-sanctioned perspective. Thus, from its beginning, it has denoted representations that invite implicit contrast with those circulated by China's national and regional media networks. The testimonies of several new documentary directors reveal that dissatisfaction with their artistic options as producers for these networks was, in fact, perhaps the most significant reason behind any decision to partly abandon them. In addition to Wu Wenguang and Shi Jian, Jiang Yue (a former Beijing Film Studio employee) claims to have moved toward television after becoming "disgusted" with the slow pace and bureaucracy of feature film production.[16] Much like Shi, Jiang had hoped to make official documentaries before exposure to the work of Shi and Wu in 1991 encouraged him to release his films—the first three of which concerned Tibetan society and religion—unofficially. Duan Jinchuan, who spent time with Jiang in Lhasa (Duan was briefly an employee of Tibet Television), would also turn to unofficial distribution after early experiences in broadcasting left him "with a hypocritical feeling," while stifling his ability to produce images that were "individualized" and "real."[17] In particular, Duan cites a 1990 meeting with Wu Wenguang as one of the decisive factors in shaping his initial preference for a career beyond the media mainstream. What these claims also suggest, of course, is that new documentary filmmaking's origins also lie in a complex web of professional associations and shared influence. While it should be noted that other directors associated with the genre—Li Hong (*Out of Phoenix Bridge*, 1997), for example—are not associated as closely with this undeniably male-centered myth of its emergence, similarities in professional background (television) and representational methods (documentary, unofficial distribution) have facilitated their inclusion in the canon regardless.

While these filmmakers, and their admirers, are often quick to emphasize the original qualities of new documentary works, it should be noted that others have attempted to suggest ways in which they can be viewed as predictable outcomes of changes in the official system itself. As media historian Fang Fang suggests, new documentary filmmakers' espousal of "outside" influences such as NHK features or non-Chinese *cinéma vérité* directors (Shinsuke Ogawa, Frederick Wiseman, Joris Ivens) should be thus understood in relationship to the search for new representational techniques that accompanied an emerging official emphasis on profits, rather than propaganda, during the 1980s. Indeed, NHK and mainland television institutions had worked together on multipart documentaries like *The Silk Road* (Sichou zhi lu, 1980), indicating that such exchanges were, by 1989, clearly a feature of mainstream broadcasting as well.[18] Other factors that clearly influenced and encouraged the search for an independent model included international film festivals and investment—options that had been available to a select group of mainland directors (Zhang Yimou and others of the "fifth generation," for example) since the late 1980s. While disputing the notion that new documentary cinema is simply an outgrowth of official institutional and aesthetic change, Lü Xinyu has also suggested that attention to contemporary reality, as well as previously marginalized or repressed subject matter, defined post-1989 art and literature in general rather than independently produced documentaries in particular.[19]

With these ambiguities in mind, I believe that what largely accounts for new documentary's privileged status as an independent, authentic perspective on reality is the rhetoric of the filmmakers themselves. In one interview, Wu Wenguang has described *Bumming in Beijing* as closely linked to the "completion" of a particular period in time, and thus reflecting changes in China between 1988 and 1990.[20] Elsewhere, he has emphasized the practice of objective "onlooking" as an organizing feature of his work. In *1966, My Time in the Red Guards* (1993), for example, divergence from official viewpoints concerning the Cultural Revolution is staged through a series of persuasive montages that include interviews with former Red Guards and borrowed footage of Red Guard rallies. For Wu, the significance of the film was that it allowed him access to a historical experience from which he often felt excluded—one in which, as he described it, "the wheel of revolution had always drove on ahead of me . . . [and] I was only able to catch up to the wake it had cast aside."[21] Although critic Rey Chow has described *1966* as attempting to re-create "the ethnic and national self-consciousness of being Chinese," it also seems worth considering that Wu envisioned the project as a history deliberately *opposed* to representations of the Cultural Revolution included in Chinese textbooks, television programming, and film.[22] A corrective to mainstream views of the 1960s that emphasized suffering, *1966* was thus intended to provide "a kind of memory that was cruel, but true"—the Cultural Revolution as a period of youthful exuberance and self-discovery (also a dominant theme in director Jiang Wen's 1994 opus, *In the Heat of the Sun*).[23] In this case, Wu further distanced "his" Red Guard era from the official account by intercutting a rock performance by the band Cobra.

Consequently, I would like to suggest that early 1990s independence also be understood in terms of the artistic strategies and goals described above—that is, as a practice aimed at recapturing the "unofficial" truth of historical or present moments. Indeed, this is exactly the sense given by Wu Wenguang in an interview with Fang Fang, when he states that "independent production is really no more than a kind of form (*xingshi*) . . . it doesn't matter whether it's on television, whether it's made for television, or [even] whether it upholds an individual viewpoint."[24] Independence, according to Wu's formulation, arises from one's relationship to the representational conventions of the mainstream. Yet as films like *Bumming in Beijing* and *1966* indicate, early definitions of independence also included the notion that reality, where it appeared, did so more truthfully by virtue of the filmmakers' close relationship to individuals. Moreover, their con- scious avoidance of official trappings intimated that insofar as these depictions *were* true, they were significant exactly for the fact of their divergence from offi- cial claims. What this means in concrete terms is illustrated by a further—albeit brief—consideration of several early new documentary works.

There is undeniably a unique, often dystopian perspective present in *Bum- ming in Beijing* (1990), *Tiananmen* (1991), *I've Graduated* (1992), *1966* (1993), *The Square* (1994), *At Home in the World* (1995), *The Other Bank* (1995), and *No. 16 Barkhor Street* (1997), all of which seem to focus on the limitations that contemporary society places on individuals, marginal and otherwise. This interpretation is supported by Shi Jian's claim that new documentary's major preoccupations were a concern with objectivity, interest in the lives of ordinary people, and the hope of providing an indirect, albeit inconclusive, criticism of official social perspectives.[25] In particular, I would suggest that what defines the new documentary "mood" is its directors' refusal to depict meaningful solutions to the complex social tableaux they observe. What the artists, Tibetans, Red Guards, students, middle-class Beijingers, and rural teenagers who populate these films share in common is an implied inability to better their chances—a condition that betrays the presence of irreconcilable tensions between aspira- tion and fulfillment endemic to Chinese society as a whole. Indeed, one of the rare moments when such tensions are briefly resolved occurs in *Bumming in Beijing*, when escape to another country becomes possible. Rather than a view of China's margins, what such films provide is a condemnation of the discrep- ancy between state rhetoric and actual experience that their directors perceived as lying at the heart of everyday life.

Seen in this context, Wu Wenguang's first three feature works have the effect of depicting a contemporary Chinese "condition" that appears rife with powerlessness and frustration. The "drifters" of *Bumming in Beijing* endure financial and mental hardship in pursuit of their art, yet by the time of *At Home in the World* (for which Wu followed them to North America and Europe), their lives overseas evidence little satisfaction beyond an increase in material comfort. Likewise, the former Red Guards of *1966* contradict each other, and often themselves, over the issue of whether to remember the Cultural Revolu- tion as a time of euphoria or suffering. Given that these films were released at a time when state officials encouraged directors to serve the people, uphold national traditions, and extol the "new era" of economic reform, they can hardly be considered part of the representational mainstream.[26] What marks such works as independent, then, is their tacit attack on official policies con- cerning Chinese society's proper depiction and their unofficial release. The fact remains, however, that this account cannot explain how new documentary works have attained such an overtly *politicized* status in the eyes of audiences. What follows is a description of how the independent position adopted by directors like Wu Wenguang was gradually translated, so to speak, into a marker defining the new documentary genre as a whole.

TRUTH AND VALUE: NEW DOCUMENTARY CINEMA ON DISPLAY

The success enjoyed by new documentary filmmakers during the mid-1990s was, of course, in no way preordained. By Wu Wenguang's own account, once the editing of *Bumming in Beijing* was completed, he attempted to contact various film festivals through a friend, but accepted a Tibetan assignment with CCTV when no immediate response was forthcoming.[27] Only later did he learn that *Bumming in Beijing* had been selected for screening at the Hong Kong Film Festival, where it was noticed by other festival representatives and Wu's career as a "Chinese independent" (funded partly by the Yamagata International Documentary Film Festival) was launched. Shi Jian and Duan Jinchuan both traveled similar paths to recognition. Indeed, a recurring theme in each case is that unofficial exhibition, and the patronage secured thereby, was crucial to these directors in making their careers economically viable. As Duan has humorously described his experience:

> I've got pretty good feelings about the [Yamagata] Film Festival. Afterward I went abroad again, and my film was selected by a series of other festival committees. Next I went to Germany, to a festival in a little town . . . where I was able to set up a panel on independent Chinese cinema.[28]

International exhibition, in other words, was clearly essential to the process by which independent or nonstate perspectives, through the conduit of unofficial distribution, first gained a visible foothold as legitimate representations of China abroad.

This account raises two important parallels where international film festivals are concerned. First, as the experiences of Wu, Duan, and other independents show, overseas screening meant access to audiences unattainable by official means. Second, if one is to take seriously Wu's own claim that, prior to his participation in a series of international film festivals during 1991, he had no idea of what a "real" documentary actually was, it seems clear that these venues shaped independent mainland directors' creative strategies by supplying categories of genre (documentary) and identity (Asian, Chinese, third world) through which their work would become comprehensible to overseas viewers. The consequences, however, have raised difficult questions for filmmakers and audiences alike.

As evidenced by his writings, such encounters left Wu Wenguang with mixed impressions. In an article provocatively entitled "The 'Poor Folks' at the Film Festival," he described the "custom" by which such festivals' claims to represent the "current state" of global cinema depended on the presence of filmmakers from all over the world, and new films which represented the "cutting edge." In the case of the Yamagata Film Festival, moreover,

> because the mainstream of documentary creation and its influential trends are formulated in Europe and America (owing to traditional, social, political, financial, and other reasons), the present situation is that the production and standards of "third world" documentaries are obviously below that of Europe and America. Thus, the label of "poor people" has become commonly affixed to those making documentaries in the "third world."[29]

Difference, in other words, was interpreted as a consequence of poverty, or underdevelopment. At the same time, insofar as a "representative" film festival required that the impoverished attend, this provided an opportunity of sorts as long as one was willing to play along by acting the "third-world director"—on some level, the relationship was a codependent one. Wu was struck by the case of several female Korean filmmakers who, representing themselves as a "Korean women's documentary movement," had received complimentary plane tickets and hotel rooms from the festival's promoters.[30] With less humor he observed while Yamagata fostered the ideal of a global documentary "family," it was difficult to escape the sense that he and other third-world directors remained, by virtue of their identities as such, a group of "poor relations" in the eyes of their first-world counterparts.[31]

Such misgivings did not prevent Wu from accepting the festival's top prize in 1993, but they do raise the question of how work viewed as "below" Euro-American or first-world standards has generated so much interest in these regions. Here, the issue of politicization takes center stage. As Yingjin Zhang has demonstrated elsewhere, international "discovery" and promotion of controversial fifth-generation directors during the mid-1980s coincided with a belief among Western critics that their responsibility concerning these films, and filmmakers, was one borne of "urgent political and moral responsibility" concerning "the advancement of freedom, democracy, and human rights in post-Mao China."[32] Thus, he concludes, "political issues have informed much of Western interest in Chinese cinema," resulting in considerable critical attention to films that, like *Bumming in Beijing*, have provoked negative state responses (becoming "banned," for example), or whose directors have claimed unofficial status. Such attention, in other words, often derives from a quixotically antistate sensibility on the part of critics and audiences alike, one which equates the Communist Party with bureaucratic totalitarianism and embattled filmmakers with enlightened individualistic ideals. In this context, directors like Wu Wenguang have not only represented important "develop-ments" in Chinese cinema, but also the promise of a China independent of the party altogether. A similar observation is made by critic Dai Jinhua, who writes that by the time *Bumming in Beijing* and Zhang Yuan's *Beijing Bas-tards* arrived on the international festival circuit, critical response to these films seemed "no longer based on given Western art standards (even Oriental-ist ones), but exclusively on the films' production style and *perceived separa-tion from the official Chinese filmmaking system.*"[33]

Without arguing that *Bumming in Beijing* was praised simply on the basis of its dissident appeal, or for a view of Chinese directors as mere pawns of foreign interests, it is undeniable that both Euro-American *and* Asian (Hong Kong, Japan, Singapore) demand for unofficial mainland films contributed to the growth of Wu Wenguang's reputation, and for the emphasis placed on its "underground" or "independent" qualities. While the result was not, as Duan Jinchuan has stated, a "movement," excitement over the new art pervaded both mainland and international documentary communities during the years 1992 and 1993—excitement that is difficult to dismiss as an effect of Western preoc-cupations.[34] Indeed, while festivals do seem to have imposed a preferred read-ing of new documentary films that stress objectivity and resistance, it is crucial to recognize that works like *Bumming in Beijing* and *Tiananmen* were con-ceived in terms that facilitated such impositions. Thus, according to Wu, his growing preference for unadorned *vérité* aesthetics implied a critique not only of mainland filmmakers' emphasis on "artistry," but also of the "distance" from reality that, in his view, plagued contemporary Chinese media of all kinds.[35]

While directors, critics, and audiences may have differed over the politics of such statements, their shared faith in the power of unofficial filmmaking to present a more truthful depiction of contemporary China has clearly defined new documentary cinema since its inception. One result of this faith was that by the mid-1990s grainy, low-budget production had become virtually synon-ymous with ethnographic (if not artistic) value. Another was that the supply of such films rapidly increased to keep pace with demand, a trend that has led Shi Jian to recall 1995 and 1996 as years during which many directors "wallowed" in derivative *vérité*-style filmmaking.[36] Yet even as new documentary cinema enjoyed success as a subversive window onto Chinese society abroad, many of its practitioners were again moving toward the mainstream at home, as a different politics—that of providing mass-oriented or "popularized" (*pingmin-hua*) depictions of society—began to take root in the mainland news media.[37] As a result, new programs like *Oriental Moment* (Dongfang shikong, first broadcast in 1993), *Real Talk* (Shihua shishuo), and *Living Space* (Shenghuo kongjian) not only received high ratings from a domestic audience apparently hungry for images of everyday experience, but actively solicited the contributions of promising independents like Shi Jian, Duan Jinchuan, and Jiang Yue to enhance their prestige. In fact, frequent movement between festival filmmaking and employment under official auspices (whether in the form of work unit affiliation or subcontracting) seems to have again become the "independent" norm during this period, exemplified by Jiang's work for the CCTV programs *Oriental Moment* and *Living Space* while completing his first major unofficial film, *The Other Bank*. As Wu recalls, by 1995 there was so much institutional demand for new images that he and a group of friends contemplated producing high-quality "professional" documentaries for theatrical release.[38]

The year 1993 thus marks a moment in which the uncertain exodus of filmmakers away from the official system quickly reversed itself, as well as one in which several traits associated with new documentary cinema—concern with the representation of everyday life, for example—were established on China's television screens. While such programming may have lacked the pessimistic "edge" that distinguished early new documentary cinema, it did provide a forum, however circumscribed, within which new representations of contemporary society could appear. For obvious reasons, it is difficult to credit high-profile independent directors alone with this change. Both foreign and domestic audiences have expressed considerable interest in images of "real" China, although the rhetoric of independence has had less currency among the latter. This does not diminish the fact, however, that *both* contexts have played an important role in ensuring the visibility of new documentary directors at home and abroad.

Likewise, as film festival politicization of independent film suggests, the terms in which new documentary filmmakers have been discussed and elevated among mainland scholars differs clearly from those deployed within "festival catalogues, popular publications and marketing literature" overseas (see Valerie Jaffee's chapter). At a 1994 Beijing conference for discussing recent developments in Chinese film, Wu and other "newborn" directors (a term referring to their lack of a generational designation) were discussed as examples of filmmakers with experience in the professional "system" (*tizhi*) who, by rejecting lush, fifth generation–style historical allegory in favor of *vérité* realism and "popularized" narrative techniques, seemed well-positioned for careers as cultural producers for mainland markets.[39] Yet while cautious optimism was voiced concerning these directors' "individual, unorthodox styles" and "independent, experimental work," considerable reservations also remained. In particular, the fact that their films appeared, in the eyes of Western audiences, as "political symbols" was seen to diminish their chances for official distribution.[40] Encouraging such interpretations, the organizers concluded, could only create an "unhealthy" atmosphere for the emergence of pluralism within the domestic film industry.[41] From a perspective of participation in the official system, international exhibition and patronage provided a kind of visibility for Chinese independents that was ambiguous at best.

Attitudes of foreign audiences seemed to undermine hopes for a popular diversity, or "multiplicity" ("the strategy by which global marketing attempts to cope with local demands"), in the eyes of mainland critics and investors alike.[42] But the very existence of this and similar conferences indicates a growing entanglement of official and unofficial spheres of cultural production, largely as a response to global competition and concomitant hopes for a "development" capable of defending the mainland film industry—a pressing concern for Chinese cultural elites throughout the 1980s and 1990s. Thus, just as the 1992 Fourteenth Party Conference declared goals of building a socialist market economy and reforming state-run enterprises, film production and distribution exhibited a reliance on "downsizing, internal restructuring, and talent outsourcing" as means of coping with international competition in the cultural sphere.[43] An ironic consequence is that even resolutely unofficial directors like Wu were recognized both for their work, which represented a potential resource for populist entertainment, and their experience as successful filmmakers abroad.

In its incipient forms, new documentary cinema emerged from attempts to supersede the mainstream and redefine contemporary views of Chinese reality. By the mid-1990s, however, many independent filmmakers had returned to official media institutions, while continuing to produce works for international release. Whether conceived in terms of artistic diversification or "selling out," the important question concerning this process remains—how, given the marginal status that most Western critics have ascribed to these filmmakers, did it occur? To briefly sum up several of the arguments so far, the articulation of an "independent" documentary form by Wu Wenguang, Shi Jian, Duan Jinchuan, Jiang Yue, and others proceeded from their efforts to formulate a new kind of cinematic representation, one that would be faithful to the experiences of ordinary people and (as in the case of *Bumming in Beijing, The Other Bank*, and *At Home in the World*) the artistic milieu of the directors themselves. Yet at no point did these efforts signal complete abandonment of the official media and its institutions. Rather, their unofficial distribution can be understood as one of several strategies employed by aspiring directors who sought recognition beyond the boundaries of existing institutional norms. First made visible within the international film circuit, and later by the growth of a populist or realist rhetoric *within* the field of mainland cultural production, these filmmakers thus also "emerged" at points where demand for new representations of contemporary China met with the possibility of their inclusion—critical junctures defined by both international and domestic patronage. While the politics surrounding this emergence created considerable tension, they also brought new images of mainland society to the fore.

AWKWARD ACCOMMODATION:
NEW DOCUMENTARY INSTITUTIONALIZED

For new documentary filmmakers, the mid-1990s were experienced as a continuation and consolidation of their earlier successes. In 1995, when his third feature-length film *At Home in the World* was completed, Wu Wenguang could even be described as an artistic celebrity, albeit one known mainly to academics, critics, and other international festival buffs. In terms of audience numbers alone, there is little basis for describing the work of these directors as a popular phenomenon. Yet *Bumming in Beijing* was still a principal attraction at international film festivals eager to appear cutting-edge (including one held in Guangzhou).[44] Likewise, Duan Jinchuan's *No. 16 South Barkhor Street*, which later broke domestic ground when it was screened at a 1997 Beijing international documentary conference, was even being circulated among provincial television stations as a template for those seeking to emulate this most recent documentary craze.[45]

One consequence of the increasingly mainstream aura was the encroachment of a new set of production values aimed at bringing independent documentary's "look" into line with industry standards. The 1997 CCTV program *Century* (Shiji), for example, employed a big-budget format to showcase directors like Duan, who also signed contracts with the BBC to produce footage for prime-time European television.[46] In short, international recognition forced filmmakers to make decisions concerning how to proceed within a market that was already exhibiting signs of growth and change. Thus even Wu Wenguang, who had publicly distanced himself from official production in the past, began to engage in projects that reflected broadening interest in documentary-style images. As a contributing editor for the short-lived serial publication *Documentary Handbook* (Jilu shouce), he promoted techniques and films that had influenced his own career. Recalling this time, Wu has commented that while the magazine seemed to bring some people closer to documentary cinema, it was also published during a period when former "documentary people" became intensely sought-after commercial directors and "kings of MTV."[47] Wu also produced and edited segments for another short-lived venture, CCTV's *Ordinary People* (Baixing jiayuan), which showcased the documentary efforts of nonprofessionals and was, in many ways, an omen of the "amateur documentary" wave that struck during the late 1990s.[48] The show was cancelled in 1999 by those who "feared what they claimed to love" (Yegong haolong)—that is, images produced by individuals outside of the professional hierarchies that dominated China's mass media.[49]

As many observers have noted, the rise of semiofficial media institutions and conglomerates of all types during the mid-1990s (many financed with state resources) seems most responsible for the party's unleashing of a campaign against "spiritual pollution" in 1996.[50] This campaign, which aimed to "limit cultural autonomy and regulate the cultural market," in practice often meant propping up China's domestic film and television industries against the encroachment of global competition.[51] These increased restrictions also meant a reining in of media content that seemed to depict the present regime and society unfavorably. In the documentary world, one manifestation of such policies was the suspension of broadcasts featuring international film-makers.[52] For directors like Wu—still frequently marketed as an independent rebel by the international media—the new atmosphere also spurred a decision to seek professional opportunities abroad.[53]

Yet as Wu's writings make clear, the growth and institutionalization of independent documentary cinema were, if anything, accelerated by this turn in domestic events, as well as by new DV technology. Writing for *City of Literature* (Shucheng), he described how 1998 and 1999 had witnessed a pro-liferation of "individual" documentaries.[54] DV productions like Zhu Chuan-ming's *Beijing Cotton-Fluffing Artisan* (1999) and Yang Tianyi's *Old Men* (1999) seemed to signal the inclusion of more and more nonprofessionals within domestic filmmaking circles, despite the fact that the works themselves would likely only see festival release. Indeed, the international festival scene had become so predictable as an outlet for young Chinese directors that, he observed elsewhere, these new "poor folks" (*qiongren*) arrived fully versed in the language of exhibition, prize money, and "future development."[55] Nor were spectators immune to the effects of repetition. A proper decorum of documentary film-going had clearly been learned, as evidenced by the unre-lenting "seriousness" with which Yamagata audiences confronted each day's depictions of hardship and violence from across the globe.[56] This type of sym-biosis had become so complete, he observed, that filmmakers now calculated the endurance of their audiences' posteriors prior to editing.[57] A few excerpts from Wu's description of the Berlin Film Festival's International Forum of New Cinema communicate, in plain language, the kind of stakes that this viewer/viewed relationship both communicated and concealed:

> If some filmmaker talks about how, while he was shooting, he didn't even think of festivals or prizes, I can be sure he's a liar. . . . Past festivals were fun, but now it's not like that. . . . The stakes people have in winning or losing brings in all kinds of emotions, but it's a brutal (*canku*) routine just to list them all: irrepressible happi-ness, deathly pale expressions, stifled joy, feigned relaxation. . . . Spike Lee, Tar-antino, Ang Lee [Li An], Hou Hsiao-hsien [Hou Xiaoxian] and others all made it big (*liangxiang chudao*) here . . . a lot of Chinese directors had their earliest works shown here as well. . . . Last year Jia Zhangke's *Xiao Wu* made a big splash. . . . Where did the first "forum" participants go? Spike Lee and Ang Lee fell in with big Hollywood producers, and Hou Hsiao-hsien works with moguls now. . . . I can't help thinking of Jia Zhangke, and where he's going to end up.[58]

Independent cinema, documentaries included, had seemingly become another step on the ladder of professional advancement.

It could easily be argued that this was always the case, and that Wu's complaints were based entirely on a deliberate misrecognition of international exhibition and its politics (although essays like "The 'Poor Folks' at the Film Festival" suggest otherwise). Yet his observations provide a clear indication of important changes in global cinema, most notably the degree to which independent, and even amateur, filmmaking had become formally incorporated into larger media networks. Thus, insofar as 1996 was China's "year of television"—referring to the number of mergers between mainland film and television studios that took place as a result of the formers' poor economic performance—it also seems to mark a point at which "independent" documentary production became recognized as a viable means of incorporating young and amateur filmmakers into the official system.[59] In addition to programs like *Ordinary People*, organizations like the Young Experimental Filmmakers' Group (formed in 1997 by Beijing Television) reflect active forays into cultivating and training young "talent" by mainland institutions.[60] As Internet resources, academic conferences, and festivals devoted to the discussion and exhibition of documentaries also indicate, this change was hardly confined to the official media alone.

The point here is that by the late 1990s, "new documentary cinema" could not conceivably be understood apart from the institutions that supported the production and exhibition of works documenting "unofficial" China. It is perhaps for this reason that the term itself, which lacked the politicized mystique of designations like "underground" and "independent," entered critical parlance on the mainland and elsewhere at roughly the same time. For those who, like Wu, emphasized the importance of preserving autonomy with respect to official forms (if not institutional systems) of representation, this new period of accommodation raised feelings of what can only be described as resistance, or awkwardness. Of his criticisms, two stand out for their assessment of the potential dangers present in seeking an official/unofficial rapprochement that left both "sides" essentially untransformed. The first is that venues *within* Beijing and other Chinese cities still failed to provide the kind of "plural space" (*duoyuan de kongjian*) that would encourage exhibition of unofficial or marginal images at home.[61] The second is that documentary filmmakers themselves had already begun to assume "professional" identities, marked by a hackneyed rhetoric of "artistry" and "fame," and defined by their attempts to "occupy" all available venues, domestic and otherwise.[62]

In short, a new hierarchy had emerged, one whose elites were content to leave the status quo essentially unchanged so long as their own careers were advanced thereby. Again, while one could argue that such advancement was always the aim, the contrast that it provided with a "new documentary

The DVD cover of Yang Tianyi's documentary
Old Men *(1999)*

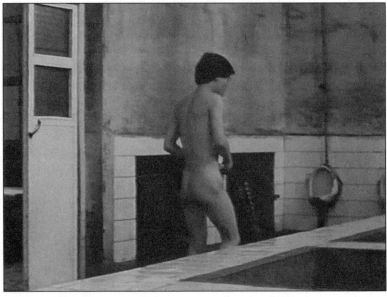

An artisan pickpocket singing alone in a public bathhouse in Jia Zhangke's Xiao
Wu *(1997)*

discourse" of sharing marginalized perspectives, reinterpreting history, and testing the mainstream's capacity for "difference"—what, for critics like Lü Xinyu, defined new documentary as a recognizable phenomena and marked Wu Wenguang, Shi Jian, Duan Jinchuan, and Jiang Yue as its most important contributors—was apparently too much for Wu himself to condone. The consequences of this strain, however, reveal a pattern of organization and exhibition that, for all of its participants' claims to innovation, appears surprisingly familiar.

REPETITION WITH DIFFERENCE:
NEW DOCUMENTARY IN THE DV ERA

By the late 1990s, the question of how one might continue to produce unofficial or independent documentary works had created a sense of crisis for Wu, which his contemporaries did not necessarily share. Indeed, this crisis seems to have emerged as a direct reaction to the official system's use of new documentary-style representation for audience-oriented aims, a trend which clearly threatened its status as both "art" and "reality." In response, Wu proposed a new style based principally on the works of Frederick Wiseman (with whom Wu spent an extended period of time during his sojourn to the United States), and which rested upon disassociation of documentary from the "professional" in favor of the "individual."[63]

First articulated in a series of essays written between 1997 and 1998, this new position emerged as Wu attempted to convey, for a mainland audience, his frustrations with film circles abroad. In "New York [and] the Loneliness of Documentary Film," for example, he attacked the "television-ready" nature and "unconvincing" realism of contemporary independent cinema.[64] Elsewhere, he derided the inability of professional directors to depict everyday life in a "moving" way—this effect, he asserted, could only be produced by the hands of the untrained—and expressed nostalgia for the days when unofficial films by contemporaries like Duan Jinchuan and Zhang Yuan were screened at private gatherings of like-minded individuals, rather than at the behest of corporate festival sponsors.[65] Recognition, it seemed, could only be equated with co-optation and boredom. Consequently, returning to a "real" form of documentary required a rejection of such recognition, and by extension the professional status that seemed to follow in its wake.

These invectives against the status quo might justifiably be interpreted as canny self-positioning, the stock and trade of a self-conscious independent claiming opposition to mainstream values as the sole proof of his works' authenticity. Yet in many ways, they concisely express a tense intellectual environment in which, at least during the early 1990s, art's privileged relationship to truth *was* in fact closely intertwined with a sense of divergence from the official media. While by the late 1990s this environment had shown signs of substantial change, Wu's artistic *mentalité* apparently had not. Indeed, as Valerie Jaffee demonstrates in her chapter in this volume, subsequent work began to align Wu closely with the so-called urban director Jia Zhangke, as well as Zhu Chuanming (*Extras*, 2001) and Zheng Dasheng (*DV China*, 2003), two recent directors also grouped under the new documentary label. In her view, the obsessive amateurism—expressive of an "impulse to challenge cultural institutions"—that these filmmakers espouse, coexists with a self-conscious interrogation of art's relationship to the self. This argument is amply evidenced by the fact that all of Wu's DV work, which includes films like *Jiang Hu: Life on the Road* (1999), *Dance with Migrant Workers* (2001), and *Fuck the Movies* (2004), features fraught depictions of artistic production as its central theme.

In the context of my discussion—which thus far has focused on the institutions and rhetoric, as well as the images, through which new documentary cinema has become a signifier for the idea of an independent and resistant documentary practice—the nature of this challenge itself deserves further scrutiny. On the one hand, films like *Jiang Hu* undeniably reflect an attempt to further the notion that unofficial filmmaking should be understood as an alternative to dominant representations, which by this point included documentary in both its official and unofficial forms. The rural performers of the "Far and Wide Song and Dance Troupe," whose lives function ostensibly as the film's subject matter, thus also serve as a mirror in which Wu performs a kind of inquiry concerning the "performer-as-self," in particular where its emphasis on socioeconomic difference is concerned. Yet if the concept of "amateurism" reveals Wu's attempt to define a new kind of authenticity and autonomy vis-à-vis an expanding documentary mainstream, it must also be expanded to account for another fundamental problematic—that of documentary's status as an index of truth. Indeed, Wu claims that while filming *Jiang Hu* he was interested in how the troupe's emblematic "big tent" might also serve as a microcosm in which one might "observe the unceasing changes of society."[66] Like *Bumming in Beijing* and *1966* before it, the film is thus very much linked to capturing a particular mode of experience. At the same time, Wu attempted to minimize *Jiang Hu*'s objective qualities, especially insofar as these might be linked to a broader social agenda, by claiming that it was the product of purely personal concerns, and thus a departure from "so-called documentary style."[67] What self-consciously "amateurish" filmmaking *also* had to offer, then, was a path to one's own subjectivity, unmediated by the burdens of criticism or omniscience. "You cannot help 'them,'" he remarked cryptically; "you can only liberate yourself."[68]

Yet clearly, confusion over what to make of the socioeconomic difference between filmmaker and his struggling subjects (as *Jiang Hu* clearly shows, the "big tent" performers are disadvantaged by their rural backgrounds and lack of formal education) clashed with such easy dismissals of documentary's pedagogical function. While hesitant to spell out the consequences, Wu did acknowledge that privileged "we" might still bear some responsibility with respect to a less advantaged "them." The issues that *Jiang Hu* raises are therefore similar to those faced by many anthropologists, and highlight the tense relationship between theories of critical observation and those of social action. In fact, by summer 1999 Wu was already likening his filmmaking to an anthropological "field investigation," one which included compiling oral histories of numerous troupe members for publication in printed works like *Jiang Hu Report* (Jianghu baogao) and *Present Scene* (Xianchang).[69] Yet ultimately, it seems that his hopes for "the movement of documentary from the public toward the private"—for a space in which artists, rather than audiences, could regain authority over the types of meaning imposed on their work—represent less cynicism than they do longing, in particular for the preservation of documentary as an "extraordinary" image, freed from its commodity status.[70] In short, Wu's anxiety over the function of documentary filmmaking, and artistic production overall, appears as confirmation that new documentary's shedding of its unofficial/independent aura (except, perhaps, in the promotional literature of international film festivals) had already precipitated its decline as a viable sign of opposition or critique.

On the other hand, questions of how to carry out this assault on mainstream values, including those of documentary cinema itself, reveal a reliance on strategies that deviated very little from those by which the latter's aura had first taken shape. First, Wu's overt rejection of professional trappings—in other words, his attempt to anger, challenge, and otherwise insult those filmmakers intent on "conquering some mountaintop" (*gongda mou ge shantou*)—was accompanied by rhetoric which carefully privileged a "real" independence, the latter defined precisely in terms of its separation from film circles, television, festivals, and awards altogether.[71] This principle was described as his second "big revelation" (the first being his discovery of nonmainland documentary filmmaking in 1991). What is true, genuine, and authentic (*zhenzheng*), Wu argued, could only come from one's own eyes and hands—in other words, from individual methods and experience.[72]

This new orientation toward privileging DV cinema in terms of its individual/personal qualities was accompanied by a concerted effort on the part of Wu and others to instantiate it as a visible practice on the cultural "scene"—essentially, an attempt to challenge one establishment through the formation of alternative networks. The opposition took place on several fronts. First, Wu

offered (generally) positive and constructive criticism of recent films by old
friends such as Zhang Yuan, and newcomers like Jia Zhangke, Wang Jianwei,
Yang Tianyi, and Zhu Chuanming on the pages of such high-brow publications as *City of Literature*, *Orient* (Dongfang), *Film Art* (Dianying yishu),
Southern Weekend (Nanfang zhoumo), and *Reading* (Dushu).[73] "Although the
reality [depicted in these works] may sound otherworldly," he wrote in one
1999 article on DV filmmakers, "they contain truly honest everyday detail."[74]
Elsewhere, in the avant-garde art publication *New Wave* (Xinchao)—which in
2001 also sponsored large-scale Beijing and Chengdu exhibitions of independent DV work—Wu published a two-part feature entitled "DV Image Handbook," explaining in knowledgeable detail which films and equipment were
worth the attention of readers looking to enter the field.[75] Together with fellow DV filmmaker Yang Zi, he was also a key organizer of the Beijing-based
"DV Documentary Group" (DV jilu xiaozu), an informal association for the
semipublic screening and discussion of its members' films before hip local
audiences.[76] Under Yang Zi's leadership, this "small group" went on to offer
filmmaking courses and sponsor festivals for the further exhibition of popu-
lar/unofficial (*minjian*) China.[77]

At the same time, and in a way that Wu could only have ignored through a
supreme act of denial, the individualized, DV-based works that he championed
were replacing their predecessors not only in terms of authenticity, but in terms
of exposure. To the benefit of many practicing the new "anti-art," 1999—the
year in which *Jiang Hu* was finally released—was also the year that DV-made
works began to garner significant recognition via the same venues that had facilitated the rise of several important new documentary directors almost a decade
earlier. Through a combination of local (including the circulation of pirated or
director-circulated copies) and international exposure, films like Yang Tianyi's
Old Men, Zhu Chuanming's *Beijing Cotton-Fluffing Artisan*, Hu Shu's *Leave
Me Alone* (2001), Wang Bing's *West of the Tracks* (2001), and Du Haibin's
Along the Railroad (2000) have all gained attention as evidence of Chinese
independent documentary cinema's progression toward new frontiers of the
"marginal" and "repressed." While the definition of such terms has shifted over
time—indeed, it is hard to argue that the artists, Red Guards, bureaucrats, and
middle-class urbanites featured in early new documentary films constitute a
group of "subalterns" *except* with regard to their relative lack of voice within
the official system—they remain fully bound up with understandings of unofficially released documentaries' independent nature. Moreover, the interviews
and uninterrupted, *vérité*-style takes that defined new documentary cinema
have remained very much a stylistic staple of these most recent attempts to
satisfy the now-established market for Chinese reality and difference.

In fact, one aspect of this "DV wave" that served to distinguish it from
past trends, especially where documentaries were concerned, was its relative

diversity of subject matter. Director Zhang Yuan released three documentaries between 1998 and 2000—one profiling a household resisting eminent domain (*Dingzi hu*, 1998), one a spokesman for recreational English-learning (*Crazy English*, 1999), and one a dancer who undergoes a sex-change operation (*Miss Jin Xing*, 2000). Likewise, the emphasis that Wu Wenguang's anti-industry diatribes placed on individual experience and style did not mean that the tacit social criticism defining his and others' earlier works had been abandoned completely. The homeless teens (*Along the Railroad*), rural performers (*Jiang Hu*), escorts/prostitutes (*Leave Me Alone*), and chronically unemployed (*West of the Tracks*) featured in post-1999 documentaries all bear witness to considerable inequalities within mainland society, providing a lurid scrapbook of modern development's persistent "other." What it did mean was that the torch of "real" independence had been passed to a new set of filmmakers, whose nonprofessional status served to distinguish them from the present establishment, official and otherwise.

Repeated claims for difference, however, could not make common ground with, and dependence on, the "system" disappear. Among the most obvious points of overlap include festival promoters' continued effort to package independent Chinese filmmakers as courageous activists, no matter how limited or professionally oriented the scope of their activities in practice. This kind of mythmaking is amply captured by a press blurb for the Pacific Film Archive's 1998 "Unofficial China: The New Documentary Movement" screenings, which proclaimed that

> when the Chinese democracy movement collapsed on June 4, 1989, it didn't vanish, it resurfaced here and there, as traces of a reforming spirit. . . . Unofficial China is a first look at these eye-opening works from what has come to be called the new documentary Movement (NDM). . . . Inspired by the portability of video, the [movement] is also known for formal breakthroughs . . . eclipsing a history of official silence.[78]

Concerning the politics of international exhibition, one producer notes frankly (if glibly) that "films that are banned in China . . . [provide] a great promotion and publicity point of attack. . . . I actually had distributors ask me if it was OK to say our films have [been] banned, even though they haven't."[79] Again, it is also important to note that directors themselves have played an active role in courting such attention, even while they may resist its more overtly antistate connotations. This bid for recognition is most often expressed in terms of a more cautious desire to provoke, as evidenced by Wu Wenguang's claim that "the point of [films like *Jiang Hu*] is to leave people unsettled and without answers," or Du Haibin's assertion that he has released *Along the Railroad* in order to "make [the audience] think of such unclear things along with me."[80] Although these filmmakers may also denounce independent cinema's increasingly commercial nature, the point here is that even oppositional gestures indicate a desire for sustained attention and established "space."

Furthermore, it remains the case that despite the contempt that some feel for this trend, documentary filmmaking is still undeniably the domain of professionals, or those with professional ambitions. Du Haibin's *Along the Railroad* was completed as the aspiring director was preparing to graduate from the Beijing Film Academy. Likewise, most members of "amateur" organizations like the DV Documentary Group were university students, or recent university graduates, for whom DV filmmaking represented an acknowledged path to exposure.[81] It should also be noted that, important exceptions like Li Dan (*Old People*, 2000) and Wang Fen (*Unhappiness Doesn't Stop at One*, 2000) aside, they were almost overwhelmingly upwardly mobile young men, although work by both sexes has featured prominently on DV-oriented programming such as *DV New Era* (DV xin shidai), a program launched by Phoenix Satellite Television (Fenghuang weishi) to showcase the incipient "new visual movement" taking place among "young Chinese everywhere."[82] Owing to lack of general audience interest in such youthful perspectives, the show was cancelled due to lack of advertising revenue in 2002. But while commercial or mainstream successes may remain difficult to attain, a recent survey by the Beijing Film Academy and sponsored by the State Administration of Radio, Film, and Television shows that the majority of China's more than one million DV users are college students who nonetheless, in the words of one interviewee, see DV-based documentary and feature filmmaking as a "route to potential fame and fortune."[83] Ultimately, it may be the establishment of "amateur" documentary practices among China's consumer elite (according to the same survey, sale of DV camcorders is increasing at a rate of nearly 30 percent a year) that appears as the most distinct trace of new documentary cinema's afterlife—that is, insofar as its realist depictions of quotidian environments and (increasingly) exoticized social groups make it difficult to separate from similar trends accompanying market- and audience-oriented "mass-ification" of the official media throughout the 1990s.[84]

CONCLUSION

Attempting to answer the question "What makes a work of art a work of art?" Pierre Bourdieu was moved to discuss the importance of Marcel Mauss's *Theory of Magic*, in which the ethnographer, pondering the riddle of magic's effectiveness, "found that he had to move back from the instruments used by the sorcerer to the sorcerer himself, and from there to the belief held by his followers . . . [to] the entire social universe in whose midst magic evolves and is practiced."[85] Likewise, in describing the emergence of new documentary cinema and its relation to the mythology of independence—in particular, by paying attention to the methods of its practitioners, the venues in which their works are exhibited, and their actual relationships to the system and state they supposedly challenge—it seems worthwhile to step back from the films themselves and toward *their* social universe. While I do not oppose readings of films by Wu Wenguang and others that stress their value as reflections of political possibility or the "real" and varied experience of living in contemporary China, I do believe that examining the production of art and its aura can tell us something about politics and reality as well.

The corpus of work subsumed under the term "new documentary" was, initially, produced by a community of directors (including several deserving others, such as Li Hong and Kang Jianning, I have not addressed) who aspired to produce a perspective on Chinese society absent from the mainstream, using formal techniques that marked this perspective as "genuine" while decrying official views as overly "distant" or "narrow." Indeed, the very term "documentary" (*jilu pian*) and the myth of its discovery indicate a sense of opposition to dominant institutions, even though the means and influences through which new documentary cinema was actually constructed were then, as now, quite complex and not limited to the kinds of unofficial or illegal methods that other terms like "independent" are understood to convey. In all cases, these early films were produced by individuals with a background in official film or television production. Moreover, they were first exhibited at international film festivals before moving—with varying degrees of willingness on the part of some directors—back toward domestic institutional spaces that signaled, if not influenced, a shift toward quotidian imagery and acceptance of unofficial credentials within the mainland media as a whole.

These observations are not particularly innovative, nor do they reach what seems to me is the real crux of the issue—namely, how it is that new documentary cinema achieved such a critical mass of "effectiveness" in the first place, to the point that an entire genre was invented through which it could be credibly marketed and discussed. There are several plausible answers to this question. On the one hand, foreign interest in any cultural production *not* explicitly associated with the Chinese state had become, by the 1990s, so diverse and widespread as to be practically overdetermined. Whether expressed as fetishism, cults of the intellectual/auteur, or sociological curiosity, the recent preoccupation with "real China" can be fit rather neatly into a pattern of cultural consumption dating back at least to the 1980s, when the fifth generation generated similar outbursts of exhibition and acclaim. Again, while arguments to this effect have also been made by critics like Dai Jinhua and Yingjin Zhang, the fact that they are so frequently ignored perhaps makes them worth repeating here. Receiving even less attention, however, is the degree to which the realist and *vérité*-style aesthetics that seem to distinguish new documentary cinema from other modes of representation have been circulated *within* the mainstream media to varying degrees since the late 1980s. In tracing this cinema's path to domestic acceptance and recognition, one would have to begin by attempting to reconstruct its interaction with agendas of market- and audience-oriented media reform on the Chinese mainland, several aspects of which (popularization and professionalization being two of the most important) this chapter has touched upon in passing.

Also deserving mention is the epistemological crisis that independent/ official rapprochement has generated among those wishing to preserve documentary's dual status as both authentic "reality" and individual expression, insofar as this crisis informs perplexing, powerful works that, like *Jiang Hu*, constitute the genre's more recent inclusions. For while the professional community has also contributed to new documentary's success—albeit in ways rarely acknowledged by those preferring instead to highlight its oppositional mystique—so has its aura of originality, or innovation. It is not so much the existence of domestic and global film markets, but the obvious devolution of new documentary cinema to the position of "just another" commodity *within* those markets that threatens to discredit its producers' self-positioning as subversives, independents, and so on. This dilemma is expressed by the specifics of Wu Wenguang's recent career, particularly his refutation of claims to professional status while, in an attempt to legitimate and further his reputation, continuing to exhibit the cinematic expressions of these sentiments before those eager for a glimpse of "raw" reality. As Bourdieu writes elsewhere, "Art cannot reveal the truth about art without snatching it away again by turning the revelation into an artistic act."[86] Yet rather than simply criticizing Wu Wenguang's uncertain position, and the practices that support it, I think it is important to remember the ways in which documentary's realist depictions might still function as a powerful medium of expression and critique. In this sense, a kind of new documentary "spirit" does persist, even as its images and icons become co-opted, canonized, replaced, or forgotten.

NOTES

1. Lü Xinyu, *Jilu Zhongguo: dangdai Zhongguo xin jilu yundong* [Documenting China: The New Documentary Movement in Contemporary China] (Beijing: Sanlian shudian, 2003).

2. These links are established not only by critics and observers, but by the directors themselves. See, for example, the filmographies and essays included in the appendix of Wu Wenguang's *Jingtou xiang ziji de yanjing yiyang* [The Lens Is the Same as My Eye] (Shanghai: Shanghai yishu chubanshe, 2001).

3. Bérénice Reynaud, "Dancing with Myself, Drifting with My Camera: The Emotional Vagabonds of China's New Documentary," *Senses of Cinema* 28 (Sept.–

Oct. 2003), www.senseofcinema.com/contents/03/28/chinas_new_documentary.html (accessed July 23, 2005).

4. Charles Leary, "Performing the Documentary, or Making it to the Other Bank," *Senses of Cinema* 27 (July–Aug. 2003), www.sensesofcinema.com/contents/03/27/performing_documentary.html (accessed July 23, 2005).

5. Ernest Larsen, "Video *vérité* from Beijing," *Art in America* (Sept. 1998), www.findarticles.com/cf_dls/m1248/n9_v86/21268565/p2/article.jhtml?term= (accessed July 17, 2005).

6. On postsocialism, see Paul G. Pickowicz, "Huang Jianxin and the Notion of Postsocialism," in *New Chinese Cinema: Forms, Identities, Politics*, ed. Nick Browne, Paul G. Pickowicz, Vivian Sobchack, and Esther Yau, 57–87 (Cambridge, England: Cambridge University Press, 1994).

7. Wu Wenguang, *Jingtou xiang ziji de yanjing yiyang*, 212.

8. Wu Wenguang, *Jingtou xiang ziji de yanjing yiyang*, 213.

9. Mei Bing and Zhu Jingjiang, *Zhongguo duli jilu dang'an* [Records of China's Independent Documentary Cinema] (Xi'an: Shaanxi shifan daxue chubanshe, 2004), 26.

10. Mei and Zhu, *Zhongguo duli jilu dang'an*, 67.

11. Lü, *Jilu Zhongguo*, 149–51.

12. Wu Wenguang, *Jingtou xiang ziji de yanjing yiyang*, 213.

13. Similarly, Chris Berry writes that new documentary cinema's most dramatic departure from the mainstream lies in its lack of an overtly "pedagogical" or "preachy" (*shuojiao*) tone; see Chris Berry, "Miandui xianshi: Zhongguo de jilupian, Zhongguo de hou shehui zhuyi" [Facing Reality: Chinese Documentaries, Chinese Postsocialism], trans. Liu Zijia and Wen Jin'gen, *Southern Entertainment* (2003), www.southcn .com/ent/zhuanti/gzart1/doc/200301140008.htm (accessed July 23, 2005).

14. Wu Wenguang, *Jingtou xiang ziji de yanjing yiyang*, 222.

15. Wu Wenguang, *Jingtou xiang ziji de yanjing yiyang*, 222.

16. Lü, *Jilu Zhongguo*, 137.

17. Lü, *Jilu Zhongguo*, 70.

18. Fang Fang, *Zhongguo jilupian fazhan shi* [History of the Development of Chinese Documentary Cinema] (Beijing: Zhongguo xiju chubanshe, 2003), 313–26.

19. Lü, *Jilu Zhongguo*, 1–23.

20. "Wu Wenguang fangtan" (Interview with Wu Wenguang), *Liulang Beijing* (*Zhongguo jilupian xilie: Wu Wenguang zhuanji zhi yi* (DVD) (Beijing: Beijing Beijing luyin luxiang gongsi, no date).

21. Wu Wenguang, *Jingtou xiang ziji de yanjing yiyang*, 202–3.

22. Rey Chow, *Primitive Passions: Visuality, Sexuality, Ethnography, and Contemporary Chinese Cinema* (New York: Columbia University Press, 1995), 31.

23. Wu Wenguang, *Jingtou xiang ziji de yanjing yiyang*, 206.

24. Fang, *Zhongguo jilupian fazhan shi*, 379.

25. Lü, *Jilu Zhongguo*, 147–53.

26. John A. Lent, Wang Renying, and Yuheng Bao, "Contemporary Chinese Cinema: A Chronicle of Events, 1978-2000," *Asian Cinema* 11, no. 2 (2000): 172–74.

27. Fang, *Zhongguo jilupian fazhan shi*, 379.

28. Lü, *Jilu Zhongguo*, 71–72.

29. Wu Wenguang, *Jingtou xiang ziji de yanjing yiyang*, 92.

30. Wu Wenguang, *Jingtou xiang ziji de yanjing yiyang*, 94.

31. Wu Wenguang, *Jingtou xiang ziji de yanjing yiyang*, 92–93.

32. Yingjin Zhang, *Screening China: Critical Interventions, Cinematic Reconfigurations, and the Transnational Imaginary in Contemporary Chinese Cinema* (Ann Arbor: Center for Chinese Studies, University of Michigan, 2002), 26–27.

33. Dai Jinhua, "A Scene in the Fog: Reading Sixth Generation Films," in *Cinema and Desire: Feminist Marxism and Cultural Politics in the Work of Dai Jinhua*, ed. Jing Wang and Tani Barlow, 72 (emphasis added) (London: Verso, 2002).

34. Lü, *Jilu Zhongguo*, 97.

35. Wu Wenguang, *Jingtou xiang ziji de yanjing yiyang*, 217–20.

36. Lü, *Jilu Zhongguo*, 142.

37. Xu Guangchun, ed., *Zhonghua renmin gongheguo guangbo dianshi jianshi, 1949–2000* [A Concise History of Radio and Television in the People's Republic of China, 1949–2000] (Beijing: Zhongguo guangbo dianshi chubanshe, 2003), 379–81.

38. Wu Wenguang, *Jingtou xiang ziji de yanjing yiyang*, 258.

39. Hei Ding and Feng Hong, "Zai duoyuan fazhan de geju zhong zou xiang xin shiji: 90 niandai Zhongguo dianying fazhan taishi yantaohui zongshu" [Moving toward the New Century amidst a Polycentric Pattern of Development: A Summary of the Roundtable on the State of Chinese Film Development in the 1990s], *Dangdai dianying*, 1994, no. 3:26–27.

40. Hei and Feng, "Zai duoyuan fazhan de geju zhong zou xiang xin shiji," 26–27.

41. Hei and Feng, "Zai duoyuan fazhan de geju zhong zou xiang xin shiji," 26–27.

42. Zhu Ying, *Chinese Cinema during the Era of Reform: The Ingenuity of the System* (Westport, Conn.: Praeger, 2003), 28.

43. Zhu Ying, *Chinese Cinema during the Era of Reform*, 75–79.

44. For a fairly exhaustive list of details concerning Wu's works, including dates and places of exhibition, see "Wu Wenguang zuopin yilan" [Exhibitions of Wu Wenguang's Works], *Xin qingnian*, May 16, 2001, http://movie.newyouth.beida-online .com/data/data.php3?db=movie&id=wwgzpyl.

45. Fang, *Zhongguo jilupian fazhan shi*, 353.

46. Lü, *Jilu Zhongguo*, 77–78.

47. Wu Wenguang, *Jingtou xiang ziji de yanjing yiyang*, 143–44. Fifteen issues of the periodical were published and released between July 1996 and December 1997.

48. Wu Wenguang, *Jingtou xiang ziji de yanjing yiyang*, 258.

49. Wu Wenguang, *Jingtou xiang ziji de yanjing yiyang*, 178.

50. See, for example, Geremie R. Barmé, *In the Red: On Contemporary Chinese Culture* (New York: Columbia University Press, 1999), 186–87.

51. Zhu Ying, *Chinese Cinema during the Era of Reform*, 88.

52. Lü, *Jilu Zhongguo*, 19.

53. Wu Wenguang, *Jingtou xiang ziji de yanjing yiyang*, 146.

54. Wu Wenguang, *Jingtou xiang ziji de yanjing yiyang*, 178.

55. Wu Wenguang, *Jingtou xiang ziji de yanjing yiyang*, 95–96.

56. Wu Wenguang, *Jingtou xiang ziji de yanjing yiyang*, 88.

57. Wu Wenguang, *Jingtou xiang ziji de yanjing yiyang*, 107.

58. Wu Wenguang, *Jingtou xiang ziji de yanjing yiyang*, 112–17.

59. Zhu Ying, *Chinese Cinema during the Era of Reform*, 85.

60. Fang, *Zhongguo jilupian fazhan shi*, 427.

61. Wu Wenguang, *Jingtou xiang ziji de yanjing yiyang*, 31.

62. Wu Wenguang, *Jingtou xiang ziji de yanjing yiyang*, 253–54.

63. Wu Wenguang, *Jingtou xiang ziji de yanjing yiyang*, 121–27. This 1998 essay, "The Lens Is the Same as My Eye," represents one of Wu's most important manifestos concerning DV filmmaking, and one of his most pointed critiques of the professional establishment.

64. Wu Wenguang, *Jingtou xiang ziji de yanjing yiyang*, 50–51. Although disappointed by the experience, Wu concluded trenchantly that "America did not end with New York."

65. Wu Wenguang, *Jingtou xiang ziji de yanjing yiyang*, 126, 141.

66. Lü, *Jilu Zhongguo*, 13.

67. Wu Wenguang, *Jingtou xiang ziji de yanjing yiyang*, 235.

68. Lü, *Jilu Zhongguo*, 21.

69. Wu Wenguang, *Jingtou xiang ziji de yanjing yiyang*, 236. See also Wu Wenguang, *Jiang hu baogao: yige dapeng wei ge'an er zhankai de tianye diaocha* [Jiang Hu Report: A Field Investigation Unfolding from the Case of the "Big Tent"] (Beijing: Zhongguo qingnian chubanshe, 2001); Wu Wenguang, ed., *Xianchang (di yi juan)* [Document: The Present Scene, Vol. 1] (Tianjin: Tianjin shehui kexue chubanshe, 2000) and *Xianchang (di er juan)* [Document: The Present Scene, Vol. 2] (Tianjin: Tianjin shehui kexue chubanshe, 2001).

70. Wu Wenguang, *Jingtou xiang ziji de yanjing yiyang*, 128–31.

71. Wu Wenguang, *Jingtou xiang ziji de yanjing yiyang*, 259–63.

72. Wu Wenguang, *Jingtou xiang ziji de yanjing yiyang*, 195.

73. These reviews are collected in Wu Wenguang, *Jingtou xiang ziji de yanjing yiyang*.

74. Wu Wenguang, *Jingtou xiang ziji de yanjing yiyang*, 179–80.

75. See issues 11–12 (Oct.–Nov. 2001) of *Xin chao* [Next Wave]: *yishu xianchang dang'an*, which is a periodical published in Sichuan province.

76. See Wu Wenguang, *Jingtou xiang ziji de yanjing yiyang*, 173–77, 183–88.

77. Mei and Zhu, *Zhongguo duli jilu dang'an*, 51–52.

78. Steve Seid, "Unofficial China: The New Documentary Movement," presented in collaboration with *Unofficial China: The New Documentary Movement* at The Pacific Film Archive, March 8–19, 1998, www.naatanet.org/Exhibition/html/sfiaaff98/programs/unofficial.html.

79. Augusta Palmer, "Taming the Dragon: Part II, Two Approaches to China's Film Market," *indieWIRE*, Dec. 8, 2000, www.indiewire.com/biz/biz_001208_Chinese PartII.html (accessed July 23, 2005).

80. Lü, *Jilu Zhongguo,* 16; Zhang Xianmin and Zhang Yaxuan, *Yige ren de yingxiang: DV wanquan shouce* [All About DV: Works, Making, Creation, Comments] (Beijing: Zhongguo qingnian chubanshe, 2003), 112.

81. See Wu Wenguang, *Jingtou xiang ziji de yanjing yiyang,* 173–77, 183–88.

82. See, in particular, Zhang Xianmin and Zhang Yaxuan, *Yige ren de yingxiang.*

83. "Recording Real Life," *China Daily* (English edition), April 5, 2004, www .chinadaily.com.cn/english/doc/2004-04/05/content_320654.htm.

84. For a persuasive argument concerning "mass-ification" and its structural causes, see Yin Hong, *Yin Hong yingshi shiping* [Film and Television Criticism in the Work of Yin Hong] (Henan: Henan daxue chubanshe, 2002), 7–33.

85. Pierre Bourdieu, *The Field of Cultural Production: Essays on Art and Literature,* ed. and intro. Randal Johnson (New York: Columbia University Press, 1993), 258–59.

86. Bourdieu, *The Field of Cultural Production,* 80.

4

"Every Man a Star": The Ambivalent Cult of Amateur Art in New Chinese Documentaries

Valerie Jaffee

Until recently, Western academic writings on Chinese underground, independent, and sixth-generation film have been lacking in both quantity and quality. This lack is especially evident when contrasted with the abundance and richness of scholarship that has been produced in the West in response to fifth-generation works. In general, the terminology and thematic foci of Western scholarship on underground works have tended to bear a strong resemblance to the descriptions of those works found in festival catalogues, popular publications, and marketing literature, much to the scholarship's discredit.

It is easy to forgive scholars' relative neglect of underground and sixth-generation cinema. After all, the phenomenon is not much more than a decade old and students of contemporary culture are not able to rely on established canonical wisdom to determine which works and auteurs are truly worthy of attention. For the time being, the growing consensus seems to be that the Chinese underground has not produced many individual works that have survived several years of critical viewing as successfully as the landmark fifth-generation works have. In my conversations with Chinese film fans and scholars of multiple nationalities, I have discovered a profound strain of skepticism regarding the aesthetic value and inherent interest of the majority of underground works. The film critic Dai Jinhua famously declared in 1994, when the term "sixth generation" was entering common parlance with a great deal of fanfare, that, to someone "still committed to the worth of art and its objective aesthetic value . . . the sixth generation ha[s] only produced a handful of original creative works."[1] Other writers have accused landmark sixth-generation films of being "narrowly constructed, capable of striking a chord with only limited audience segments" or, in the case of *Beijing Bastards* (1993), "vacuous and technically inept to a fault."[2] Today's observer is indeed forced to wonder whether anyone will be watching these films, and thus whether anyone will want to read about them, decades from now. This nagging question has grown all the more troublesome in recent years, as the term "sixth generation"—whose very existence could have served as a convenient device for ensuring the movement's place in history—has been attacked as a misleading simplification.[3] Meanwhile, most of the successful underground filmmakers of the 1990s, including Zhang Yuan and Jia Zhangke, have begun making "aboveground" films in full cooperation with bureaucratic authorities, challenging both the equation of the term "sixth generation" with the term "underground" and the very significance of the concept of an "underground" in China today.[4]

My aim in this chapter is to diverge in several crucial respects from what I see as the majority of Western scholarly approaches to the topic of Chinese underground cinema, in the hopes of making more thorough progress toward proposing a plausible answer to the questions of whether Chinese underground cinema exists, and whether it is a deserving object of critical attention. First, I am interested in concentrating on the thematic concerns that are *relatively unique* to Chinese underground cinema. What I mean by this is best explained by example. A striking number of the explanations of what distinguishes sixth-generation or underground cinema have referred to an urban/rural binary, associating the sixth generation with urban life and culture in contrast to the fifth generation's interest in rural topics. Broadly accurate though this association may be, it fails to encompass the diversity within and historical acuity of underground film (many recent examples of which are actually concerned with small towns or with migrant workers, both of which by their very existence corrupt the neatness of the urban/rural dichotomy). More importantly, a simple opposition between urban and rural concerns seems inherently doomed to tell us little about what makes the underground movement unique. The contrast between the urban and the rural constitutes one of the oldest and most commonplace dialectics of twentieth-century Chinese culture, and thus it is difficult to identify a single cultural movement that cannot somehow be placed alongside one or the other of its poles. My choice of focus for this chapter—amateur art—is, in contrast, a topic that comes up with much less frequency in modern Chinese literature and film. If present-day underground filmmakers have something to contribute to the development of Chinese film aesthetics, then their contribution will likely be related to issues like this one.

Second, most observers of Chinese underground cinema have taken as their main point of departure the opposition between that movement and other institutional or artistic fields—the works of the fifth generation, state-run studio films, market-oriented mainstream cinema, and so on (see Chris Berry's chapter). In doing so, these observers often cannot help but neglect the internal diversity and consequent complexity of the creature we tentatively call "underground cinema." I, on the other hand, want to take as my point of departure not the many sociocultural phenomena that underground film is *not* but, instead, the conflicts and contrasts evident *within* the movement. I will discuss at length three recent works that belong in the category of "new documentaries," generally regarded as an important subset of the independent film movement: Wu Wenguang's *Life on the Road* (aka *Jiang Hu*, 1999), Zhu Chuanming's *Extras* (2001), and Zheng Dasheng's *DV China* (2003). These three films are similar in subject matter and in certain stylistic features but are also strikingly, and tellingly, different where tone, production details, and eventual reception are concerned. These differences only skim the surface of the actual diversity of postures and practices to be found within the Chinese cinematic underground.

IN PRAISE OF AMATEURS

It seems only natural that a cinematic movement that began as a movement of outsiders would sooner or later express an interest in the concept of amateur art (*yeyu yishu*). But in fact an explicit concern with the state of outsider-hood *with regard to art and cinema proper* postdates the early-1990s birth of the sixth generation by about half a decade. The Chinese film world's earliest and most direct pronouncements on the possibility of the amateurization of filmmaking come from the director Jia Zhangke. Jia's first three feature films—*Xiao Wu* (1997), *Platform* (2000), and *Unknown Pleasures* (2002)—are, in the details of their production, clear inheritors of the novel "tradition" established by Zhang Yuan and Wang Xiaoshuai.[5] Certain broad stylistic preferences also link Jia's films to the flagship films of the sixth generation: low budgets and technical minimalism, on-site shooting, and a focus on daily life in contemporary society. But Jia's choice of subject matter represents a conscious departure from his recent forebears. While Zhang Yuan's and Wang Xiaoshuai's landmark films—*Beijing Bastards* and *The Days* (1993), respectively—focus on the lives of urban, relatively well-educated rock musicians and artists, the main characters of Jia's films are individuals whose walks of life are closer approximations of the Chinese "average": all live in or are from towns of lower rank than provincial capital, none have college educations or the hope of attaining one, and none occupy the extraordinary social position of the professional artist.

While not naming names and (mercifully) without declaring the need for the rise of a new numbered "generation" of Chinese filmmakers, Jia has, in public statements, rejected the attitudes of his immediate underground ancestors. In many ways, his rejection is more pointed than the sixth generation's

A small-town pickpocket "dating" a KTV hostess in Jia Zhangke's Xiao Wu *(1997)*

rejection of the achievements of the fifth. Like virtually every important feature film director to emerge in China between 1980 and 1995, Jia is a graduate
of the Beijing Film Academy (BFA). However, as a student in the Film Literature Department from 1993 to 1997, he felt locked out of the inner circle of
privilege that was the school's more prestigious Directing Department. Since
Jia's days at the BFA, the ranks of Chinese filmmakers have been filled out
by a significant minority of participants who have never been connected with
the BFA.[6] Compared to these individuals, perhaps, Jia is an insider. But in the
mid-1990s, and in his own opinion, he was an outsider, and in interviews he
has expressed indignation at the snobbishness and parochialism he observed
in his schoolmates and the institution itself: "Some people were saying, 'Oh,
these days every Joe Schmo on the street wants to be become a director.' I was
really angry when I heard this; I thought, what's wrong with every Joe Schmo
on the street wanting to be a director?"[7]

Jia Zhangke's article "The Age of Amateur Cinema Will Return" first
appeared in the newspaper *Southern Weekend* (Nanfang zhoumo) in 1999.
In this essay, Jia decries the domination of the film world by "professionals"
who fervently guard an established cinematic canon and are "very concerned
about whether or not their works will demonstrate their so-called professional
attainment; for example, their compositions must be as elegant as an oil painting, or they must exhibit the same degree of control as Antonioni." He finds

A bicycle ride to nowhere in Jia Zhangke's Platform *(2000)*

an alternative to this insularity in the idea of "amateur directors." However, the examples through which he explicates this concept indicate that he is not exactly talking about actual amateurs—untrained individuals for whom film-making is an activity outside of their main profession—but is instead extolling a certain mode of self-presentation among directors who are, by all conceivable standards, professionals. Jia cites Krzysztof Kieslowski's designation of himself as an "amateur director from Eastern Europe" and Akira Kurosawa's declaration that "even with all the films I have made, I still don't know exactly what film is and am still searching for a film aesthetic." Modesty, then, and a deliberate posture of outsider-ness are what Jia is talking about. He also associates amateurism with disregard for established convention and the pursuit of originality; directors in the amateur spirit "don't care about so-called professional styles." His examples of this spirit are, again, drawn from a rather indisputable canon of influential directors: Eric Rohmer, R. W. Fassbinder, Jean-Luc Godard, and Roman Polanski.[8]

Amateurism for Jia, then, is primarily an attitude, not a lifestyle condition—an attitude composed of self-deprecation and disinterest in convention. But Jia also makes a point, and a vaguer one, of connecting this attitude to the possibility of the rise to the status of filmmaker of individuals lacking conventional credentials:

> Who's to say that the Chinese Quentin Tarantino couldn't emerge from among the crowds hanging out in VCD stores? . . . Film should never again be the privilege of a minority of people. It belongs by rights to the masses. In Shanghai, I met a group of film lovers. Those people, who make their livings repairing airplanes and producing ads, might well represent the future of Chinese film.[9]

At stake here is the question of who may have the legitimate means and opportunity to become a filmmaker. Jia is identifying and praising a complex social and economic phenomenon that is arguably on its way to influencing all sectors of Chinese professional life: the decline, under the influence of free-market reforms, of a social system in which individual life-paths are determined by education and state demands, and the replacement of that system by one in which personal ambition and market demands instead circumscribe more broadly the ways in which an individual can earn a living and identify himself. Social and occupational mobility, and a film industry that will accommodate such mobility, is the crux of the culture of amateurism Jia identifies; the example of Quentin Tarantino, a onetime video store clerk, is perhaps the clearest indication of this.

The specter of broader social transitions and political import haunts Jia's essay in other ways as well. The piece is peppered with words that suggest a political manifesto as much as a statement of aesthetic direction. "The spirit of amateurism encompasses the values of equality and justice," Jia writes. In another essay that covers related ground, on growing access to opportunities for viewing and making films in China due to the spread of digital technology, Jia describes the proliferation of VCD in China as a sign that "we are reclaiming our rights."[10] Justice, equality, rights—the actual political significance of any of Jia's statements is oblique at best; what matters is his choice of terms from political discourse to describe directions in the aesthetics and sociology of cinema. Jia is trying to identify and recommend to Chinese cinema a spirit that I will go so far as to call *democratic*. Those with privileges within the system—professional filmmakers—ought to be humble about and not take for granted those privileges; those who lack them—amateurs—ought to have at least the hope of acquiring them. Access to cinema is conceived of as a *human right*—that is, a privilege that should be universal.

As Jia's comments about his classmates at the Beijing Film Academy indicate, the egalitarian polemic in favor of the amateur is as much one young filmmaker's attack on other young filmmakers as it is the mass of young filmmakers' attack on any larger or less progressive institutional system. In many ways, this elevation of amateurism is underground cinema's rebuke *to itself* rather than to the censorship system or mercenary markets to which critics more often contrast the movement.

In a recent book about China's "new documentary movement," Fudan University professor Lü Xinyu relates an anecdote that suggests a fascinating shift in concern between the underground documentaries of the early 1990s and those of more recent years. In 1995, one of the main subjects of Wu Wenguang's documentary *Bumming in Beijing* (1990), a theater director named Mou Sen, attracted the attention of another documentarian, Jiang Yue. Mou was staging the experimental play *The Other Bank* in Beijing and had recruited a group of teenagers from rural areas to serve as his cast; Jiang was recording the proceedings.

After a break in the shooting, Jiang returned to the cast and crew to find a situation that made him deeply uneasy. Mou Sen ran into problems with funding sources for the continuation of the project, and he was having trouble feeding and housing the teenagers in his care. With regard to the predicament of these teenagers, who were enthusiastic, not particularly privileged economically or well-educated, and utterly unfamiliar with Beijing, Mou displayed a callousness that shocked Jiang Yue. Mou allegedly remarked dismissively that the actors did not interest him, since they were incapable of understanding the deconstructionist ideas behind his play, and he suggested to one of the broke teenage girls that she prostitute herself. After these episodes, Jiang Yue decided to move the focus of his documentary away from Mou and the play and toward the young people in its cast instead. The film that resulted, also called *The Other Bank* (1995), was completed in 1995. Lü opines that this anecdote "reflects a transformation in [Jiang's] position."[11] From the perspective of this chapter, it is a telling transformation indeed—a shift in focus, prompted by a sense of moral outrage, from the established professional artist (and not just any professional artist, but one whose voice and image had helped bring to life the Chinese underground documentary movement) to the amateurs over whom he held a not-entirely-benevolent power.[12]

Lü Xinyu's account never actually uses the words "amateur" (*yeyu*) or "professional" (*zhuanye*). These terms do appear fairly regularly in discussions of underground film, particularly those discussions that focus on the new digital video movement.[13] But it is very rare to find them applied to specific films, and the jump I am about to make in my own discussion, from this discourse to individual films, is a somewhat daring one. More to the point, a contrast that emerges even in the texts discussed above needs to be addressed here: Jia Zhangke's optimistic manifesto is about *amateur filmmakers*, while Jiang Yue's and Lü Xinyu's statement of moral priorities has to do with *the filming of amateur-made art*. The three documentaries I am about to discuss all serve the latter function, and only one is actually about an amateur filmmaker.

Be that as it may, Jia's polemical use of the term "amateur" seems highly relevant to a subgenre that has developed in recent underground, and particularly documentary, films. This subgenre consists of films concerned with the lives of socially marginalized people who, in some way or another, participate or try to participate in artistic endeavors, without the training or recognition that distinguishes professional artists. These people's artistic endeavors, and filmmakers' interest in them, may not be precisely the kind of activity that Jia Zhangke is calling for in his essay. However, it seems fair to speculate that the sentiments and convictions that inspired Jia to write the essay are broadly similar to those that inspire the makers of these films.[14] All three films, as well as Jia's manifesto, are animated by a deconstructive impulse directed at institutions through which Chinese society circumscribes the zone of legitimate cultural production. To a greater extent than the manifesto, these films are concerned with the human impact of that circumscription.

AN ARTIST'S MEA CULPA

An evolution in the perspective and focus of Wu Wenguang, who helped to found the underground documentary movement when he filmed the lives of Mou Sen and other itinerant Beijing artists for *Bumming in Beijing*, parallels the transformation in Jiang Yue's interests that Lü Xinyu describes. When asked what he thinks about his early documentaries—*Bumming in Beijing, At Home in the World* (1995), *1966, My Time in the Red Guards* (1993)—Wu declares unequivocally that he thinks they are "rubbish," at least in comparison to the (at the time) new documentary on which the interview is largely focused.[15] That newer work, called *Life on the Road*, portrays a traveling performance troupe, made up mostly of individuals from peasant backgrounds, that earns a scant living putting on large-scale variety shows involving singing, dancing, and lip-synching, for mostly middle- and lower-class audiences in suburban areas and small towns.

The actual Chinese title of this film is *jianghu*, a word that defies easy translation into English. *Jianghu* literally means "rivers and lakes," but it also has the related metaphorical meaning of "all corners of the country." From this meaning comes the tertiary meaning of "an itinerant, a wanderer"; as an extension of *that* meaning, the word takes on its common popular usage of "crafty, untrustworthy; a swindler, a quack." Given the layers of cultural assumption accumulated in the term, "gypsy" (as broadly used in popular parlance, without ethnic connotation) seems a worthy English translation.[16] In an interview conducted by none other than Wu Wenguang himself, Jia Zhangke told a story about his BFA entrance examination that was meant to illustrate the subtle class discrimination to which he was subject at that institution. Apparently one of Jia's examiners told his colleagues that he thought Jia had "something of the gypsy about him."[17] The word I translate as "gypsy" here is, of course, *jianghu*. This convergent use of terms may be merely a charming coincidence. But it might also point to the discursive echoes and the common values through which an emerging cinematic underground is defining itself.

Wu Wenguang's background makes his work a particularly interesting channel through which to approach the theme of amateur art. Wu made *Bumming in Beijing* with his own resources, without the support or permission of any institution or bureaucratic organ, before pioneer independent fiction film directors like He Jianjun, Zhang Yuan, and Wang Xiaoshuai had begun working in this fashion. In the early 1990s, when most underground filmmakers had been trained at the BFA, Wu stood out for having received no formal education in filmmaking.[18] Finally, *Bumming in Beijing* is about self-declared, self-employed artists struggling to survive in Beijing without residence permits, jobs, or any institutional affiliation.[19] These individuals were all friends of Wu's before the filming commenced, and his lifestyle at the time was largely similar to theirs. Thus, *Bumming in Beijing* can be tentatively read as an artist's self-portrait.

Yet, while he was making *Life on the Road*, Wu came to think of that indirect self-portrait as "rubbish." In an interview of Wu conducted by Lü Xinyu, an intertwined set of issues emerges as justification for that dramatic statement. The filmmaker and the scholar express a number of shared attitudes toward the subject matter of the documentary; upon close examination, those attitudes form an awkward array, neither contradicting one another nor quite coexisting comfortably. First, Wu's disavowal of his earlier work is accompanied by a general distaste for intellectuals and artists of all stripes. He claims that his time in the circus-style tent that serves as shelter and stage for the traveling performers in *Life on the Road* made him feel that his "life in Beijing was shallow, very unreal, especially the contemporary artists in Beijing. . . . I feel that the current art scene in China is icy, divorced from reality, even has something cruel about it." His criticism of that world, and of his own position in it, is reminiscent of an old-fashioned party intellectual's mea culpa: "I discovered that for the past ten years I've lacked an understanding of the truly most basic pulse of China."[20]

Wu expresses the contrast between urban, educated, artistic people like himself and the mysterious mass of individuals who live less rarefied lives through the metaphoric dichotomy of inside and outside. Beijing city regulations prohibit traveling performers from working within the major city limits: "From the perspective of geography, they can never enter the city; they're forever stuck outside the Fourth Ring Road, and the roads of the city are closed to them."[21] If urbanity is the inside that these outsiders are denied entry to, then *professionalism* is another, parallel inside.

> Wu: . . . I don't want to rest on my status as a member of a profession . . .
>
> Lü: [You mean] turning documentaries into something professional, specialized.
>
> Wu: And then acting high and mighty because of that . . .
>
> Lü: Or trying to turn yourself into a documentary expert . . .[22]

Later in the interview, Wu openly endorses an alternative to a professionalism that "emphasizes intense mobilization of resources, scale, and deliberate obscurity"; he calls that alternative "amateurism" (*yeyu*).[23]

An old theme is reappearing in Wu and Lü's lionizing of his subjects and Wu's potshots at the Beijing art world. The performance troupe members are "a group located at society's margins." They are people who do not fit in anywhere: "One of the people in the movie says to the camera that he didn't want to do hard labor in the fields, and working in a factory wasn't right either; he couldn't find a place for himself, so he has to muddle through life this way."[24] Wu Wenguang says that he was "very much moved" when the troupe resumed its performances after police harassment had kept it from performing for days at a time.[25] Ten or even five years ago, if one had posed as a riddle "a group of Chinese artists who feel they don't fit in the paths their society delineates for them and are eager to express themselves despite direct and indirect suppression from state authorities," the obvious answer would have been, "people like the artists portrayed in *Bumming in Beijing*." Now, though, Wu proffers a group of lip-synching peasants as the more legitimate inheritors of that tradition. They seem to have stepped into the sociological and mythological position vacated by the group of painters, avant-garde theater directors, and video artists of which Wu is a member. It is perhaps worth noting here that *Bumming in Beijing* is subtitled *The Last Dreamers* and that, of the five artists it portrays, four had left China for more affluent lives abroad by the time the documentary was released. Wu Wenguang, who in 1994 was one of seven underground filmmakers officially barred from making further films in China but who in succeeding years has watched several of the other members of that group of "seven gentlemen" enter the fold of official Chinese filmmaking,[26] may well have good reason to react with particular force, and perhaps a bit of nostalgia, to the sight of people who want to sing and dance actually being prevented from singing and dancing. In the world of Chinese art proper, that situation is increasingly rare, thanks to pirated films and books, the occasional generosity of capricious bureaucrats, and the paths forged by pioneers like Wu himself.[27]

But Wu's impulse to name his performance troupe as the rightful inheritors of a title that he and his compatriots have proven themselves unworthy of—the title of romantic and struggling artist—also seems dampened by a visceral distrust and fear of the actual activities for which the performers are sacrificing security, status, and home. My single viewing of *Life on the Road* actually surprised me a bit, after the ringing rhetoric in Wu's own words on the film. Despite Wu's intimations that *Life on the Road* may be read as a new self-portrait overwritten upon his older ones, the intimacy that *Bumming in Beijing* very successfully established between audience and subject is notably absent in the later documentary. Given Wu's more recent acquaintance with these performers and the social chasms between him and them, that is more or less to be expected. But the lack of intimacy in *Life on the Road* occasionally turns into something more drastic, a sense of true alienation of audience and camera from filmed subject. The overarching tone of the film emerges through three main subtopics.

The first is highly subtle and is perhaps best described through the subtle concept of *class*. Wu's concern with the performers' class status, made evident in the interview cited above, is conveyed through complicated and intriguing codes. Early in the film, we get several close-up shots of the body of the boss of the troupe, Old Liu, which show his large, unwieldy cell phone and then his pack of 555 cigarettes, two items that code this man as a provincial upstart. Throughout the film, such meaningful close-ups create a sense of a private conversation between filmmaker and audience about—and maybe sometimes at the expense of—the filmed subjects. Physicality and haphazard sexuality are part of the complex of impressions that help define these people's class status. In scenes of the tent being assembled or taken down, Wu often provides close-ups of the sweat-soaked torsos of the men performing this labor. The camera also lingers on the performers, both male and female, as they wander through the coeducational environment of the tent half-dressed or change costumes in full view of each other backstage. An ethnographic curiosity seems to inform many of these shots, and the effect is one that leads to alienation of audience from subject.

The second subtopic enforces, though perhaps in less direct ways, that effect of alienation. This subtopic is the *performances* that define the lifestyle of these individuals. These nightly revues are an endearing postmodern mélange that resembles the content of the televised variety shows that have long been popular in China. Female performers dance in scanty clothing, and singers, mostly male, perform songs originally made famous by such diverse sources as the revered rock musician Cui Jian, the Hong Kong pop singer Richie Ren, and the film *Titanic*. The camera's attitude toward all this is difficult to discern. On the one hand, certain performances, generally by the male singers, are characterized by what seems to be genuine enjoyment and gusto. On the other hand, Wu makes a point of showing us the very bored and lackluster expressions on the faces of dancing girls. This same ambiguity emerges in Wu's verbal statements and writing on the subject. In his interview with Lü Xinyu, he describes, with an almost naive fascination, the extent to which this sort of popular culture serves as a "comfort" to its fans, and he uses the first-person plural to describe the sort of people who are affected by popular songs and soap operas.[28] The second component of his *Life on the Road* project, a compendium of the oral narratives he recorded among the performers, contains several autobiographical statements from troupe members who seem driven by a passionate desire to perform.[29] In other words, sentiments which could be regarded as positive, as "elevated," or as "artistic" are not absent from the performers' approaches to their work. But at the same time the intellectual's standpoint that Wu and Lü both decry is evident in portions of their discussion and leads to a rather more negative appraisal of the creative activities that go on inside the troupe's tent:

> Lü: When you first said that you were shooting a traveling performers' tent, I immediately thought you meant a traditional troupe. But in fact pop culture has now entered those tents. . . . Multiple forms of the discursive power of the center are using all kinds of methods to penetrate the margins, to control the margins, producing a kind of centripetal force, producing a kind of imitation of the center.
>
> Wu: What I found most striking was that these popular songs are all about tender love, broken hearts, life-and-death struggles, aesthetic beauty, and the expression of emotions. . . . But then on the other hand [these people's] reality is nothing but trash strewn on the ground. But they need the kind of illusory contentment [the songs provide].[30]

These conflicting attitudes toward the troupe's performances get right to the core of the ambiguities surrounding the topic of this chapter. Can the activities of this troupe be considered "amateur art"? A certain commonsense perspective says yes; the performers are engaging in activities (singing, dancing) that society would most certainly lump under the category of artistic pursuit, at least if those engaging in them were trained to do so. As argued above, Wu Wenguang clearly perceives in the performers' lifestyle a purer and more genuine inheritor of the undeniably artistic lifestyles portrayed in *Bumming in Beijing*. But the fact remains that the performances aspired to here are, first, only performances and not compositions and, second, inspired by cultural strains whose status as "art" remains in dispute. Perhaps most telling of all is the fact that the performers lump together the probably "artistic" (the songs of Cui Jian) and the probably-not (dances to disco beats by girls in bikinis) in selecting their program. All things considered, what the entire *Life on the Road* phenomenon accomplishes is the asking of a pressing question: What qualifies as art?

That question is every bit as relevant to this particular chapter in Wu's biography as to the subjects of the documentary. The film *Life on the Road* is perhaps the roughest and least-polished of his works. It is meant to be accompanied by a print volume (the self-narratives of the troupe members) that is more like a reference work than like discrete reading material and that evidences little to no intervention by Wu, its purported "creator." Perhaps most significantly for all of Chinese underground film, *Life on the Road*, like many other such films, has barely been shown and has not been distributed in China or abroad, so that it is entirely possible that more people have *read* about it than will ever see it. In other words, the documentary is, in its ambivalent relationship to named genres and the assumptions that accompany them, emblematic of the contradictions and discipline-confounding complexity that characterize Chinese society today. In this respect, *Life on the Road* and its subject, the Far and Wide Performance Troupe, have a great deal in common.

I have discussed Wu's use of close-ups and curiosity shots and the sense of alienation of audience from subject that these create. The third subtopic that dominates *Life on the Road* is the crux of the portions of the film in which that alienation is reversed. This subtopic is another complex assemblage of themes that, for simplicity's sake, I will call "compulsion." The *compulsion* detailed in the film is manifold. The father and son who manage the performance troupe are constantly worrying about the troupe's commercial prospects and its ability to clear requisite hurdles with local authorities. Meanwhile, the performers and workers have not been paid their wages for some time. Many want to leave the fiscally underperforming troupe, but the bosses hold onto their ID cards to prevent them from leaving, and they are reluctant to leave without receiving the wages owed to them. It is during discussions of these pressing issues that Wu seems to achieve a higher level of intimacy with his subjects, many of whom are eager to initiate one-sided "interviews" in which they air their grievances.

Related to the troupe's instability and the anxieties it causes is the implication of potential criminality inherent in its very existence. Local authorities look askance at the presence of such a large party of transients in their domain, and a common accusation leveled at this and similar troupes is that they feature "liberated" (nude) dancing. During one performance, several troupe members perform a "prisoners' dance." They hang around their necks placards on which their own names and the names of crimes they have not actually committed are written, and then they do a group recital, augmented by descriptive dancing, of a traditional prison song. This act acknowledges and satirizes the performers' shadowy legal status and the vague sense that, in their work and existence, they are at odds with social norms. A good deal of Wu's interest in and respect for these people seems to be related to this status and sense.

All things considered, Wu's relationship to the lives of these amateur performers is related to a narrative of change that feels familiar, even archetypal, in all artistic movements described as subversive or underground. After producing an influential work that conveys the dangerous, unconventional, impoverished, and unusual conditions of a world of which his art qualifies him as an inhabitant, Wu eventually came to dismiss himself and that world as members of a new "establishment," also capable of intolerance, complacency, and narrow-mindedness. He then placed his hopes of renewing and revivifying the Chinese underground on works like *Life on the Road*, which raise the threshold for documentary subjects that can properly be called "marginal." Yet the difficulty of achieving these aims is highlighted by the class- and culture-based distance between Wu and his subjects, even though this distance is of course what attracted him in the first place. That distance shrinks when Wu focuses on their sheer marginality, on their uncomfortable relationships with legal and economic centers; but it gapes uncomfortably when the amateurish creative works of his subjects are highlighted. These performers' love for international hit songs reminds the audience (and perhaps Wu) that pure "amateur art" is a rare and fleeting commodity. The troupe members are amateurs, but they are striving with full sincerity to be professionals, just as Wu Wenguang strives with full sincerity to get in touch with a world outside of art proper but cannot, logic tells us, efface entirely the fact that everyone who has heard of him knows him as an artist—presumably, a professional one.

SEX, SUFFERING, AND SHOW BUSINESS

Underground Chinese films of similar quality and with similar subject matter can experience very different fates in the tumultuous film market. Like *Life on the Road*, Zhu Chuanming's *Extras* is an unofficial project shot on digital video about the lives of lower-class pop-culture devotees in and around Beijing. However, while Wu's film has been shown only a few times in China and abroad and is virtually unavailable in portable copies in China, Zhu's has been distributed on VCD by a private local distribution company. The difference in Wu's and Zhu's life stories also highlights the diversity among young underground directors. Wu was born in 1960; while he began his career as something of an autodidact, his success over the past decade means that few people would instinctively think of him as an "outsider" to the Chinese film world anymore. Zhu's biography, on the other hand, contrasts sharply with the lives of the earliest underground directors but follows a pattern that is increasingly prominent among younger directors.[31] Born in 1971, Zhu attended technical school instead of high school and spent five years working in a petrochemical plant in Jiangxi province before being accepted by the BFA, thereby becoming the first person from his hometown to attend a four-year college.[32]

The extraordinary fact of *Extras* having been commercially distributed in the mainland (VCDs of the documentary began appearing in stores in late 2003 and early 2004, over two years after it was made) is probably attributable at least in part to the unusual degree of controversy the film has stirred up among the small, generally quite appreciative and tolerant Chinese audience for independent works (see Seio Nakajima's and Yingjin Zhang's chapters). Online rumor currently has it that, when the film was made available for download from the Internet, certain viewers condemned it as "fascist"; and its few public showings are supposed to have prompted audience members to walk out before it was over.[33] (The version of the film that prompted these reactions is apparently not the one released on VCD; the former, 120 minutes long, was turned into a seventy-minute cut for distribution.[34]) While the claims of "fascism" are a bit bewildering, the minor controversy sparked by *Extras* is generally easy to understand and is probably related to two major factors. The words with which I choose to denote those two factors in the subheading of this portion of the chapter—sex and suffering—are a bit grandiose and not perfectly descriptive, but they capture the general idea: the film's somewhat upsetting sexual content is one factor, and the pathetic situations and confessions of its main subjects, unusual even for the generally quite pathetic genre of Chinese underground documentaries focusing on lower-class individuals, are the other.

To a much greater extent than Wu, Zhu zeroes in on three major "characters" and allows the audience to develop intimate relationships with them. This is accomplished in part by a slightly more proactive documentary practice than that used by Wu. Zhu introduces each of his major characters with subtitles, and a hefty portion of the film is taken up with individual monologues by lone subjects speaking directly to the camera. The three main subjects are all young people, in their late teens or their twenties, and all of them are members of the crowd of erstwhile film extras who spend their days waiting outside the Beijing Film Studio for short-term acting work. One, Bao Hehua, is a young woman who has forsaken her Zhejiang migrant family's unglamorous but prosperous seafood business to pursue this line of work. The second, Wang Gang, has come from Hubei province in the hopes of attaining fame and fortune through this route. By the time Zhu films him he seems rather saturnine

The VCD cover of Zhu Chuanming's documentary Extras *(2001)*

about his prospects, but he is reluctant to give up and return home without something to show for his time in Beijing. The third character, Li Wenbo, is also the oldest and most sophisticated. He earns his living as a sort of agent for the extras, processing and meeting the studio's requests for extras of particular descriptions. None of the three is earning a particularly extravagant living. They share a bare-bone, "coeducational" rented place on the far outskirts of Beijing.

The extras' living situation is responsible for the film's sexual content, which in the distributed cut is fairly tame but still quite difficult to watch. Bao Hehua, the only woman in the group, serves repeatedly as the butt of sexual jokes and of teasing that wavers between flirtation and actual cruelty. In one scene, she, Li Wenbo, and two other young men are in bed together, clothed, in their rented house. Li suggests, with a sly glance at the camera, that he shoot a porn film starring Bao; and a number of jokes about whom Bao has slept with are batted around. In a scene not long after, we see the same subjects in bed together again; someone says, "Let's go to sleep," the lights go out, and Zhu continues filming while they produce kissing sounds and groans of passion for the camera's benefit, punctuating these noises with giggles. A later scene in the rented house features the extras watching television. First they watch popular music videos, then Li Wenbo turns on a pornographic video and urges Zhu to zoom in on a very explicit scene. Zhu complies.

As these descriptions indicate, at least in the final cut, the "hormonal atmosphere" that Zhu Chuanming claims he aimed to reproduce in the documentary does not in itself help us understand why the film caused such an uproar.[35] More enlightening may be a related critique, leveled online, that the lack of respect for the privacy and dignity of the subjects inherent in these scenes is more significant than the scenes themselves:

> The slices of life that Zhu Chuanming exhibits in his film, particularly in a few shots of the girl Bao Hehua and the male extras, earned the disgust of some viewers and judges, who thought that the director's indiscriminate exhibition to the audience of shots that demonstrated the ignorance and stupidity of his subjects stemmed from a lack of compassion and was an affront to those subjects.[36]

This tendency of *Extras* to capture and highlight the harshness of its subjects' lives and their personal flaws links the film's mild prurience to its quality of pathos, which is equally or more taxing for the viewer. The male characters' endless jokes about Bao Hehua's sexual proclivities are punctuated with even more juvenile bouts of mock violence and jokes about her bad skin; the whole complex of mockery at her expense comes across at times as these men's hapless and nervous attempts at flirting. But Bao is the one more deserving of sympathy in this situation. The nervous broad smiles she casts at the camera whenever one of her male friends makes a dirty joke directed at her are downright heartbreaking and lend credence to the accusation that this film is guilty not just of voyeurism but of producing another layer of harassment; the presence of the camera is obviously helping to increase Bao's discomfort in these situations.

Even when Bao Hehua and the sexual high jinks she inspires are ignored, the documentary is still saturated with pathos, most of it centered on the extra Wang Gang. Very early in the film, Zhu captures him in front of the Beijing Film Studio looking at movie posters and complaining to the camera about a martial-arts actor named Huang Wenhao who monopolizes the parts Wang himself dreams of playing. An interview that follows has Wang telling the camera that he is too ashamed at his shoddy progress in becoming a star to phone his family. Wang adds that he would like to go home but is unwilling to unless he has at least ten thousand yuan to show for his labors. Then he launches into a description of the situation he dreams about, one in which his family can read news reports about him and feel proud. At the film's conclusion, however,

Wang Gang's dreams have predictably come to naught. Zhu captures him desperately searching for a job that will help him survive the Beijing winter, then suffering violent illness as the result of his outdoor work as a security guard, and finally recounting narratives of going hungry for days at a time in a dingy basement room he rents for two hundred yuan (about US$25) per month. As he leads the camera-toting Zhu into that rented room, Wang warns him in advance, with visible embarrassment, that it is small. He then points out proudly, in one of the film's most melancholy moments, the small air freshener he has bought to keep the smell of dampness at bay.

In other words, the disturbing effect of the sexual content of *Extras* is at least in part related to the reactions the film elicits in its audience of pity for the main subjects and suspicion that the fact of their being filmed has made them somehow more pitiful. But the sexual content serves another function as well, one that is perhaps more in line with Zhu Chuanming's intentions for the film. The destitution and dissolution of the extras can be read as a rebuke to and subversion of the mainstream cinematic world—represented by the Beijing Film Studio—around whose corners they spend their lives lurking. Thus Zhu asks: "Why did I choose to film this group of people—the extras? Could it be because their professional identity is not unrelated to that of actors, [because of their] awkward position as the story behind, the backside of, the big stars?"[37] Both the lewdness and the misery of the extras make for a sharp contrast with the heroic martial-arts epics and sentiment-infused pop songs that are the backdrop of their lives and the fuel for their absurd dreams.

Zhu frequently shows us the extras watching television, often panning or cutting from their sullen faces to the sensational images (war films, music videos, New Year's variety shows) on the screen. At one point, we see Bao Hehua in her mother's house, singing along to a love song whose video is being shown on television. Zhu then cuts from this shot of her to one of the drab courtyard of the house, which presents a meaningful contrast to the still-audible song. In one of the documentary's rare violations of its strict and unadorned verisimilitude, a long shot of the run-down house where the extras live is immediately followed by a shot of the main gate of the film studio, with the same peppy pop song played over both shots: a meaningful contrast and connection seem to be implied here. In another sequence, Zhu cuts quickly from a shot of Li Wenbo and several other young men watching a music video—one more shining and sanitized exemplar of pop-cultural modernity—to a shot of Li playing a pornographic video. Li then says to Zhu, "Go ahead and record this." That line, coupled with other attempts by the extras to involve Zhu's camera in their bawdy play, points to another effect of the hormones and humiliation rampant in the documentary. In addition to a desublimation of the mainstream popular culture industry, they also represent a similar effect of desublimation directed at the very different cinematic and cultural movement that Zhu Chuanming represents. That is, they represent a violent attack on an underground director's earnest attempt to draw attention to and identify himself with the darker, less privileged, and more exotic sectors of Chinese society.

All in all, *Extras* feels like a disrespectful film, though the currents of disrespect running through it are complicated enough that it is hard to pin down exactly whom the disrespect is originating with and at whom or what it is directed. However, just as Bao Hehua and Wang Gang are the respective centers of the film's filthy and pathetic content, Li Wenbo is the center from which much of its disrespect radiates. He initiates many of the harshest sexual jokes about Bao, he turns on the pornographic film, and he tells Zhu and the camera over a meal that he believes the film industry he once wanted so hard to break into is about nothing more than money and connections. Indeed, the documentary's most direct assaults on that industry come from him, as do most of the moments at which Zhu's camera itself becomes the object of ridicule. Toward the end of the film, Li begins working for a company that claims to be a professional placement agency for aspiring actors. An intertitle at the end of the film informs us that the company has been shut down, and Li has been arrested, for claiming to be working for Feng Xiaogang, China's most prominent director of commercial comedies. All the subversion inherent in the film *Extras*, and in the very existence of these extras themselves, is summed up nicely in that incident: these people encroach upon the glory of a popular culture that is perhaps the most powerful authority in China today. Their devotion to that culture has the counterintuitive effect of detracting from its authority.

The contrast between *Life on the Road* and *Extras* tells a fascinating story about the recent evolution of the independent documentary movement. Wu Wenguang's description of his film is peppered with attacks on artistic establishments, including the avant-garde establishment of which he himself is a member. Yet the vast distance between the subjects of *Life on the Road* and the avant-garde establishment results in a sort of estrangement of the film from those attacks. Wu's attempt to represent the establishment that inspires these amateur artists—that is, Chinese popular culture—is foiled by the director's own ambivalence about and lack of familiarity with it. Yet pop culture's omnipresence in the film leaves the viewer feeling as if it, and not the performers, is the film's true yet absent subject, left unapproachable, mysterious, and unconfronted at the film's end. The same three major foci—the amateur artists, the popular establishment, and avant-garde practice—are present in *Extras*, but in this film the three are integrated into a more complete triangle. The sexuality and suffering of the amateurs serve as an effective critique of the popular establishment, and at the same time, on a less obvious level, they assault the dignity of avant-garde practice. This assault may be partially responsible for the criticism leveled at the film.

For observers like Jia Zhangke, Wu Wenguang, and Lü Xinyu, all of whom bemoan in their own ways the prospect of the Chinese avant-garde and underground film community crystallizing into a community exclusive both in its membership and in the range of its vision, Zhu Chuanming ought to represent a beacon of hope. As mentioned above, he migrated into the BFA and Beijing's independent documentary community from a working-class background. Both of his two films to date—*Extras* and his earlier piece, *Beijing Cotton-Fluffing Artisan* (1999), on which he collaborated with Du Haibin—have focused on lower-class subjects. He decries the "hegemonic position" that documentary directors might be tempted to assume and, in language echoing Jia Zhangke's, he has declared that what he gained through his education at the BFA was "the *right* to make films."[38] Unlike the work of Wu Wenguang, Zhu's documentary about outsiders to the film world qualifies as outsider art in its own right.

It is therefore wildly ironic that *Extras*, which thanks to all these factors ought to be a perfect exemplar of the kind of "democratic" filmmaking that the discussion of amateurism is calling for, comes across as a "fascist" film. The packaging of the VCD version features the following statement, presumably by way of advertisement: "Even while audiences praised the picture, they thought it 'raped its subjects.'" The efforts of an undeniable "artist" like Wu Wenguang to out-subvert a once-but-no-longer subversive avant-garde seem intuitively doomed to simple failure. But the efforts of a relative outsider like Zhu Chuanming to accomplish the same thing seem to have succeeded, albeit in a perverse way. The moral charges that Wu levels against his peers are not nearly as effective at discrediting them as is Zhu's own (perhaps willful, perhaps accidental) embodiment of the worst ethical violations one might accuse the underground documentary movement of committing. Moreover, Zhu's film contains direct rebukes, in the indomitable form of vulgar comments, to underground cinema *as a practice*, rebukes that originate with lower-class outsiders—exactly the sort of thing Wu Wenguang might have wanted to achieve through gentler means.

At the same time, though, Zhu's film arguably does a decent job of reviving and strengthening the genre of the independent documentary *as a product*. The controversy stirred up by the film, and rumors of bawdy or voyeuristic content, almost certainly helped increase its viewership, and its small-scale VCD distribution in China allows it to reach a wider audience than many more canonical works in that genre, most of Wu Wenguang's works included.[39] Perhaps most telling of all, the discussion generated by *Extras* has revolved around documentary ethics, around the question of what the privilege that Zhu describes as "the right to make films" should carry with it in the way of responsibilities. All in all, the hypothesis espoused above by Wu, Jia, and Lü and intimately tied to what I call the *amateur* spirit, the hypothesis that the Chinese cinematic underground can survive as such only by taking cues from outsiders and by understanding filmmaking in terms of rights and power, perhaps garners some proof in its favor from the phenomenon that is *Extras*. What the framers of that hypothesis might not have imagined, however, are the levels of violence, disturbance, and irony that the advent of the amateur spirit might have to entail.

THE TRUEST DV ARTIST

I began with a discussion of the Chinese underground film movement's treatment of the idea of amateur art. Zheng Dasheng's *DV China* is at once more and less appropriate as a case study on this issue than the other two films: more appropriate because it actually deals with the practice of truly amateur filmmaking, less appropriate because it does not exactly qualify as an "underground" film where production and distribution are concerned and because stylistically it has little in common with the vast majority of Chinese underground documentaries. If sheer credentials can divide professionals from amateurs, Zheng Dasheng is by far the most "professional" of the three directors discussed. He studied theatrical directing at the Shanghai Academy of Drama, did graduate work in film production at the Art Institute of Chicago, and is currently employed as a director with the Shanghai Film Studio. *DV China* is an "aboveground" production, financed in part by the China Film Group.[40] It has not been distributed on DVD but has instead followed the route of the vast majority of traditional (nonunderground) Chinese documentaries and gone straight to television; the film aired on the Chinese Central Television (CCTV) network's movie channel in late 2003 and early 2004. Still, *DV China* has been placed on the rosters of recent Chinese documentaries of interest to audiences who seek works outside the mainstream. A recent exhibition in France of "independent Chinese documentaries" included *DV China*, and a March 2003 documentary festival organized in Beijing by the independent-minded Fanhall Studio likewise included *DV China*, alongside the works of staple underground documentarians like Ying Weiwei, Pan Jianlin, and Zhu Chuanming.[41]

In reality, *DV China* is just one of multiple recent phenomena that emphasize the flexibility and haziness of the borders between underground and nonunderground documentary filmmaking. The symbiotic and relatively harmonious relationship between the worlds of independent, unofficial documentarians and the official field of television documentary has been noted by multiple scholars, as has the role of mainstream institutions like the newspaper *Southern Weekend* in supporting filmmaking that bypasses traditional channels (see Matthew Johnson's chapter).[42] *DV China*'s dual identity—aboveground yet "independent"—is described well by its two titles, English and Chinese.

Digital video has constituted a powerful rallying cry for recent Chinese underground filmmakers, and one expects a film called *DV China* to exemplify that movement's values in at least some measure. But the Chinese title, and the one with which the film was identified when it was shown on CCTV, is *A Peasant's Career as a Director* (Yige nongmin de daoyan shengya). This title is evocative less of millennial urban fashion than of other chapters from recent Chinese history, of ideological imperatives that demand, and do not merely encourage, the expansion of the realm of art to include people who have been excluded from that realm.

I have suggested before that the theme of amateurism was an excellent lens through which to view underground film because of the fact that a concern with amateurism represents that movement's relatively unique contribution to contemporary Chinese cultural discourse. The phenomenon of *DV China*, however, points to a potential and surprising antecedent for that concern: the Communist Party cultural policy. As it turns out, the main subject of *DV China* is, like its director Zheng, an employee of the party-state apparatus. Zhou Yuanqiang is the head of the party-run cultural center in a village near Jingdezhen, in Jiangxi province. Fiercely dedicated to his job, Zhou sought to cultivate villagers' interest in "culture" through a variety of methods. As television began to saturate their daily lives, he obtained a home-use video camera and began shooting major events in the villagers' lives for broadcast on local television. Then, in 1993, he began writing, producing, and directing homemade versions of television serials, casting villagers in all roles and distributing the finished product on VCD for noncommercial local viewings.

In early 2002, when Zheng Dasheng arrived to film him, Zhou Yuanqiang had already been the focus of some national media attention. Until then, Zhou's works had consisted mostly of war serials, loaded down with references to the glory of martyrdom for the party, with story lines drawn from the actual experiences of local people during the War of Resistance against Japan and the civil war against the Nationalists. In 2002, though, Zheng arrived just in time to capture Zhou's first stab at making a martial-arts serial. While Huang Feihong films starring Jet Li make an appearance in *DV China*, the overwhelming majority of its references is to a popular culture more readily associated with party-approved "main melody" entertainment than with the chaotic collection of market-oriented errata that was the inspiration of the characters in *Life on the Road* and *Extras*. If Zhou's subject matter is a bit archaic, his technical basis is, from the standpoint of the digital-age viewer, possibly even more so. He has used the same camera—a Sony Hi8 video recorder—since 1993, which in fact complicates somewhat his titular designation as a DV practitioner and reminds the viewer that certain activities that the mythology of digital video occasionally touts as newly possible are actually a bit older than the era of DV.

In addition to differing from the other two films I discuss in its level of official legitimacy and in the sociohistorical "sites" it references,[43] *DV China* is also a very different kind of film where style is concerned. All three documentaries were shot on digital video; but while the first two strove for a hypertrophied version of *cinéma vérité* style, *DV China* relies on a less philosophically consistent bag of tricks to get its message across. In both *Life on the Road* and *Extras*, long takes are the norm. Characters generally deliver monologues in medias res, while engaged in life activities in which they would presumably be engaged even if the documentarian's camera were not rolling. Most importantly, the documentarian's camera never violates the strictest rules of realism. But in *DV China*, Zheng relies heavily on rapid takes and montage. He makes use of carefully staged, "talking-head" interviews, accompanies many scenes with nondiegetic music, and frequently inserts curt intertitles, generally conveying no new information but simply naming what a coming segment of the film is about. Several sequences in the film use montage to create the illusion of a "god's-eye view" for the camera; for example, in a scene in which major characters are rowing a boat down a river, Zheng cuts from a shot taken from within the boat to one taken from the distant riverbank and then cuts back again.

Zheng's stylistic strategy is thus surprising and ironic for the film that has been presumptuous enough to claim the title *DV China*. *Life on the Road*, and *Extras* in particular, are far more representative of the style of flagrant technical modesty that has dominated Chinese DV work, be it the documentaries of Du Haibin, Jia Zhangke, and Wang Bing, or experimental semifiction films by directors like Cui Zi'en and Andrew Cheng. The overwhelming dominance of this self-effacing style looks especially prominent in the face of an exception like *DV China* and is in all likelihood related to the polemic of amateurism that has surrounded the use of digital video in China from the very beginning. Because DV obviates the need for a certain amount of funding (associated with institutions) and a certain degree of technical know-how (associated with education), it is readily equated with movements and sentiments that might prefer to eliminate the influence of institutions and education in the film world altogether. But *DV China*'s blatant disregard of the equation of DV works with technical simplicity and hyperrealism, coupled with the film's apparent ability to "pass" as an independent work at exhibitions and the like, points to a potential problematization of that equation, with uncertain implications for the underground that has put so much stock in it. But perhaps the most threatening aspect of *DV China* comes from the fact that the film both uses cinematic technique to create illusions in its rendering of reality *and* is peppered, with a postmodern glibness, with occasional references to the fact that it is a film. A member of Zheng's crew is at one point called out from behind Zheng's camera to help with a scene that Zhou Yuanqiang is shooting, and the final scene takes place against the backdrop of Zheng and an assistant editing footage from *DV China*, footage the audience saw in the guise of recorded reality not so long ago.

The action of *DV China* is oriented around Zhou Yuanqiang's attempts to produce his first martial-arts picture. Along the way, the audience absorbs details of his life story and learns a great deal about the process by which he succeeds in getting his serials made, from his appeals to bureaucratic "investors" for financial assistance to his primitive editing technique (two VCRs) and his creative methods for achieving special effects (for example, a hypodermic needle full of red liquid squirted at an actor makes "blood" appear on the cue of simulated gunshots). Occasionally Zheng highlights Zhou's influences by cutting between Zhou's works and the professional productions (Lin Nong's *Daughter of the Party* [1958], the Huang Feihong pictures) that serve as his models. As the documentary progresses, interviews with those who know Zhou, and pointed cuts between shots of him at work and shots of the villagers who are his collaborators, emphasize the intensity of his obsession with his creative work. In particular, the contrast between Zhou's solemnity in approaching tasks like figuring out how to make it appear as if an actor in martial-arts dress is leaping over a seven-foot high wall, and his collaborators' relatively relaxed and enjoyment-oriented attitude toward the enterprise, divides the film's interest in amateurism into several layers. On the one hand, Zhou is an amateur filmmaker; on the other hand, the relationship between him and his actor-collaborators is representative of two visibly different approaches to the production of creative works, perhaps corresponding to the difference between professionalism and amateurism. The documentary subtly drives home the point that Zhou is not the only amateur artist in his hometown by including lengthy scenes of villagers singing folk songs and practicing traditional operatic dance steps. Gradually, the audience begins to wonder who the true "amateur" spirit belongs to: the martinet-like Zhou or his more casually creative constituents. The potential complexity of the concept of amateurism is thereby highlighted.

Commentary on the documentary by both Zheng Dasheng and viewers is flavored with the same kind of value system—art belongs to all—that was professed by Jia Zhangke in his essay and by Wu Wenguang in his mission statement for *Life on the Road*. In an interview, Zheng Dasheng compares himself to Zhou Yuanqiang ("we are both filmmakers; one's professional status doesn't matter, nor does the kind of equipment one uses . . . all that matters is that a person begins to engage with images, that he has begun to engage in self-conscious creative activity") and declares that Zhou's work, and not that of young, urban, independent directors, represents the true "sprouting of a DV era."[44] According to Zheng, Zhou is also as much a relic, a "fossil," as he is the harbinger of a new era. His methods force film practitioners to reflect on the origins of filmmaking, on the primitivity of technique to which the process may, with imagination, be reduced.[45] One online commentator takes the obvious step of placing the middle-aged, rural, state-sponsored Zhou alongside the more familiar world of Chinese "amateur" film practitioners and hints that the goals typically ascribed to the latter are better fulfilled by Zhou:

> Right now, given the paucity of film funding, it will be difficult to ensure Chinese film output and to satisfy audience needs. Thus, a group of cutting-edge young directors is taking advantage of low budgets and making fiction films with realist topics. Now compare them with Zhou: putting aside the question of what the advantage of low budgets really is, isn't it clear that none of them can out-low-budget him?[46]

The same author then goes on to explain that he has invited Zhou to show his works at a festival of DV television production in Beijing. It seems, then, that *DV China* has helped in some degree to further the mandate mentioned above: opening the eyes of the professional world to sites beyond its own borders.

All in all, *DV China* offers a curious response to underground filmmakers' recent calls to action regarding how "art" should be circumscribed, conceptually and sociologically. Voices from the independent film movement have been pleading the cause of amateurs dabbling in artistic activity in the undeniably professional forum of art-film producers and audiences that overlaps broadly with the independent documentary community in China today. None of the documentaries discussed here as potential answers to that plea functions as a dutiful and unambivalent advocate for the union of underground and amateur. *DV China* is perhaps the richest and most laudatory portrait of amateur art among the three, but it performs the curious trick of dissolving the concept of an amateur underground in much the same way as underground voices may have hoped to dissolve the concept and reality of professional art. It does not look like a Chinese underground documentary and yet it has in several venues been allowed to pass for one. Like the early fifth-generation films, the works of Zhou Yuanqiang, whose job exists only because of the party's mandate to involve itself in cultural life, are supported at least in part by state money and institutions; yet Zhou ends up being painted as the ultimate independent artist. The budgets that finance this state employee's film projects are glaringly low even in comparison to the budgets of underground filmmakers, and this fact serves to remind viewers that state and other institutions, typical straw men of first resort for movements that seek to break down boundaries, can in fact be incredibly diverse and fragmented themselves. The consequent deconstruction of a unified concept of the "aboveground" must send a few tremors through the self-image of any underground that defines itself in opposition to it.

CONCLUSION: SELF, OTHER, AND THE BURDEN OF ART

The earliest Chinese underground films were about artists: freelancers in Wu Wenguang's *Bumming in Beijing*, musicians in Zhang Yuan's *Beijing Bastards*, painters in Wang Xiaoshuai's *The Days*. Perhaps this fact is related to the underground's more recent interest in amateur art, and perhaps this observation can shed light upon the precise role and meaning of Chinese underground cinema in its broader context.

Recent critical narratives about the rise of the underground sixth generation tend to stress the "personal" aspect that one cannot help detecting in films made by young artists about young artists; some observers have described this personal aspect as "narcissism."[47] At the same time, intimations that these films as aesthetic objects never quite deserved the attention that was lavished upon them, and that the real object of foreign and scholarly interest in them was always the historical and political factors surrounding the directors and their "bankable dissent" against authority, only support the statement that the most important focus of early Chinese underground cinema was the *selves* of the filmmakers. Another commonplace observation about the Chinese underground is that its films are concerned with the "lives of the marginalized."[48] The first and best-known Chinese underground films can fairly be described as portraits of self as marginalized. In all the exemplary cases named above, the portrait of self is also a portrait of self *as artist*, an identity that seems to encompass more than (and may have little to do with) the actual production of artistic works.

So, Chinese underground film has been about artists from the very beginning. The shift described at the beginning of this chapter—Jia Zhangke's disparaging remarks about his predecessors, a shift in subject matter from urban artistic types to working-class folk—has inserted a self-conscious discourse of "amateurism" into the fray but does not actually seem to have altered that emphasis. Amateurs, after all, are still people whose lives are bound up with artistic practice. But that shift does appear to have opened a chasm between these filmmakers' conceptions of self and their conceptions of artists. In these later films an obsession with *the Other*—with impoverished people speaking in exotic dialects and living at the mercy of socioeconomic forces—has led to what I see as the heart of this discourse of amateurism: an attempt to lodge the aura of art in the Other, and to redefine the self in so doing.

In both *Life on the Road* and *Extras*, the "self" in question is less an individual filmmaker than it is underground cinema in general—and art and artists in general. The attempt just described, therefore, is rather a desperate one in these films. Wu Wenguang's attempt to name the performers in *Life on the Road* as the more deserving heirs of the artists portrayed in *Bumming in Beijing*—to name these Others as a new and improved self—falters because the confusing question of *what art is* vanishes underneath the weight of his ambitions. Zhu Chuanming's film casts a pall of violence and exploitation over the relationships between art and Other, and between self and Other. While this allows the film to function very well as a dutiful postmodern self-critique, it also threatens all of the elements in the equation with imminent destruction. Finally, Zheng Dasheng's *DV China* does appear at first glance to succeed in achieving the most basic formulation of the task under discussion: allowing the Other to partake of art. But the fraudulence associated with the creative activities of the principals in *Life on the Road* and *Extras* makes a milder reappearance in the background of this film. The filmmaking agent in this film is not really the Chinese underground but is rather a branch of the filmmaking and political establishment that has been remarkably successful at commandeering the language, themes, and aims of the underground. A film interested in amateur artists may generally be expected to break down the boundaries dividing art from non-art, but *DV China* does something a little bit different, by effacing the boundaries between the underground and the "establishment." In so doing, it reiterates the threats of annihilation that have assaulted that movement from multiple corners for years: the state has long said that it has no right to exist, its purported practitioners claim not really to be a part of it, scholars suggest that it does not exist and never has.

In summation, a harrowing dialectic of self and other, professionalism and amateurism, art and non-art, has developed in underground documentaries. This dialectic embodies the sense of difficulty and crisis that has both haunted and vivified Chinese underground film from the beginning. It is also a fine illustration of the *self-consciousness* that animates the cinematic underground and that perhaps constitutes its most valuable contributions to Chinese aesthetic discourse as a whole. As shown in the discussions above, the commentaries generated by underground documentaries extend to multiple corners of Chinese culture. Amateurism, or the impulse to challenge cultural institutions, has been a characteristic of Chinese underground cinema since its inception. More recently, however, it has become something closer to an obsession. And it has gained new interest from the connection, fostered by Jia Zhangke, between amateurism and democracy, through political terminology that turns an orientation toward amateurism from an option into an ethical mandate. In any case, the new emphasis on amateurism, on the impossible ideal of art not made by artists, supports the conclusion that the recent underground's engagement with amateurism is a variation on the straightforward "narcissism" of the first underground films. It is a variation that may properly be called that narcissism's opposite, a variation that in the end ensures—just as well as the narcissism did—that the figure of the artist will remain an important subject—perhaps the only truly important subject—of Chinese underground cinema.

I began this chapter with a reference to the skepticism that surrounds the topic of Chinese underground cinema—questions about the validity of the topic's terminology, doubts about the worthiness of the individual works. This chapter does not seek to overturn that skepticism entirely, but it does seek to mute it by emphasizing the underground movement's broader significance for Chinese artistic discourse and even Chinese society as a whole. My hope is that this chapter has revealed, and helped to uncover some kind of order within, the very real *diversity* of the Chinese underground, and the invigorating conflicts that may well fuel its future evolution. Underground filmmaking, particularly the production of documentaries, remains a lively and viable practice in China today. In spite of (or perhaps because of) the self-consciousness that has continuously characterized underground films, the movement has raised countless questions, concerns, and polemics that have aesthetic, social, and ethical implications for worlds beyond its own.

NOTES

1. Dai Jinhua, "A Scene in the Fog: Reading Sixth Generation Films," in *Cinema and Desire: Feminist Marxism and Cultural Politics in the Work of Dai Jinhua*, ed. Jing Wang and Tani Barlow, 77 (London: Verso, 2002).

2. The first quotation is from Ying Zhu, *Chinese Cinema during the Era of Reform: The Ingenuity of the System* (Westport, Conn.: Praeger, 2003), 166; the second from Geremie R. Barmé, *In the Red: On Contemporary Chinese Culture* (New York: Columbia University Press, 1999), 195.

3. See, for example, an interview in which the new underground director Li Yang, often lumped in casually with the other members of the "sixth generation," denies the validity of the term. See Stephen Teo, "'There is No Sixth Generation!': Director Li Yang on *Blind Shaft* and His Place in Chinese Cinema," *Senses of Cinema* 27 (July–Aug. 2003), www.sensesofcinema.com/contents/03/27/li_yang.html (accessed July 23, 2005).

4. For example, see Wang Xiaoyu, *Zhongguo dianying shigang* [An Outline History of Chinese Cinema] (Shanghai: Shanghai guji chubanshe, 2003), 246–47.

5. Jia's recent film, *The World* (2004), is an aboveground work produced under the auspices of the Shanghai Film Studio.

6. Most of these individuals are documentary or experimental filmmakers. But in recent years a limited number of feature filmmakers with no connection to the BFA have risen to significance as well. These include Li Yu, the female director of the lesbian-themed *Fish and Elephant* (2000), whose background is in television; Li Yang, who made *Blind Shaft* (2002) and who studied briefly at the Beijing Broadcast Institute but completed his education in Germany; and Zhang Yang and Shi Runjiu, two graduates of the Central Academy of Drama whose films have enjoyed widespread domestic and international popularity. Other feature directors of recent years are affili-

ated with the BFA only through its less prestigious graduate or continuing education programs; these include Zhang Ming, Wang Chao, and Liu Hao.

7. See Wu Wenguang, ed., *Xianchang (di yi juan)* [Document: The Present Scene, Vol. 1] (Tianjin: Tianjin shehui kexue chubanshe, 2000), 188.

8. Jia Zhangke, "Yeyu dianying shidai jijiang zaici daolai" [The Age of Amateur Cinema Will Return], first published in *Nanfang zhoumo* in 1999, in *Yige ren de yingxiang: DV wanquan shouce* [All About DV: Works, Making, Creation, Comments], ed. Zhang Xianmin and Zhang Yaxuan, 306–8 (Beijing: Zhongguo qingnian chubanshe, 2003).

9. Jia, "Yeyu dianying shidai jijiang zaici daolai," 308.

10. Jia Zhangke, "Youle VCD he shuma shexiangji yihou" [Now That We Have VCDs and Digital Cameras] in Zhang Xianmin and Zhang Yaxuan, *Yige ren de yingxiang*, 309.

11. Lü Xinyu, *Jilu Zhongguo: dangdai Zhongguo xin jilu yundong* [Documenting China: The New Documentary Movement in Contemporary China] (Beijing: Sanlian shudian, 2003), 1–4.

12. A slightly different perspective on the relationship between Mou Sen and his actors in *The Other Bank* can be found in Charles Leary, "Performing the Documentary, or Making it to the Other Bank," *Senses of Cinema* 27 (July–Aug. 2003), www .sensesofcinema.com/contents/03/27/performing_documentary.html (accessed July 23, 2005).

13. A fairly representative such use of these terms comes from Zhang Xianmin and Zhang Yaxuan, both BFA professors and prominent experts on underground film. They write that the term "DV doesn't just refer to all form of digital visual recording; instead, it refers mainly to a form of visual recording that is semi-professional." They prefer the term "semi-professional" to "amateur" but use the former in ways largely interchangeable with the latter; the quality of DV films can, in their opinion, "be described as amateur, or, more pleasant to hear, as semi-professional." See Zhang Xianmin and Zhang Yaxuan, *Yige ren de yingxiang*, 1.

14. Another objection that is sure to be raised to my delineation centers around the definition of "art." In at least the first two documentaries I discuss, the activities of the main subjects may strike some readers as something other than "art." To this intuitive reaction, I offer the following rhetorical questions, which hopefully will serve as rebuttals to the train of intuition that creates that reaction: first, if the performers in *Life on the Road* were putting on equally formulaic productions of well-known traditional operas, would there be much doubt about their status as artists? Second, if the main subjects in *Extras* were trying to secure minor roles in plays, wouldn't their status as aspiring artists be similarly secure? And isn't it almost certainly the case that a small role in certain films by director Zhang Yimou would be exactly the sort of thing the extras are dreaming of?

15. See Lü, *Jilu Zhongguo*, 8.

16. When I suggested this translation to Wu Wenguang in a casual conversation on March 9, 2004, he was unconvinced, and his argument was that the English "gypsy" denotes a voluntary wanderer while many of the performers in *Jiang Hu* are kept from their homes against their will.

17. Wu Wenguang, *Xianchang (di yi juan)*, 186.

18. In his chapter in this volume, Matthew Johnson emphasizes the relative professionalism of Wu Wenguang's background by focusing on his experience working in
television. Johnson's and my differing emphases make sense when one remembers
that he is identifying Wu as an insider to the world of Chinese documentary filmmaking in the early 1990s, a world populated by fairly anonymous television workers,
whereas I am comparing Wu to the mass of international festival–attending *auteurs*
of fiction films.

19. While this sort of lifestyle is common enough in urban China today, in the late
1980s, when the film was shot, it represented a substantial anomaly and all sorts of
untold risks for those who adopted it.

20. Lü, *Jilu Zhongguo*, 8–10.

21. Lü, *Jilu Zhongguo*, 13.

22. Lü, *Jilu Zhongguo*, 11.

23. Lü, *Jilu Zhongguo*, 27.

24. Lü, *Jilu Zhongguo*, 18.

25. Lü, *Jilu Zhongguo*, 20.

26. The other six were Tian Zhuangzhuang, Zhang Yuan, Wang Xiaoshuai, He
Jianjun, Ning Dai, and Wang Guangli.

27. My hypothesis that Wu is looking upon these performers as potential channels
for a new, substitute self-portrait is also presented in Bérénice Reynaud's remark:
"Even though Wu depicts a counter-society further away from him than the marginalized artists of *Bumming in Beijing*, certain identification continues to take place"; see
Reynaud, "Dancing with Myself, Drifting with My Camera: The Emotional Vagabonds of China's New Documentary," *Senses of Cinema* 28 (Sept.–Oct. 2003), www
.senseofcinema.com/contents/03/28/chinas_new_documentary.html (accessed July 23,
2005).

28. Lü, *Jilu Zhongguo*, 12.

29. One former cook named Zhao Xin, for example, describes loving music from
childhood, having at one point been willing to sing for a performance troupe in his
spare time for no pay, and suffering penury and hunger in his attempts to find employment with a troupe. Another, Xue Long, also harbored dreams of being a singer and,
before joining the troupe, attempted suicide when he failed to test into a school that
prepares young people to be members of official performance art organizations. See
Wu, *Xianchang (di yi juan)*, 253–56, 264.

30. Lü, *Jilu Zhongguo*, 26.

31. Many of the sixth-generation directors, like Zhang Yuan, Wang Xiaoshuai,
and Lou Ye, came from "college-preparatory" backgrounds and grew up in artistic
or intellectual families in large cities. Even Wu Wenguang was enough of a member
of the higher social stratum to be classified as an "educated youth" during the Cultural Revolution. For biographies of sixth-generation directors, see Cheng Qingsong
and Huang Ou, *Wode sheyingji bu sahuang: xianfeng dianying ren dang'an—shengyu
1961–1970* [My Camera Doesn't Lie: Documents on Avant-garde Filmmakers Born
between 1961 and 1970] (Beijing: Zhongguo youyi chuban gongsi, 2002).

32. See Zhu Chuanming, "Zhu Chuanming zishu: naxie wo yuanyi zhushi de ren: guanyu wo de liangbu jilupian" [Zhu Chuanming in His Own Words: The People I Am Willing to Pay Attention to: My Two Documentaries], *PC Online*, April 28, 2003, http://arch.pconline.com.cn/digital/textlib/other/buy/10304/156657.html   (accessed July 23, 2005).

33. Xia Dongmei and Du Yongli, "'Xu . . . xu . . .' Yong xusheng wei xiaoyuan DV guzhang" [Cheering for College DV with Boos and Hisses], *PC Online*, May 6, 2003.

34. See the appendix to Zhu Chuanming, "Zhu Chuanming zishu."

35. Zhu Chuanming, "Zhu Chuanming zishu."

36. "DV, li dianying you duoyuan" [DV, How Far Away from Film?], *Xinmin Zhoukan*, Nov. 20, 2001, www.kpworld.com/xb/news/pn48013.html.

37. Zhu Chuanming, "Zhu Chuanming zishu."

38. Zhu Chuanming, "Zhu Chuanming zishu."

39. As of the time of writing, video stores in China offered only a few domestic documentaries on DVD or VCD: *Extras*, Wu's *Bumming in Beijing*, and Yang Tianyi's *Old Men* (1999). Also available in homemade VCD copies were Du Haibin's *Along the Railroad* (2000), Ju Anqi's *There's a Strong Wind in Beijing* (2000), and Hu Shu's *Leave Me Alone* (2001).

40. Li Bin, "Yingxiang yu zhenxiang: jilupian *DV China* daoyan Zheng Dasheng fangtan" [Image and Reality: An Interview with Zheng Dasheng, Director of the Documentary *DV China*], *Beijing dianying xueyuan xuebao*, 2002, no. 6:67.

41. The French exhibition in question was "Brut de Chinese: documentaires independants Chinois," held in Paris in September of 2003. More information about the Fanhall festival can be found at http://ent.tom.com/Archive/1002/1011/2003/3/27-22714.html.

42. Both of these phenomena are mentioned in Zheng Wei, "Jilu yu biaoshu: Zhongguo dalu 1990 niandai yilai de duli jilupian" [Documentation and Expression: Mainland Chinese Independent Documentary since 1990], *Dushu*, 2003, no. 10:82, 86. In September 2001, *Southern Weekend* teamed up with an experimental Beijing film group to present an exhibition of independent documentaries that included *Extras* (see Yingjin Zhang's chapter).

43. I use the term "site" here following Yingjin Zhang's call for "site-oriented investigations" of Chinese cinematic works, understanding Zhang's use of the term as referring to something along the lines of a generic, historical, economic, or technological milieu conceived of in spatial terms; see Yingjin Zhang, *Screening China: Critical Interventions, Cinematic Reconfigurations, and the Transnational Imaginary in Contemporary Chinese Cinema* (Ann Arbor: Center for Chinese Studies, University of Michigan, 2002), 40.

44. Li Bin, "Yingxiang yu zhenxiang," 67, 71, 68.

45. Li Bin, "Yingxiang yu zhenxiang," 69.

46. "Bieren yanzhong de Zhou Yuanqiang" [Zhou Yuanqiang in other people's views], *Our DV*, March 8, 2004, www.tosin163.com/xinwen/html/dv_r%5C2004-3-8/200438213634.shtml.

47. Ying Zhu writes that early sixth-generation films "offered mostly personal accounts of [the filmmakers'] adolescent experiences"; see her *Chinese Cinema during the Era of Reform*, 166. The term "narcissism" is used in Dai Jinhua, "A Scene in the Fog," 95.

48. Sheila Cornelius, with Ian Haydn Smith, *New Chinese Cinema: Challenging Representations* (London: Wallflower, 2002), 111. I have frequently found this observation less than enlightening because of its failure to take into account the difference between subjects who exist at the *margins* of society because they represent a social *minority*—the protagonists of *Beijing Bastards* or *Bumming in Beijing*—and subjects who, from a Western perspective, live socioeconomically *marginalized* lives but actually represent a *majority* of their society—for example, the protagonists of Jia Zhangke's films.

5

Independently Chinese: Duan Jinchuan, Jiang Yue, and Chinese Documentary

Chris Berry

> Why was it always "underground" and "independent" back then? Because we had no opportunities.
>
> —Jiang Yue

This chapter asks what it means to be an independent filmmaker in the People's Republic of China by examining the careers of Chinese documentary filmmakers Duan Jinchuan and Jiang Yue, as well as their colleagues and peers Li Hong and Wu Wenguang. All have been active independent documentarians for over a decade, making it possible to trace changes in independent practice through their careers. Despite Jiang's seemingly dismissive remark, he and Duan still consider themselves to be independents. But what that means for them has clearly changed. The Soviet model of independence as dissent was frequently invoked in the early days of Chinese independent film culture, although not, I must emphasize, by documentarians like Duan and Jiang. Today, the American experience of corporate independence is also in the air. In this essay, I acknowledge that both are relevant to the Chinese context, but note that neither of them fits exactly. Rather, Chinese documentarians define themselves in relation to a three-legged system, composed of the party-state apparatus, the marketized economy, and the foreign media and art organizations that have built up a presence in China today. Furthermore, both the American and Soviet models are also conceptually inadequate. They are grounded in an understanding of independence as freedom from power rather than something produced through power. Only by beginning from this different understanding of power can we hope to grasp the qualities of Chinese independent film production today, where Jiang and Duan's experience indicates that contrary to commonsense assumptions, working with state institutions, large corporations, and foreign organizations may help to sustain independence rather than compromise it.

Duan Jinchuan rose to prominence in the 1990s. Together with independent feature filmmaker Zhang Yuan, he directed a celluloid documentary in the Direct Cinema mode about Tiananmen Square called *The Square* (1994). In 1997, one of the films in his "Tibetan trilogy," *No. 16 South Barkhor Street*, became the first Chinese film to win the Grand Prix at the Paris Cinéma du Réel documentary film festival. Duan's future colleague Jiang Yue made a remarkable documentary called *The Other Bank* (1995), which focused on an experimental theater event directed by one of the artists featured in Wu Wenguang's film, *Bumming in Beijing* (1990). This 1990 *cinéma vérité*–style documentary about alienated artists living on the outskirts of the capital had already won Wu international attention. And their friend Li Hong debuted with a film about Beijing maids up from Anhui province called *Out of Phoenix Bridge* (1997), which went on to be broadcast by the BBC and distributed in the United States by Women Make Movies. All these documentaries were made independently in the observational mode.[1] All the documentary makers have known each other since the early 1990s, when they began their independent careers outside their television station jobs.

What does it mean to say these documentaries were made "independently?" Chuck Kleinhans offers this insight into the nature of "independence" in the context of an essay on recent American independent film: "'Independent,' then, has to be understood as a relational term—independent in relation to the dominant system—rather than taken as indicating a practice that is totally free-standing and autonomous."[2] He draws our attention to two factors. First, what is the "dominant system" that independent filmmakers in a cinematic culture use to define themselves? For Chinese independents, it is clear that the dominant system is not the same as for American independents. As will be detailed below, the early careers of established Chinese independents like Duan Jinchuan confirm that the state system was dominant in China. But, contrary to the assumptions of many foreign commentators and journalists, they also demonstrate that independent filmmaking in China has never been a Soviet-style dissent culture. Furthermore, in recent years, marketization and globalization have both complicated the picture of the dominant system for Chinese filmmakers, creating a triumvirate of larger forces for them to negotiate: the state, corporations, and foreign sources of funding and exhibition opportunities. The American experience of independence is becoming ever more relevant to understanding the Chinese context, but it is still far from an exact match.

Second, when Kleinhans comments that this relational approach to independence is contrary to the usual understanding of it as "autonomous" and "free-standing," he raises the question of how we should understand independence itself. Kleinhans implies that in defining oneself against something, one is also simultaneously caught up with it and shaped by it, even if only in a resistant sense. Despite all the rhetoric of standing alone (*duli*), it may be more than just a play on words to note that "independence" is also "in dependence." Extending this insight, a Foucauldian approach to power as productive enables us to see how contemporary practices of independent Chinese filmmaking are not achieved solely in a negative mode—freedom from something else—but also in a positive mode as enabled and shaped by the changing power dynamics operating in the People's Republic.[3]

It is important to grasp this different approach to independence from the outset because it changes even our understanding of a resistant subculture such as Soviet-style dissent culture. At first glance, dissent culture seems to be a clear case whose existence is produced as a kind of autonomy or freedom from power. But even Soviet dissent culture was within rather than outside the overall power system operated by the state. It was shaped by its necessarily clandestine operations that poached upon the state monopolies and depended upon silent cooperation amongst dissenters: it used state equipment such as mimeographs to produce samizdat publications and depended upon anonymous and untraceable modes of distribution such as hand copying and person-to-person transmission. Furthermore, it also depended conceptually on knowledge of another cultural mode than the following of the party-state's directives that was the norm in the Soviet Union. Even though our own knowledge of the operations of corporate power may complicate what we think goes on in "the West," the belief that an individual writer or artist could initiate and control the content of a project formed a very important enabling concept for dissent culture.[4]

In the United States, the "dominant system" Kleinhans writes about has always taken the form of large corporate capitalism known as Hollywood. Historically, the state system has been dominant in the People's Republic, as it was in the former Soviet Union. To this day, an independent Chinese film is generally understood to be one that was initiated and controlled by the filmmaker her- or himself and not made within "the system" (*tizhi*). In other words, it is not part of the approved internal annual production schedule of either a state-owned film studio or television station. Indeed, when they began their independent careers at the beginning of the 1990s, the state was the sole force that Chinese filmmakers had to define their independence in relation to. Like many other independent documentary makers, Duan, Jiang, and Wu all began their careers in state-owned and run television. Duan graduated from the Beijing Broadcast Institute in 1984 and went to work for Lhasa Television in Tibet.

"Lots of people thought I must be a very dedicated comrade, but actually it wasn't quite like that!" Duan laughed when I asked him in a 1997 interview why he chose Tibet. "There were a number of Tibetans amongst my classmates, as well as some Chinese who had been working there. We were good friends and they were always telling me stories about how unique Tibet was, so I thought it would be fun to go."

The years 1983 and 1984 were also the height of a fashion among Chinese arts graduates for dropping out and going to Tibet.[5] "As I remember 1984, in places like Beijing life was still on a pretty tight leash, but we knew that Tibet was a very free place at that time," Duan continued. "And when I got there, I felt that it really was the freest place in China then. In fact, I had the idea of making a film called *Barkhor Street* as early as 1987. Back then, I planned a film that would give some of the history of the place, as well as the Tibetan rites that are held there." Barkhor Street is a central ring road in the shape of an octagon in Tibet where pilgrims come to circumambulate. Number 16 is the location of the local government offices and also the local police station. "For example," Duan continued, "when a girl has her first period, she comes to Barkhor Street for a ceremony, and so on. But we never finished that film because the situation changed in 1987 and 1988 and Barkhor Street became the very center of the independence activities. We couldn't shoot there and we had to give it up."

It is not only in this autobiographical narrative that Duan sets up the state as the force in relation to which he becomes independent. The rhetoric of his work also marks itself out from the typical work associated with the state-run studios. State-produced celluloid and video documentaries, known as *zhuanti pian*, tended to take the form almost of an illustrated lecture with a clear pedagogical aim. In contrast, *No. 16 South Barkhor Street* eschewed narration altogether, abandoning the pedagogical project in favor of pure observation.[6]

If the dominant system in the People's Republic is the state system, does this mean that independent culture in China is like dissent or underground culture in the Soviet Union? Duan's remarks about his early desire to make a film about Barkhor Street and the impossibility of doing so because of political censorship could be interpreted within a "dissent" framework. Indeed, journalists and academics alike often assume that the situation in the People's Republic must be similar to what they believe the former Soviet Union was like. From this perspective, to be independent is not only assumed to be a dangerous and possibly illegal activity, but also defined as a freedom produced by eluding power. In China itself, the term "underground film" (*dixia dianying*) is often used to describe independent filmmaking, and seems to invoke this kind of image.

Furthermore, just like Soviet dissenters, Chinese independent filmmakers often "borrowed" the facilities of the state monopolies to make their work. Li Hong, the director of *Out of Phoenix Bridge*, also worked by herself, but borrowed her equipment from the television station where she continues to work to this day. And just as an image of the West informed dissent culture, so early contacts with foreign television program makers who had come to China were important for China's future independent documentarians. Indeed, Wu, Duan, and others have told me that they first heard about the idea of independent production through such encounters when they were working for Chinese state-owned television stations that were hosting such visitors. Later, when they were invited to attend festivals such as the Yamagata International Documentary Film Festival in Japan, both Duan and Wu saw the observational filmmaking that they appropriated into the Chinese context.

In academic writing, the dissent framework was frequently used from the post-Mao years until about a decade ago in order to understand independent culture in China. For example, in his 1999 book, *In the Red*, Geremie Barmé borrows the term "velvet prison" from Hungarian author Miklós Haraszti's samizdat novel, claiming it as "one of the most insightful, albeit irreverent and often tongue-in-cheek, guides to mainland China's post-1976 'new age' of culture."[7] Barmé also borrows other terms from the discourse of oppositional culture in the former Soviet bloc, such as "dissident" and "dissent," and invokes figures from Stalin to Havel.

The model of Soviet dissent culture certainly can be applied to certain forms of textual production in China. Those who took photographs of the 1976 Tiananmen protests that followed Zhou Enlai's death, those who posted on Democracy Wall in 1978 and 1979, and those who participated in the 1989 Democracy Movement were persecuted by the state and in many cases killed. Even today, there is the case of Liu Di, who was detained for over a year after using the pen name "Stainless Steel Mouse" to write Internet articles critical of the government. This indicates that the Soviet model of independence as dissent culture cannot and must not be dismissed too easily in the Chinese context.[8]

However, few if any underground or independent filmmakers have been actively persecuted or jailed by the state authorities. In these circumstances, many people in and out of China have become skeptical. They see "banned in Beijing" or "underground film" as little more than a marketing tool that helps to sell the films to foreigners.[9] Even the editors of the 1989 volume *Unofficial China*, Perry Link, Richard P. Madsen, and Paul Pickowicz, note in the introduction to their 2002 follow-up, *Popular China*, that, "although Party and government officials still exercise supervision and censorship, the vigorous proliferation of [new media] has greatly loosened state control."[10]

In fact, although they may have benefited from the "banned in Beijing" rhetoric, neither Duan Jinchuan nor any of his colleagues have ever worked in the clandestine manner that would warrant describing their films as "dissent culture" and they themselves do not claim such a status for their work. Whereas the former Soviet Union was more or less isolated and the state attempted to monopolize the right to initiate and control cultural production, independent production in China has coincided with the rise of the market economy and globalization. Both of these elements have played an important role in shaping Chinese independent production.

First, in regard to the films themselves, the "opening up" (*kaifang*) associated with globalization has, as noted, helped the filmmakers to find models to appropriate. Duan's work on Tibet is exemplary here. He took the observational style associated with American Direct Cinema filmmakers such as Fred Wiseman—whose *Central Park* (1989) directly inspired *The Square*—for use in the Chinese context.[11] However, what makes this model appealing is not its power to produce a dissent culture, but rather its ability to produce an independent perspective *without* simultaneously producing something that could easily be construed as dissent. Although these filmmakers may push the envelope in terms of acceptable subject matters and styles, they are also careful to avoid anything that could be seen as oppositional or "counter-revolutionary" (*fan geming*) in the language of the People's Republic. With this mode of documentary, there is no narration or added music, and the filmmaker can always claim to be literally only showing what happened. The meaning of scenes included in the film is very much open to an audience member's interpretation. In *The Square*, for example, Duan and Zhang film state television program makers interviewing children who are visiting the square. They tell them what to do and what to say, eliciting suitably patriotic and revolutionary sentiment from them. Is this just footage of the program makers doing their jobs? Or is it an ironic contrast with the pure observation pursued by Duan and Zhang, exposing the fabricated reality of conventional state-sponsored documentary modes? It is up to you to decide.

However, the choice of this careful technique also shows how the independent documentarians' practice continues to be shaped by and in response to the power of the state. Independence does not only appear because certain filmmakers want control over the making of their own films, but also because the state no longer insists that it will guide and initiate all activities within the borders of the People's Republic. In these circumstances, what it will tolerate shapes the kind of films that the filmmakers can initiate and retain control over, and in the People's Republic the threshold for punitive intervention would be anything that could be considered "counter-revolutionary."

Second, it is by no means clear that video production outside the state-owned system is or has ever been in itself either illegal or forbidden by regulation. In my discussions with Duan, Wu, Jiang, Li, and other independent documentary and feature filmmakers I have spoken to over the last decade, two points have been repeatedly emphasized in relation to China's complex regulatory environment. First, video and celluloid film production, distribution, and exhibition are regulated by separate branches of the ministry now called SARFT (the State Administration for Radio, Film, and Television). This explains, for example, how it is possible that some Chinese films that have not been passed for exhibition in the movie theaters can be legally available as a VCD or DVD on the shelves of every neighborhood store. Second, the main mechanisms of state regulation designed to control both film and video are the various censorship mechanisms within the state film studios, television stations, and ministries. These are concerned with passing films for release or television programs for broadcast. If a film or video maker produces a work independently but does not attempt to release it in the commercial movie theaters or broadcast it on television, then it is not subject to any censorship mechanism. Most of the films described as "banned in Beijing" by foreign journalists have never been near a censor.

This gray area has greatly facilitated the growth of civil society in the People's Republic, which was not encouraged in the former Soviet Union. In the early days, many independent filmmakers took on freelance activities such as making promotional videos or MTV-style music videos to raise funds. They then used these funds to buy their own equipment and support the projects they wanted to make. This is the background to Duan Jinchuan and Zhang Yuan's *The Square*. Civil organizations have also sponsored the independent filmmakers' work in some cases. The primary source of funding for Duan's *No. 16 South Barkhor Street* was an independent group called the Tibetan Culture Communication Company.

Success at festivals overseas, such as Duan's prize at the Cinéma du Réel festival, generated foreign interest in independent Chinese documentaries and some sales outside China. In the case of Li Hong's *Out of Phoenix Bridge*, the international documentary agent Jane Balfour took on international sales for the film and also negotiated for the BBC to send an editor to Beijing to work with Li on a new edit suitable for broadcast.

With developments of these kinds, significant changes have begun to occur within the structure of independent production in China. Well into the 1990s, the state sector was the dominant system in China. As far as filmmaking and video production were concerned, the private sector was limited to small organizations, and overseas possibilities were a rare but vital help they were only too happy to work with. However, with increased marketization and globalization, the "dominant system" for Chinese independents may now be a three-legged one composed of the party-state apparatus, the domestic market economy, and overseas connections. How do these components relate to each other? What can the independent documentary filmmaker do to preserve independence?

Similar questions and a corresponding range of practices have also been found in the United States. As Chuck Kleinhans points out, "Independent production and diffusion . . . was the norm when cinema was starting," simply because there was no dominant player. Once Hollywood was established, a variety of companies established themselves outside the Hollywood studio system. Some of them catered to specialized markets from ethnic communities to taste cultures ranging from varieties of exploitation film to art cinema. Others produced B movies for the major studios.[12]

For some writers, it is not enough to have corporate autonomy alone, as was the case with the first American independent company, United Artists, set up in 1919. "Such independents," writes Jim Hillier, "were neither truly independent—since they relied on the major studios for distribution—nor trying to make films that were significantly different from those of the major studios." Applying this standard to measure independence in the United States, Hillier notes that "the acclaim that greeted Steven Soderbergh's *sex, lies and videotape* at Sundance in 1989 has been taken by many to mark the advent of American independent cinema as a major force in the landscape of US moviemaking. In retrospect, it may represent the assimilation of that cinema."[13]

If we transfer Hillier's approach to the output of Chinese independent filmmakers, similar issues could be raised. In coming "aboveground"—in other words, starting to work with the censorship system and produce films that can be released in the People's Republic—feature filmmakers such as Zhang Yuan and Jia Zhangke have moved toward less "edgy" subjects and styles that can be accommodated more easily both by the censors and the market. Is this assimilation? Are they still "independent," and in what sense? The world of feature films falls outside the scope of this essay, but has been discussed widely elsewhere.[14]

In the documentary sector, Wu Wenguang steadfastly refuses to work with either "the system" in China or overseas corporate players such as the television stations. Instead he maintains a very low-budget production system and shows his films at independent venues, such as cafés, bars, and universities in China, and at film festivals and museums overseas. In this way, he can be said to have taken up the position of the artist, working with the expectations of the art world to maintain his independence. Indeed, he emphasizes that "documentary filmmaking is not my profession—I do not depend on documentary," signaling that this enables him to be truly independent.[15] However, the price for this independence is, of course, limited audiences and limited production resources (see Matthew Johnson's and Valerie Jaffee's chapters).

From the perspective of this artist model of independence, trying to earn a living as a documentary maker and cooperating with television stations overseas and the system in China signifies loss of control over one's work. However, Duan Jinchuan and Jiang Yue have been willing to work with both major overseas organizations like the BBC and Chinese television stations like CCTV (the China Central Television). They do not see this as some sort of backdown or compromise. Indeed, it is in this context that Jiang Yue made his comment, "Why was it always 'underground' and 'independent' back then? Because we had no opportunities." Now that the opportunities to work with both internationally and domestically dominant organizations have opened up, Duan and Jiang have seized them as a way to develop and expand their independent output. If independence is understood as retaining the power to initiate and control the work, how are Duan and Jiang trying to negotiate their way through China's new three-legged dominant system to achieve this?

First, two elements of the new dominant system are in an ever-closer relationship today. Marketization and the party-state system were implacable enemies during the Maoist era and had a tense relationship during the 1980s. But now they are like two sides of the same coin. While the physical plant and equipment of the film studios and television stations remain state-owned, their day-to-day activities are entirely funded and driven by the marketplace. Documentary makers are most likely to come into contact with television stations. Now, only 0.5 percent of CCTV's income still comes from the government, which is less than it pays in tax back to the government.[16] Ratings are provided by ACNeilsen and CVSC Sofres Media Peoplemeters, and television's share of all expenditures on advertising rose in the 1990s from 27.7 percent at the beginning of the decade to 72.9 percent in 1997.[17] Although national CCTV advertising rarely exceeds eleven minutes per hour, local stations such as those in Shanghai can carry as much as eighteen minutes of advertising per hour.[18]

Jiang and Duan explain that the proliferation of television channels in China has created a demand for programming that is difficult to meet with in-house production alone. Since 1998 and particularly in the last two or three years, television stations have been taking more and more independently produced local material. Now they estimate that perhaps 10 percent of documentary programming is independently produced. But, recalling Hillier's discussion, is this kind of independent work still "true" independence?

Jiang and Duan have been eager to produce work for the television stations, and in particular CCTV, with which they have a good relationship. Sometimes they are contracted as individuals, but if the sums of money involved are larger, this is not acceptable anymore. Therefore, together with another documentary filmmaker, Kang Jianing, who is also a retired vice head of the Ningxia Television Station, they have formed a company called China Memo Films. "We wanted to call it the Three Represents," Duan explained wryly. However, the pun on former President Jiang Zemin's so-called theory of the Three Represents did not go down well with the section of the Ministry of Industry and Commerce responsible for registering new companies.

When I interviewed Jiang and Duan in September 2004, they were working on a series about Chinese opera for CCTV. Contrasting the nationally approved Beijing opera form with the more popular but also risqué and disapproved *errenzhuan* form found in northeast China, it consists of twenty-five parts, each thirty minutes long, and is an oral history. The year before they had completed another oral history series on the liberation of various Chinese cities by the Communists in the late 1940s. Both series were initiated by Duan and Jiang—they had the ideas and took them to CCTV. This is what makes them different from commissioned work. The fate of *Liberated* (Jiefang ah!) reveals the negotiated relationship between the independent documentary filmmaker and the television stations, and also demonstrates the complexity of maintaining independence.

"When we finished it, it didn't make it through the censorship process," Duan explained. "They said there was a problem with our stance, but they still wanted to broadcast it because they'd spent the money. It aired at two thirty in the morning, and lots of people were unable to see it. But we really didn't care when they broadcast it. Two thirty in the morning was OK with us. First, we made some money, and the censors are getting more and more relaxed. Second, we shot the footage and so we don't have to worry about that. The people we filmed are in their eighties and nineties." Both Duan and Jiang reiterated that this was particularly important to them as independent filmmakers: by working together with the system, they could get the resources to record material. Even if not all of it proved acceptable to the system, it would be useful for posterity and it would be in their hands rather than inside the system.

As for the overseas organizations, China Memo also contracted with a consortium of foreign television stations including the BBC, TV2 of Denmark, and Arte of France, to make a series. Broadcast under different titles in different countries, it included Duan's own *The Secret of My Success* (2002) about village elections in northeast China, and Jiang's *This Happy Life* (2002), about two men who work at the Zhengzhou railway station and their negotiation of China's marketization process. Both films are still made in the observational mode, although unlike their early work, they include extensive footage of the main subjects talking directly to the camera and in some cases some of the filmmakers' own conversations with their subjects. Jiang explains why they work with both CCTV and the BBC: "I've compared them. It's easier to get the money in China, because there's such a large demand. With the BBC, we can make more individual works, because they don't make demands on you about the contents."

However, while Duan and Jiang are comfortable working with organizations like the BBC, we must note that doing so has its pitfalls. For example, Li Hong also made a film in this series, *Dancing with Myself* (2002), about the people who practice ballroom dancing in Beijing's parks. The film was axed from the series. When I spoke with Li, she explained that the BBC's editors wanted either a social issue film or a film focused on one or two individuals. Her film is about everyday life and has a large number of subjects. Li retained her independence because when she refused to change the film substantially, the BBC tried to do that for her.[19] However, precisely who has control over the

Enjoying the triumph of a village election in Duan Jinchuan's documentary The Secret of My Success *(2002)*

work remained a mystery at the time we spoke, and it was unclear if Li could distribute it herself. Similarly, Wu Wenguang recounted his experiences of helping to judge a Discovery Channel competition for independent documentaries sent in by viewers. He found his judgment constrained by a Discovery Channel aesthetic of drama and fast editing very different from his own.[20] Duan Jinchuan also noted that while foreign audiences are focused on the election story in his film, Chinese audiences are more interested in the personalities, and both he and Jiang acknowledged that foreign television stations are most interested in documentaries from China that can be understood as being about social issues.

In these circumstances, we can conclude that independent filmmaking in China never was a dissent culture, and it is becoming less and less similar to one as marketization and globalization proceed apace. Furthermore, the range of opportunities and options for independent filmmakers is increasing. But, within an understanding of power as productive, this does not mean

A poster of Jiang Yue's documentary This Happy Life *(2002)*

that independent filmmakers are increasingly free from power. Rather, as their experiences with overseas television channels have demonstrated, these opportunities are themselves produced in and conditioned by relations of power. The more active they become and the more opportunities they explore, the more complex are the negotiations and relationships they have to develop with others in the matrix of power in order to remain independently Chinese.

NOTES

This chapter is based partly on interviews conducted with Duan, Jiang, Wu, and other Chinese documentary makers since the mid-1990s. The most recent interviews were conducted together with Lisa Rofel and transcribed by Zhang Mingbo and Zhang Shujuan as part of a research project supported by a grant from the University of California Pacific Rim Research Program. All translations are my own.

1. The observational mode aims at spontaneity and pure observation, without adding narration, music, and so forth. In the American Direct Cinema, it took on a fly-on-the-wall form, whereas the French *cinéma-vérité* form included the filmmaker in the film and often also included interviews. For further discussion see, for example, Brian Winston, *Claiming the Real: The Griersonian Documentary and Its Legitimations* (London: British Film Institute, 1995), 147–52.

2. Chuck Kleinhans, "Independent Features: Hopes and Dreams," in *The New American Cinema*, ed. Jon Lewis, 308 (Durham, N.C.: Duke University Press, 1998).

3. The primary work in which Foucault argues against the "repressive hypothesis" is his *The History of Sexuality, Vol. 1: An Introduction*, trans. Robert Hurley (London: Allen Lane, 1979), 15–49.

4. For a recent discussion of the self-made publication or samizdat, see Serguei Oushakine, "The Terrifying Mimicry of the Samizdat," *Public Culture* 13, no. 2 (2001): 191–214.

5. Among feature filmmakers, Tian Zhuangzhuang represents this tendency best, with his *Horse Thief* (1986), more recently followed up by his documentary *Delamu* (2003). See Yang Ping, "A Director Who is Trying to Change the Audience: A Chat with Young Director Tian Zhuangzhuang," in *Perspectives on Chinese Cinema*, ed. Chris Berry, 127–30 (London: British Film Institute, 1991); and Dru C. Gladney, "Tian Zhuangzhuang, the Fifth Generation, and Minorities Film in China," *Public Culture* 8, no. 1 (1995): 161–75.

6. I have discussed the filmic characteristics of the early documentaries in more detail in "Getting Real: Chinese Documentaries, Chinese Postsocialism" (in *The Urban Generation: Chinese Cinema and Society at the Turn of the Twenty-first Century*, ed. Zhen Zhang [Durham, N.C.: Duke University Press, 2006]). My aim here is to focus more on mode of production than text, and so I will not go into detailed discussion of individual films.

7. Geremie R. Barmé, *In the Red: On Contemporary Chinese Culture* (New York: Columbia University Press, 1999), 7.

8. "Stainless Steel Mouse that Roared," *Wired News*, Dec. 1, 2003, www.wired.com/news/politics/0,1283,61420,00.html?tw=wn_story_related (accessed Feb. 20, 2005).

9. See, for example, Dai Jinhua, "A Scene in the Fog: Reading Sixth Generation Films," in *Cinema and Desire: Feminist Marxism and Cultural Politics in the Work of Dai Jinhua*, ed. Jing Wang and Tani Barlow, 71–98 (London: Verso, 2002). For a less hostile discussion of the phenomenon, see Valerie Jaffee, "Bringing the World to the Nation: Jia Zhangke and the Legitimation of Chinese Underground Film," *Senses of Cinema* no. 32 (July–Sept. 2004), www.sensesofcinema.com/contents/04/32/chinese_underground_film.html#4 (accessed Feb. 21, 2005).

10. Perry Link, Richard P. Madsen, and Paul G. Pickowicz, eds., *Popular China: Unofficial Culture in a Globalizing Society* (Lanham, Md.: Rowman & Littlefield, 2002), 2.

11. For a detailed discussion of the formal features of Wiseman's work, see Bill Nichols, *Ideology and the Image* (Bloomington: Indiana University Press, 1981), 208–236.

12. Kleinhans, "Independent Features," 311–13.

13. Jim Hillier, ed., *American Independent Cinema: A Sight and Sound Reader* (London: British Film Institute, 2001), xiv–xv.

14. See Jaffee, "Bringing the World to the Nation."

15. Interview conducted with Lisa Rofel on Dec. 15, 2003.

16. Li Xiaoping, "Significant Changes in the Chinese Television Industry: An Insider's Perspective," Working Paper of the Center for Northeast Asian Policy Studies, the Brookings Institution, Washington, D.C., August 2001, *Columbia International Affairs Online*, www.ciaonet.org/wps/lix01 (accessed Sept. 10, 2002).

17. *Broadcasting & Cable's TV International* 7, no. 21 (Nov. 1, 1999): 5.

18. Andrew Green, "More Quality, Less Quantity," *China Economic Review* 8, no. 6 (June 1998): 35.

19. Interview conducted with Lisa Rofel on Dec. 15, 2003. For further discussion, see Bérénice Reynaud, "Dancing with Myself, Drifting with My Camera: The Emotional Vagabonds of China's New Documentary," *Senses of Cinema* 28 (Sept.–Oct. 2003), www.senseofcinema.com/contents/03/28/chinas_new_documentary.html (accessed July 23, 2005).

20. Interview conducted with Lisa Rofel on Dec. 15, 2003.

6

Trapped Freedom and Localized Globalism

Tonglin Lu

If we borrow the concept of global empire in Michael Hardt and Anthony Negri's controversial book *Empire* as a point of departure, we can distinguish globalization from modernization at least in one area: the absence of a center of reference.[1] Although many scholars still consider globalization to be an intensified continuation of modernization,[2] the distinction is pertinent if we observe the recent global expansion of capitalism from geopolitical areas outside the traditional center of modernity: the role of the West, for example, in China. Modernization outside the West was often considered tantamount to Westernization, namely, remaking non-Western culture in the image of Europe, which represented progress, rationality, and modernity. Since the May Fourth Movement of 1919, political parties and schools of thought in China have found reference points in the West across a wide ideological spectrum, from nationalism to communism. In this sense, we can say that modernity is measured not only by chronological development from past to present, but also by spatial distance from peripheries to the center. Thus, the modern age has also created the image of Europe as the center of the world, or the center of reference of "universal" values. At the same time, this centralized position corresponded to the age of military conquest of new territories, or the age of colonization, as Enrique Dussel explains.[3]

By contrast, led by multinational corporations and relatively free from the restrictions of national boundaries, globalization has a decentralizing effect as capital flows toward maximum profits. In this context, decentralization does not imply democracy, but merely indicates the absence of a moral center as the ultimate reference. Although such decentralization is designed to benefit the financial power of multinational corporations, the amorphous nature of this power has also gradually freed the collective imaginary in the developing world from the cultural complex created by the myth of modernity, Eurocentrism. As a result, instead of looking for salvation in the implicit or explicit center of ultimate reference, cultural products in the developing world, which are often shaped by globalization, may question the value system of their own production, global capitalism, as in the case of some Chinese independent films.[4]

Sponsored by domestic and multinational private corporations, many Chinese independent films are cultural products of globalization. But instead of praising the new world order, they often question the process that has given birth to their own production and question the value system that has formed the basis of their existence — the capitalist mode of production — by portraying the "localized" lifestyle of an underprivileged urban population.[5] In their documentary or documentary-like portrayals of ordinary Chinese urbanites, they debunk the myth of China as a success story of globalization, a myth disseminated by both the official media in China and the "free press" in the West in order to advance the interests of both the Communist state and multinational corporations. Further, independent films often question the centrality of the West, not in terms of history or tradition, as in the case of earlier fifth-generation predecessors,[6] but in terms of an existential reality. In other words, the opposition to traditional China and the preoccupation with the modern West that have absorbed generations of modern Chinese intellectuals have been deconstructed in independent works. What is left is a gritty Chinese urban reality that belongs to the decentralized global village. In these films, the West has lost its glow either as an implicit model that will provide solutions to Chinese problems or as a powerful enemy before whom the Chinese became powerless victims. Instead, the mythical West of the past has become part of the daily problems of China today — insidiously and insipidly.

Among independent filmmakers, Jia Zhangke, a Beijing Film Academy (BFA) graduate from Fenyang, a small provincial town in Shanxi province, has persistently problematized the process of globalization in his works. In an interview with Luisa Prudentino, Jia asks the following questions:

> The process of globalization is closely related to cultural values. Youngsters in *Unknown Pleasures* have lost faith in their cultural system. At the same time, they live in an information age; they receive more and more information on everything else in the world, except for that on their own lives and on their environments; in short, the information that matters to them the most. In this context, how should one position oneself vis-à-vis economic development? Who truly benefits from the outcome of this development? What should one say about globalization? . . . These questions preoccupy me tremendously.[7]

Since Jia directed *Unknown Pleasures* (2002) with these questions in his mind, we can partly consider this film an inquiry about how the process of globalization has influenced the living conditions of a provincial town. By analyzing his film closely, I would like to consider the following questions:

what does *Unknown Pleasures* mean in its cultural context? In what way is the titular "pleasure" related to globalization? To what extent does this film offer a vision of reality that haunts Jia Zhangke and his fellow independent filmmakers? In fact, they are the first generation of Chinese filmmakers in the era of globalization. Their life experiences are shaped by China's integration into the global market and their films are often sponsored by overseas investors. Not surprisingly, most of their works focus on the effect of globalization. As a vocal spokesman of his generation, Jia provides with *Unknown Pleasures* a test case of the problematic relationship between independent filmmakers and a dominant mode of production that shapes their existence: global capitalism.

XIAO WU, UNKNOWN PLEASURES, DRAMATIZATION, AND REALISM

Zhang Yuan, reputedly the first independent filmmaker in the People's Republic, claims: "I make films because I'm interested in social reality. I don't want to be subjective; my strength is in my objectivity."[8] If the Cultural Revolution played a crucial role in shaping the fifth generation's perception of the world (see Yingjin Zhang's chapter), we can say that two major factors have determined the vision of reality for the new generation of independent filmmakers. First, as students themselves at the end of the 1980s, they were traumatized by the crackdown on the student demonstrations of 1989. Unlike the Cultural Revolution, which has been publicly criticized as a national disaster, open discussion of the Tiananmen Incident still remains a taboo in China. Precisely because it is off limits, the trauma has haunted the collective unconscious even more powerfully. Various forms of violence that dominate underground films can be considered symptoms of this repressed trauma. Second, having grown up with China's rapid integration into the global market, independent filmmakers were initially hopeful of, and later became disillusioned with, the impact of globalization on China. The political crackdown was brutally traumatizing, and globalization has imposed a radical break between them and their parents' generation in terms of working environment, lifestyle, and value system. Rapid economic transformation combined with the ideological vacuum in the post-Mao era has shaken any cultural basis for the formation of a stable community in contemporary China. As a result, individuals must face alone a world turned topsy-turvy by the worship of the material god, money. Further, the generation of independent filmmakers has suffered from the consequences of strict censorship imposed on Chinese cinema after the Tiananmen Incident and the financial restrictions of a declining film market. In other words, they are caught between the political control of a Communist regime and the financial pressure of global capitalism. Skeptical of any idealism, independent filmmakers rarely romanticize harsh reality in their works.

Following this generational logic to the extreme, Jia's hyperrealistic films portray youngsters in provincial towns. As he explains: "In China, the difference between the big cities and small towns, between the coastal area and inner land is shocking. That's why I believe it's useful to show my films in Beijing, to make people aware of realities of small towns."[9] At the age of 27, Jia directed his first feature, *Xiao Wu* (1997), a low-budget underground film that has attracted international attention. Subsequently, Jia directed two other underground films sponsored by multinational corporations: *Platform* (2000) and *Unknown Pleasures*. Recently, because the Chinese government has somewhat eased up on film censorship, Jia directed *The World* (2004), his first film publicly released in China. His goal was to reach a broader audience (see Paul Pickowicz's chapter). Except for *The World*, all Jia's underground features are set in Shanxi, his native province, but investments in his films have mostly come by way of Hong Kong.[10]

According to Chinese critics, Jia Zhangke used a much less realistic approach in *Unknown Pleasures*, and some even consider this film surrealist. For the director, however, this "surrealism" is in fact "realistic" in China today.[11] In order to respond to these critics, Jia explained in an interview:

> I have the impression that a surrealist atmosphere prevails in China today, because the entire society faces an enormous pressure to speed up. As a result, many strange and unimaginable events have occurred in reality. As they say, "reality is more exceptional than fiction." The surrealistic elements sound unbelievable to most of us, but they are part of reality. It is precisely because I tried to catch such an allegedly surrealistic atmosphere that I have decided to direct this film.[12]

Further, Jia believes that the English title accurately captures what the film tries to communicate: "Under this enormous pressure, people are in a state of unknown agitation and unknown excitement. This state results in an irrational attitude. Sadly, because many people do not believe they have any future, they splurge on excessive enjoyment, as if life might end tomorrow. The entire film tries to recreate this atmosphere."[13]

Jia's definition of "realism" apparently differs from that advanced by most critics, a difference partly due to the ambiguity inherent in the Chinese notion of realism. According to socialist conventions, a realist film must be verisimilar and credible, not too distant from commonsense imagination. These conventions still remain implicitly influential among Chinese critics. If Jia uses a different concept of realism to defend *Unknown Pleasures*, his definition is closer to that articulated by André Bazin. Although Bazin measures films in terms of realism, his notion of realism often appears self-contradictory,

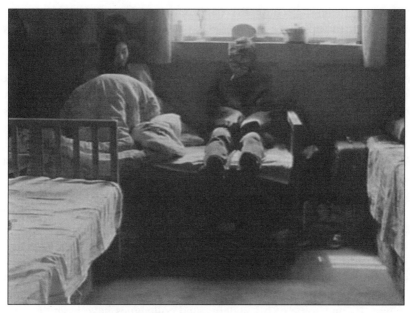

A pickpocket visiting a sick KTV hostess in Jia Zhangke's Xiao Wu *(1997)*

because for him film art is a priori "a lie" (*mensonge*).[14] In order to achieve what Bazin calls realism, or to capture a phenomenological sense of reality, a filmmaker must tirelessly struggle against cinematic illusion by means of formal innovations. On several occasions, Tian Zhuangzhuang has acknowledged Bazin's influence on the fifth generation when they were students. Although reality appears different to Jia Zhangke and his generation, we can still detect similar influences from Bazin in Jia's representation of reality, in particular his resistance to cinematic illusion by rejecting jaded filmic conventions. Bazin's notion of realism might have influenced Jia either directly during his BFA studies or indirectly through exposure to the early works of the fifth generation.[15] Jia justifies his claim to realism by reference to the notion of phenomenological reality, which also links his film to the postwar European modernist cinema.

CENSORSHIP, UNDERGROUND, AND MAINSTREAM

In an April 2004 interview in *Nanfang dushi bao* (Southern Metropolis Daily), Jia expressed his desire "to enter into the mainstream."[16] What does "the mainstream" mean in this context? In China, film was the most carefully censored cultural medium following the crackdown on the student demonstrations of

1989. Nevertheless, because the bankruptcy of Communist ideology has deprived censorship of firm ideological grounds, censors do not have any tangible criteria to follow. Further, even the party line has become ambivalent because it has been vacillating between the influence of global capitalism and the heritage of the centralized state authority. As a result, censors can no longer rely on any political guidance; their main guide is their own political intuition, shaped by the many political movements of the past. Censors are mostly retired officials, and they base their decisions mainly on one factor—whether the film risks undermining the last shreds of their political power upon its release. If anything looks ambiguous, they tend to require filmmakers, especially those younger and less known, to make changes until everything looks crystal clear. This piecemeal censorship has often deterred filmmakers of the younger generation from expressing their artistic visions or even releasing their films publicly in China.

Although Jia's first three films were shown overseas, they are available in China only in semiunderground videos and VCDs. Like several other young filmmakers, Jia chose to bypass censorship during the 1990s for fear of compromising his artistic expression. At the beginning of the twenty-first century, however, Jia and some of his underground colleagues have begun to change their minds—not necessarily because of political changes in China but because of economic changes, although it is true that film censorship has been a bit less severe recently. In other words, he gradually shifted his attention from personal expression to mass reception and commercial success in the vast local market. As he states in an interview, the "dramatization" in *Unknown Pleasures* aims to "reduce the distance between the film and its audience."[17] In this sense, *Unknown Pleasures* can be considered a transitional step from an underground film about personal expression to a publicly released film (like *The World*) that requires various compromises. Jia states, "If I want to reach a wider audience, I have to go through the system"; further, he claims that the official process offered him "respite from the pressure of producing a film entirely on his own."[18]

Even before Jia made *The World*, he may have already reached a broader audience by way of a detour, cleverly inserted as an episode in his *Unknown Pleasures*. Binbin, the protagonist, has become a peddler of pirated VCDs in order to pay back a high-interest debt to Xiao Wu, a small-time criminal who has the same name as the protagonist in Jia's first feature. One day, Xiao Wu comes by to examine how his debtor conducts business and asks Binbin whether he carries *Xiao Wu* and *Platform*. To Binbin's negative answers, Xiao Wu expresses disappointment: "How can you make money without such artsy films?"

This humorous episode contains references to three Xiao Wus: the protagonist in *Xiao Wu*, the film entitled *Xiao Wu*, and a minor character called Xiao

Wu in *Unknown Pleasures*. The first reference points to a petty thief who believes nevertheless in the outmoded value of true friendship. The second reference conveys Xiao Wu's determination to go against the stream, commercial and political, to preserve his artistic integrity. The third reference conjures up a new Xiao Wu who no longer shows sympathy for the first Xiao Wu's idealism and who only wants money, even when it means making occasional death threats. The "progress" made by the two characters named Xiao Wu in Jia's works casts an ironic light on the director's own transformation in an increasingly commercialized society. Even the choice Jia made in the past to preserve artistic integrity has become marketable in the new environment because underground movies are considered "fashionable" and thus profitable. Censorship has inadvertently brought both money and audience in this case, however limited. Like Xiao Wu in *Unknown Pleasures*, Jia has gone to the mainstream to cope with the reality of the consumer society and the market economy.

It appears as if financial incentives have succeeded where political coercion may have failed, for several directors of Jia's generation have likewise decided to emerge from the underground.[19] In the process of globalization, China has become a frenzied mixture of Communist ideology and global capitalism, and it is global capitalism that seems to work best for the Communist state. Ellen Meiksins Wood describes the nature of capitalist power when it is separated from political coercion:

> One of the most important consequences of this detachment of economic power from direct coercion is that the economic hegemony of capital can extend far beyond the limits of direct political domination. Capitalism is distinctive among all social forms precisely in its capacity to extend its dominion by purely economic means. In fact, capital's drive for relentless self-expansion depends on this unique capacity, which applies not only to class relations between capital and labor but also to relations between imperial and subordinate states.[20]

By absorbing the investments of global capitalism, the Chinese government has also quietly absorbed the capitalist value system. This absorption is mutually beneficial because it has not only allowed the smoother integration of investments from multinational corporations, but has also helped the Chinese government to reach its goals through apparently less coercive means in a territory always difficult to control: the field of cultural production.

WIGS, HEPATITIS, FANTASY, AND REALITY

In *Unknown Pleasures,* Qiaoqiao, a freelance model and dancer, often wears a wig, as if for some inexplicable reason she cannot show her hair in public.

Occasionally, her wig substitutes for her body as the object of male desire. Once, she performs a Mongolian dance without a wig following her breakup with Qiao San, her former gym teacher turned lover whose shady financial deals have made him a powerful local entrepreneur. Her dance is stiff and unattractive, in contrast to her usual graceful and sensual movements. In this sense, we can say that the wigs serve as aphrodisiacs for Qiaoqiao, and different wigs represent different forms of her sexual appeal. In short, her sexuality is closely related to her wigs.

Qiaoqiao's first wig is a loose copy of the hairdo of Mia Wallace in Quentin Tarantino's *Pulp Fiction* (1994). Significantly, Xiaoji, an unemployed young man, falls in love with Qiaoqiao in large part because this wig reminds him of the fashionable American actress. Nevertheless, when the young suitor tells Qiaoqiao the story of this film in a restaurant, he seems to misplace Mia's wig on the head of Honey Bunny. At the beginning and the end of *Pulp Fiction*, Bunny discusses with her boyfriend Pumpkin whether they should rob a bank, a coffee shop, or a restaurant. Their decision is to rob the restaurant where the discussion takes place. One can identify two images of ego in Xiaoji's (deliberate or inadvertent) confusion of Mia, the trophy wife of a gangster, and Honey Bunny, a clueless first-time criminal. Like Pumpkin, Xiaoji has neither power nor a previous criminal record. Xiaoji's ideal ego is the powerful gangster, Marcellus Wallace, Mia's overprotective husband. But he can only identify with Pumpkin in reality, as an amateur robber, because he has nothing like the clout of Marcellus. In this case, the wig has merged with his identity as a loser, with his ideal ego as a big-time mobster, and with his misidentification of a wholesome country girl as a glamorous queen of the underworld. Through the confused eyes of her admirer, this wig links Qiaoqiao to the center of the global empire, the United States. Like the dollar bill discussed below, Qiaoqiao has become a surrogate of fetishistic American values, representing the two Hollywood actresses simultaneously: one is sweet and ordinary, whereas the other appears cool and glamorous; one lovingly urges Xiaoji to commit a "heroic" crime, while the other captures the fantasized beauty enhanced by the best cosmetics money can buy.

Through her association with two actresses in *Pulp Fiction*, Qiaoqiao symbolizes freedom in a global context in the eyes of her teenage suitor, who applies imaginary American values to the Chinese context ("if I had been born in America, I would have become rich a long time ago"). Xiaoji wants to become rich by any means possible. Since no other means are available to this jobless teenager, he emulates the American hero by attempting a bank robbery. Ironically, if Qiaoqiao represents American glamour in the teenager's eyes, the Chinese equivalent of his ideal ego, Marcellus Wallace, cannot be anyone else but Qiao San, Qiaoqiao's sugar daddy, an illegal money lender. In this sense, Xiaoji's anticipated crime is meant not only to impress Qiaoqiao, his dream lover, but also to emulate Qiao San, his hated rival. Xiaoji wants to become like Qiao San through acquiring money and possessing Qiaoqiao's body.

Qiaoqiao's wigs also serve as indexes of her desirability. If her first wig connects her to the heart of the global empire in her lover's wild imagination, her second wig, a light blue short one, suggests tawdriness and exposes her life as a prostitute. The two wigs form a striking contrast, black and light blue, long and short, natural-looking and flashy-fake. Near the end of the film, Qiaoqiao appears with her second wig in the same theater box where she first encountered Qiao San. In both scenes, she watches the same traditional Chinese opera from the same angle. The identical setting suggests similar activities. Indeed, both sequences implicitly end with sexual intercourse with a man who pays for the service. Nevertheless, her wigs underscore the difference between the past and the present. By its naturalness, the wig given by Qiao San hides the mercantilism of Qiaoqiao's sexuality, while the second wig exposes her sexuality to the light of day. Thus, the wigs have become the essence of Qiaoqiao's attractiveness, if not of her personality.

As prostheses, the wigs also indicate the fetishistic nature of her attractiveness. If she represents the object of male desire par excellence, what men desire in her is not her body but only prosthesis, a detachable part that she can change at will. As the object of men's desire, Qiaoqiao signifies the void inherent in their desire for "unknown pleasures" or unlimited freedom. In reality, the object of their desire is not necessarily a living body, but the aura created by lifeless merchandise. As Žižek explains, "The enjoyment is what cannot be symbolized, its presence in the field of the signifier can be detected only through the holes and inconsistencies of this field, so the only possible signifier of enjoyment is the signifier of the lack in the Other, the signifier of its inconsistency."[21] As prosthesis, the wig is the signifier of lack par excellence. Further, the title of the film seems to have a Žižekian touch: pleasure is possible as long as it remains unknown, and freedom can be unlimited so long as it is situated in fantasy space.

Another kind of fantasy is expressed in the form of "anachronistic nostalgia," as in the case of Binbin (Xiaoji's unemployed friend) and his highschool sweetheart sharing a love for *The Monkey King*, an animated feature released in the 1960s. Born from a rock, the legendary Monkey King does not have parents. Nobody can tell him what to do, not even the heavenly emperor. As a result, he personifies unlimited freedom in the Chinese folk tradition. His freedom contrasts with the actual situation of Chinese teenagers in onechild families, where their parents watch them so carefully that they have little freedom to make decisions on their own. Not surprisingly, both jobless, Xiaoji and Binbin are from single-parent families and express a wish to be parentless on several occasions, and it may even imply that they equate freedom to no parental control.

Ironically, when the teenage lovers watch the cartoon about the Monkey King's rebellion against the heavenly emperor, they seem restricted by the watchful eyes of their absent parents. Unlike the parentless Monkey, the two teenagers cannot fulfill their desire. Instead of facing each other, they speak while facing the television (or the camera), as if an exchange of gaze might cause a dangerous explosion of desires. Unfortunately, even this highly restricted love affair in front of the television does not last. In contrast to the Monkey King who obtains immortality though rebellion, the lovers are restricted not only by their parents and by society, but also by their health. In order to join his college-bound girlfriend, Binbin decides to enroll in the army but is rejected because he is diagnosed with hepatitis B (an incurable and contagious disease said to be shared by 10 percent of the Chinese population). The official who informs Binbin of his test result warns him against infecting his girlfriend. Painfully, then, Binbin decides to sever their relationship, and this decision reveals his affection for the girl.

In preparation for their separation, Binbin wants to buy a cellular phone for his girlfriend, an expensive gift from a jobless teenager. First, he tries to borrow money from his mother, who has been laid off and has nothing to spare. Then, he requests a loan from Xiao Wu, the underworld character who charges high interest. Meeting his girlfriend in the deserted waiting hall of a bus station, Binbin offers the gift in silence. When the girl asks him to call her in the future, Binbin mumbles: "Where is the fucking future?" She asks: "What's wrong?" Getting no response, she urges him to sit beside her, but he refuses. She moves to his side, and bends her head on the table, inviting him to kiss her, but he does not move, either. She repeatedly asks him to leave with her, but he abruptly refuses and keeps silent. The girl stands, picks up her bicycle, and rides around the empty hall. When she stops in front of him and waits for minutes, he refuses even to lift his eyes. Finally, the girl leaves him alone, plagued by his incurable disease and a high-interest debt. Rumor has it that when Jia Zhangke watched his own film in Cannes, at one point he burst into tears. This must have been the scene.

PLEASURE AND FREEDOM

Borrowed from the title of a popular song, the Chinese title of *Unknown Pleasures* literally means "unrestricted freedom." The song, originally composed for a film, expresses love, regret, frustration, and nameless longing in the voice of a hero from a humble family. Significantly, the song's title derives from Zhuangzi's famous fable, "Wandering Freely" (*Xiaoyao you*), to which Qiaoqiao refers vaguely in a bedroom scene with her teenage lover. A tattooed butterfly has "landed" on Qiaoqiao's chest: a reminder of Zhuangzi's dream in another fable. Her questionable understanding of Zhuangzi is based on hearsay information provided by Qiao San, an understanding limited to one simple sentence: "Do whatever makes you feel good." In this film, the songs, the cartoons, the reference to a Hollywood film, the advertisements, and the arias from *La Traviata* repeatedly sung by a madman (played by the director himself), all seem to suggest the same theme: unrestricted freedom.

This freedom represents ultimate pleasure, which nonetheless remains "unknown." Apart from the Zhuangzi references, the notion of unrestricted freedom is often associated with global culture. Just like the familiar one dollar bill, globalization represents unlimited possibilities to people in this small town. The townspeople hold the American dollar in awe, with the same blissful ignorance they feel when excited by the news of the choice of Beijing as the site of the 2008 Olympics. They celebrate the announcement with firecrackers as if it were the Chinese New Year. Then the camera cuts to a deserted ground piled with garbage. The contrast of the two scenes suggests that if globalization has brought prosperity to some areas in China, it has left Datong virtually untouched, except for negative consequences. In fact, this process has led to the bankruptcies of numerous state-owned enterprises, the town's main source of employment in the past, and has made the impoverished town look dreary compared to the slick and hypermodern coastal cities of China. The camera repeatedly shows narrow hallways, dirty streets, and ground piled with refuse. These scenes have little to do with China's economic prosperity brought about by its integration into the global market. Furthermore, Datong, a declining industrial city, is forsaken not only by society but by nature itself. Jia's camera does not capture any signs of life, not even a green tree; instead, it reveals a vista of gloomy human faces. These dreary scenes make us wonder: if the last two decades of economic prosperity have not benefited Datong, how will the dollar bill or the Olympic Games in Beijing be able to change its barren and gloomy outlook?

If the dollar bill inspires false hope among the locals, globalization also gives them empty promises. The townspeople are trapped in a local version of globalization, a version that promises enjoyment through images of global consumerism. Like the international news repeatedly broadcast on television, globalization appears only as remote and fragmented spectacles unrelated to the population of this run-down industrial town. Furthermore, the spectacle of an event that appears to be positive at a national level is decisively associated with a negative local event. For example, the Olympic news follows an unhappy incident in the life of the two protagonists: the only fight between Xiaoji and Binbin. Immediately following their fight, a crowd on the street enthusiastically applauds the Olympic Committee, regardless of the woes of the two dispirited friends. People are excited by a distant event that has little to do with their lives, but they remain indifferent to what is happening to the members of their own community. The camera cross-cuts frequently from the television news to fragments of local life and emphasizes the disconnection between the two. Confined within the screen, the promise of the global economy remains a distant lure for the townspeople. But this lure is powerful precisely because they fail to understand the true effects of globalization on their own lives. In a Žižekian sense, global capitalism has become a powerful ideology in the impoverished provincial town:

> This is probably the fundamental dimension of "ideology": ideology is not simply a "false consciousness," an illusory representation of reality, it is rather this reality itself which is already to be conceived as "ideological"—*"ideological" is a social reality whose very existence implies the non-knowledge of its participants as its essence*—that is, the social effectivity, the very reproduction of which implies that the individuals "do not know what they are doing."[22]

The farther away these people are situated from the prosperity created by the process of globalization, the more attractive every connection to this fantasy space becomes. In other words, the reality of global capitalism in Datong is ideological in that "the individuals do not know what they are doing." It is difficult to imagine that the dollar bill would have become such a powerful symbol of wealth in another place slightly more familiar with global culture. Precisely because of the locals' ignorance, global capitalism has occupied a powerful space of collective fantasy, a space that encourages imagination about unlimited freedom or unknown pleasures.

Despite its Chinese title, freedom in the film is not just restricted but also fantastic. Fantasy exists in Chinese tradition, but here the tradition is transformed and integrated into contemporary popular culture, as in the case of Zhuangzi's philosophy. His Daoist philosophy has been reduced to "do whatever makes you feel good" in Qiaoqiao's explanation, eroticized as a butterfly tattooed on her chest, and popularized in the title song. As two elements closely related to the notion of freedom, Qiaoqiao and this song make their first appearance together in the film when she performs a modern dance to advertise Mongolian liquor. Curiously, when this song starts, the object hidden behind a large piece of red silk is not the advertised merchandise, but the dancer herself. In other words, Qiaoqiao is not only the object of desire for men but also a commodity herself. The flashy dance is intended not only to advertise liquor, but also to market Qiaoqiao's body, a hidden treasure seductively revealed behind the red silk, accompanied by the title song. As if to reinforce the impression of her commodification, in the following scene Qiaoqiao visits the director of the troupe to ask for her payment. The association between the song of freedom and the object of male desire provides a sexual undertone to an otherwise abstract notion, as if freedom can be reached mainly through sexual pleasure, or pleasure that remains "unknown." As suggested in the Chinese and the English titles of the film, freedom and pleasure are interchangeable.

Although the butterfly on her chest may symbolize sexual freedom, Qiaoqiao herself is trapped in her relationships with the opposite sex: the rich playboy gym teacher, the destitute teenage suitor, and the suitor's father in possession of an American dollar. In search of freedom, she is prepared to leave Qiao San for her teenage suitor, even if it means enduring the physical violence inflicted by her jealous owner (who is probably responsible for her black eye). However, her freedom becomes even more restricted later, as she has to sell her body to the worst possible customer, the father of her teenage suitor, for one American dollar, a symbol of global wealth. Both the dollar bill and Qiaoqiao circulate as objects of desire for the townspeople, and the two finally meet each other and merge into one entity. Qiaoqiao and the bill mirror each other as both engender illusions of freedom associated with sexual pleasure and with expectations of unlimited wealth.

In reality, the tattooed butterfly on Qiaoqiao's chest reveals her sexual dependency, because it reminds her of Qiao San, the first owner of her body. Qiao San is responsible for her understanding of Zhuangzi's dream—his explanation of this classical fable was perhaps the way the gym teacher seduced his adolescent student. If her understanding is vague, this ownership is unequivocal; she carries the symbol of his ownership in her heart more meaningfully than the desire for freedom she keeps in her mind. On the surface, she symbolizes unrestricted freedom and is the object of male desire, but in reality she is imprisoned by her sexuality. This contradiction becomes a metaphor for the entire filmic world. Qiaoqiao's association with the symbol of unlimited freedom (the butterfly) provides an illusion for the men chasing after her, as if the possession of her body could reveal the truth of "unknown pleasures," the truth behind all the glamour. Predictably, momentary gratification has not enhanced the life of any of her sexual partners. Qiao San dies in an accident. Xiaoji escapes from a criminal investigation by abandoning his only friend, Binbin, and his beloved possession, a motorcycle. Xiaoji's father returns to his depressing life after a brief interlude of excitement. In short, to each of these pleasure seekers, pleasure remains unknown, but suffering is inescapable.

Unlimited freedom remains a collective fantasy that traps everyone in unrealistic expectations of enjoyment. In the same vein, the theme song that praises unlimited freedom seems to entertain people as they move, knowingly or not, toward entrapment. In the last scene, for example, the handcuffed bank robber Binbin is forced to sing the title song under the watchful eyes of a police guard. The film concludes with the song as a metonymy of imprisonment.

RESTRICTION AND ENTRAPMENT

The sense of entrapment is further reinforced by the director's approach to movement. In the prologue, Binbin rides on a motorcycle borrowed from his friend Xiaoji. In a prolonged tracking shot, the camera moves along with the protagonist, keeping the angle and the distance almost unchanged. Although the frame is changing, the tracking shot creates the illusion that the protagonist is trapped in the same position and in the same location, despite his spatial displacement. Regardless of how fast Binbin moves, he can never break away from the frame imposed on him. Later, the penultimate sequence portrays Xiaoji in the same position, riding his motorcycle for several minutes after the failed bank robbery and before his vehicle breaks down in the middle of the highway. These two symmetric tracking shots create the impression that both teenagers are trapped in a dead end—no exit, no future, and no hope.

Xiaoji's motorcycle, however, does not break down only during his escape. In the middle of the film, after a discussion of Qiao San's death with Binbin, Xiaoji rides to an empty lot littered with garbage, and his motorcycle gets stuck at the edge of the lot. He leaves the vehicle behind, climbs to a high spot, and looks over the deserted area. The camera cuts to the next sequence in which Xiaoji's father visits Qiaoqiao in a box in the local theater in order to buy her sexual services for 50 yuan plus the famous dollar bill. In both cases, the breakdown of the motorcycle marks a major failure in Xiaoji's life. First, he fails in his sexual relationship, and the object of his desire has marketed herself to his father. Second, he fails in the bank robbery, an act through which he could identify with the heroes in *Pulp Fiction*, and his failure prevents him from searching for freedom according to his hazy understanding of American values.

If Qiaoqiao's implied relationship with her lover's father marks Xiaoji's sexual failure, it also represents an imprisonment for Qiaoqiao herself. At the beginning of the film, when she has a date with Qiao San for the first time, it takes place in the same box—a place where her unfaithful lover is showing off his wealth to impress the women around him. When they leave the box, a female singer asks him for money. Unlike Xiaoji, his destitute rival, who just refused her request, Qiao San playfully places a 100 yuan bill on his own face, until this bill falls into the hands of the happy singer. After a long journey, Qiaoqiao seems to return to her point of departure. Her struggle to break away from Qiao San's control does not change her circumstances, except for one minor difference: the price her potential client offers her is only half the value of the bill her former lover casually threw away to a stranger. In this film, wealth appears to be the only door to salvation. In order to reach this door, Qiaoqiao must sell her body, either as a model who ingratiates herself with powerful men by posing with them, or as the lover of a rich playboy like Qiao

Zhao Qiaoqiao and Xiaoji racing a motorcycle along the highway in Jia Zhangke's Unknown Pleasures *(2002)*

San who plays with women as if they were his toys. If worse comes to worst, she will plainly sell herself to anybody willing to pay the price.

Everyone in the film seems trapped. Jobless teenagers are trapped by their limited financial means, and two of them attempt to rob a bank. Their act is ridiculous in the sense that it appears incredible to them even before they act. The act proves tragic because it expresses the desperation of two youngsters from humble families. Although the title song repeats: "A hero is not deterred by his humble family origin" (*Yingxiong bu pa chushen tai danbao*), the film shows no hope for youngsters born with neither money nor power.

If financial needs trap the townspeople, wealth does not free the few rich from servitude, either, for it only intensifies their desires. The loudspeaker on the street repeatedly promotes lottery tickets, as if the only hope for most Chinese is winning a lottery. Ironically, just as the loudspeaker promises a wonderful future, two policemen arrest Xiao Wu in a public phone booth. Apparently, like Qiao San, Xiao Wu has become relatively well-to-do through murky financial dealings. Later, Xiao Wu tells Binbin that he spends his time either roaming the streets or residing in jail, as if he can barely distinguish one from the other. In this sense, wealth brought by dirty money has something in common with the jail that punishes people for enriching themselves illegally. Both are forms of entrapment. Even if rich people temporarily acquire the objects of their desire, the objects immediately lose all their previous glamour because they are too closely identified with a fantasy space. "In the fantasy-scene the desire is not fulfilled, 'satisfied,' but constituted . . . *through fantasy, we learn how to desire.*"[23] According to Žižek, the fantasy space also serves as a defense against the desire for the Other: this space allows the constitution of desire by preventing its fulfillment. Thus the desires of the rich, like those of the poor, remain forever unsatisfied, since the essence of their pleasure is "unknown."

For the Communist Party to survive in a global context, it needs global capital. Catering to the demands of multinational corporations, the Chinese government has been surprisingly successful on the economic front. In 2002, for example, mainland China alone attracted 75 percent of foreign investments in Asia. The inflow of money has brought with it the value system of global capitalism, which has gradually become an important part of official discourse in China. Influenced by radical changes in the infrastructure and in official discourse, China has embraced the values of global capitalism—namely, equating wealth with happiness. Two decades of economic reform have transformed China from an isolated socialist country to an emerging global power. *Unknown Pleasures* offers a realistic (or hyperrealistic) portrayal of this paradoxical world. Instead of broadcasting quotations from Mao's little red book, the loudspeakers on the street repeatedly advertise lottery tickets. Although the social structure of China has changed, the loudspeakers continue to voice the party line, since the state still has a monopoly on most radio broadcasts. The worship of Mao has been replaced by the worship of money, with an equal intensity. At the same time, only a few among the more than one billion Chinese can become really rich, and the few lucky rich are not necessarily happy.[24] Because money only has exchange value, there is no upper limit as to how much a person can or should possess. The standard according to which an individual is judged to be wealthy varies in different contexts. As this slippery value has become the measurement of happiness, it is difficult, if not impossible, to "know" pleasure, because the standard of measurement is itself unknowable.

In this sense, everyone is imprisoned, rich and poor alike. They are imprisoned by their financial needs (Binbin and Xiaoji), by their frantic actions (Qiao San, Xiao Wu, and Qiaoqiao), by their madness (the amateur opera singer), or by the concept of "unknown pleasures" or "unlimited freedom" as illustrated in the final scene, a scene of ultimate irony. Like handcuffed Binbin singing the title song in a police station, people are entrapped by the search for "unknown

An airplane flying over a high-rise building under construction in Jia Zhangke's The World *(2004)*

An animated sequence of a "flight attendant" flying freely over the city in Jia Zhangke's The World *(2004)*

pleasures," an illusory promised land created by global consumerism. This land is unreachable. If pleasure is unknown, it is because it does not exist.

Through its gloomy portrayal of everyday life in Datong, *Unknown Pleasures* indirectly answers Jia's own question: how should we position ourselves vis-à-vis the globalization process? The film seems to suggest that like the Communist revolution, global capitalism has not provided a solution to China's problems. For most Chinese far from the financial centers and from the coastal cities, the dazzling effect of globalization remains an unknown or unknowable pleasure. Its promises have made many Chinese hopeful, but in most situations hopes remain unrealized or unrealizable, like so many floating versions of the American dream. According to Jia, globalization in China has "a connotation of Americanization," which "has been translated into a ridiculous attempt to imitate Hollywood in Chinese cinema."[25] In this context, Jia's choice of independent filmmaking can be interpreted not only as resistance to censorship in China but more importantly as resistance to Americanization in the Chinese film industry. Following this interpretation, did his recent rise aboveground with *The World* mark an instance of political and cultural compromise? Is the price Jia paid "to reach a wider audience" too severe? Since a film cannot exist without an audience, the dilemma faced by the characters of *Unknown Pleasures* parallels the one confronting Jia Zhangke and Chinese film culture: how can one experience pleasure that is unknown or perhaps unknowable?

NOTES

1. In this chapter I will use the expression "globalization" restrictively, by treating it as an economic phenomenon, which has recently developed on a monumental scale through the expansion of global capital or through the expansion of "Empire," to bor-

row the title of a controversial book. See Michael Hardt and Anthony Negri, *Empire* (Durham, N.C.: Duke University Press, 2000).

2. For example, see Masao Miyoshi, "'Globalization,' Culture, and the University," in *The Cultures of Globalization*, ed. Fredric Jameson and Masao Miyoshi, 247–70 (Durham, N.C.: Duke University Press, 1998).

3. For an insightful critique of Eurocentrism inherent in the notion of modernity, see Enrique Dussel, "Beyond Eurocentrism: The World-System and the Limits of Modernity," in *The Cultures of Globalization*, ed. Fredric Jameson and Masao Myoshi, 3–31 (Durham, N.C.: Duke University Press, 1998).

4. "Independent film" has a much narrower definition in China compared to its generally accepted meaning. In the past, the state-owned studio system was the sole financial backer for all films. After the economic reforms, especially after the crackdown on the student demonstrations in 1989, filmmakers in China have looked for other sources partly to avoid strenuous censorship and partly because various financial sponsors, national as well as international, have become available. In this case, independent film in China is, strictly speaking, independent only from the state-owned studio system, despite its possible financial dependency on multinational corporations (see Chris Berry's chapter).

5. According to Zygmunt Bauman, if globalization creates mobility for the metropolitan elite, it also localizes a large proportion of the population: "A particular cause for worry is the progressive breakdown in communication between the increasingly global and extraterritorial elites and the ever more 'localized' rest" (Bauman, *Globalization: The Human Consequences* [New York: Columbia University Press, 1998], 3).

6. Jia Zhangke explains: "The fifth generation directors situate individuals in relation to their communities. They are always connected either to history or to tradition. But for us there are only individuals." See Luisa Prudentino, *Le Regard des ombres* (Paris: Bleu de Chine, 2003), 98.

7. Prudentino, *Le Regard des ombres*, 100–101.

8. Zhang Yuan, "Production Notes of *Mama*," *Catalogue of Hong Kong Festival* (Hong Kong: Urban Council, 1993), 67; quoted by Bérénice Reynaud, *Nouvelles Chines: Nouveaux cinema* (Paris: Editions cahiers du cinéma, 1999), 87.

9. Prudentino, *Le Regard des ombres*, 95.

10. *Xiao Wu* was produced on a shoestring budget, 280,000 RMB. By contrast, *Unknown Pleasures* was sponsored by four overseas sponsors in Hong Kong, Japan, France, and South Korea, and its budget was about five million RMB. Considering that a budget for an independent film in China is often far below one million RMB, *Unknown Pleasures* was a big-budget movie, especially shot in digital format.

11. See www.wuhuaxingqiwu_zhongguowang.htm, accessed August 2003.

12. www.wuhuaxingqiwu_zhongguowang.htm.

13. www.wuhuaxingqiwu_zhongguowang.htm.

14. André Bazin, *Qu'est-ce le cinéma?* (Paris: Les Éditions du cerf, 2002), 270.

15. Despite his criticism of the fifth generation's later works, Jia acknowledges the influence of their early works on his filmmaking, especially Chen Kaige's *Yellow Earth* (1984). See Prudentino, *Le Regard des ombres*, 98.

16. *Nanfang dushi bao*, "Daoyan Jia Zhangke fangtan: dui zhuliu de tuoxie" [Interview with Director Jia Zhangke: Compromise with the Mainstream], *Nanfang dushi bao*, April 14, 2003.

17. For a report on the lift of the ban on Wang Xiaoshuai's *Beijing Bicycle* (2000), see *China Daily*, "'Underground' Movie Directors Emerge," *China Daily*, April 26, 2004.

18. See "Jia Zhangke's The World": www.china.org.cn/english/NM-e/97624.htm.

19. *China Daily*, "'Underground' Movie Directors Emerge."

20. Ellen Meiksins Wood, *Empire of Capital* (London: Verso, 2003), 12.

21. Slavoj Žižek, *The Sublime Object of Ideology* (London: Verso, 1989), 122.

22. Žižek, *The Sublime Object of Ideology*.

23. Žižek, *The Sublime Object of Ideology*, 118.

24. Recent statistics indicate that China now has at least one thousand billionaires. Since this is measured by Chinese yuan, and US$1 roughly equals 8 yuan, each of these Chinese billionaires has more than US$125,000,000. In other words, only about one out of a million Chinese is truly a multimillionaire worth US$125,000,000. See *Guoji lianhe zaobao* (International United Morning News), Feb. 12, 2005.

25. Prudentino, *Le Regard des ombres*, 101.

7

Chinese Underground Films:
Critical Views from China

Chen Mo and Zhiwei Xiao

In the last decade, the Chinese underground film movement has been featured periodically in the Western press and has become a subject of research in Western academic circles. The current book is itself evidence of growing scholarly attention to this new development in Chinese cinema. Consequently, many savvy moviegoers and avid readers are aware of the critical acclaim Chinese underground film has received at prestigious international film festivals. But few people in the West have any idea of how underground film has been received in China and viewed by Chinese film critics. In many ways, their insider views provide a much-needed perspective for the Western audience. This chapter is a summary of representative discussions of underground film contained in leading publications in China.

Three points must be made clear at the outset. First, the views sampled in this paper are culled from scholarly writings by Chinese academics and film scholars. As such, they do not necessarily represent the Chinese government's position. But given the government's tight grip on most venues of publication in China, it should be assumed that views totally opposed to the official stance probably could not be published. Although Internet activity increasingly has been challenging the government's control of public discourse, this survey focuses on the more conventional venues of publication, including books and magazines, because despite occasional high-caliber articles, most Internet discussions of underground film suffer from poor documentation, and the writing quality varies considerably, thus failing to produce any consistency in format or style (see Internet Resources following the bibliography).

Second, scholars and academics in China often resort to coded language when discussing sensitive subjects. The unsettling nature of underground film demands extra care in the choice of vocabulary. Consequently, certain expressions, words, and terminology used in the discussion of underground film must be carefully deciphered. For instance, the frequent reference to "enlightenment" (*qimeng*) in Chinese academic writings may seem odd at first glance because Chinese intellectuals are often obsessed with "catching up" with all that is new and trendy in the West, yet the term harkens back to the eighteenth-century French Enlightenment. However, upon closer examination it becomes clear that the term "qimeng" in the Chinese context really goes beyond its original meaning and is a subtle reference to individual autonomy, liberalism, and democracy.

Finally, Chinese film scholars and critics have used several alternative labels to identify underground film, terms such as "newborn generation film" (*xinshengdai dianying*), which stresses the generational factor of the cinematic movement; "sixth-generation films" (*diliudai dianying*), an apparent attempt to distinguish underground filmmakers from fifth-generation filmmakers whose international success is well known and well documented; and "independent film" (*duli dianying* or *duli zhipian*), which focuses on the manner in which new generation filmmakers operate. As a result, these terms are interchangeable in our survey, which covers public discussions under any of the labels mentioned above and is not limited to underground film exclusively. However, our chapter does not include new media productions using DV technology, a recent current in the underground film movement.[1]

UNDERGROUND FILM IN CHINA: AN OVERVIEW

The group of filmmakers associated with underground film consists mainly of graduates of the Beijing Film Academy (BFA) or the Central Drama Academy. Still in their twenties and thirties, they were engaged in making films mostly outside the conventional venues of film production and distribution under state control. Typically, they raised production capital from private sources, conducted filming activities without being affiliated with established film studios, and refused to submit finished work to the government censors for approval—all of which are considered unorthodox practices in China. Consequently, their films have no institutional or legitimate status in China and cannot be publicly screened or distributed, hence, the "underground" designation.

It should be pointed out that many underground filmmakers are employed in the mainstream film industry and have done well within the conventional film establishment. A film scholar with intimate knowledge of the underground filmmakers categorized them into four groups. Some of them, like Hu Xueyang, Guan Hu, Lou Ye, Wang Rui, Jiang Ge, and Lu Xuechang, have jobs inside the state film industry. Others, such as Zhang Yuan, He Jianjun (He Yi), Wu Di, and Wang Xiaoshuai, are not associated with the state-operated studio system. In addition, there are also those who move freely between the two worlds. Finally, a number of people like Li Jun, who are on the state studio payroll, moonlight by taking on independent film projects.[2]

Because of the illegitimate nature of underground film, there has been no widely accepted official label for the movement. Generally speaking, film critics in China prefer to deemphasize the heretical implications of the term "underground film" by using alternative references. The underground film-makers' refusal to render their service to the state, their relative disinterest in commercialism, and their claim to artistic pursuit have encouraged the perception of their work as "individualistic film" (*geren dianying*), "art film" (*yishu dianying*), "avant-garde film" (*xianfeng dianying*), "auteur film" (*zuozhe dianying*), or "new wave film" (*xinchao dianying*).

The history of scholarly attention to underground film in China has gone through three phases, marked by three important publicly held symposia exclusively dedicated to discussion of underground films. Several individuals stand out in promoting public awareness of this movement and fighting for official recognition and acceptance of underground film. As early as 1991, journalist and film critic Zheng Xianghong first began to write about underground film. In the June issue of *Dianying gushi* (Film Synopsis), Zheng published a story on Zhang Yuan's *Mama* (1991). Two years later, in the same magazine, he published a translation of British film critic Tony Rayns's essay. The article endorsed Zhang Yuan's *Mama* in the strongest terms and was accompanied by Zheng's own detailed report on the then little-known underground film movement. Along with these articles, *Dianying gushi* also published a synopsis of two other underground films, *Beijing Bastards* (1993) and *The Days* (1993), as well as photos of leading personalities in the underground film movement. In his article, Zheng stresses the importance of the new generation of film-makers and the need for his readers to be aware of this development. For his time, Zheng's articles offered the most detailed account of the new generation of filmmakers and their representative work. In many ways, Zheng's articles marked the beginning of scholarly attention to underground films in China.[3]

Later in the decade, Cui Zi'en, a playwright at Beijing's Youth Film Studio and professor at the BFA, had emerged as a new critical voice endorsing underground films by contributing a series of articles to mainstream magazines such as *Hibiscus* (Furong) and *Music and Performance* (Yinyue yu biaoyan). To date, Cui's articles remain some of the earliest comprehensive overviews of the underground film movement in China.[4]

In addition, Cheng Qingsong and Huang Ou have contributed significantly to public understanding of underground film by publishing in 2002 a coauthored book on underground film entitled *Wode sheyingji bu sahuang: xianfeng dianying ren dang'an* (My Camera Doesn't Lie: Documents on Avant-garde Filmmakers). Among other things, the book compiles the biographies of eight leading underground film directors born in the 1960s and 1970s, including Zhang Ming, Jiang Wen, Zhang Yuan, Wang Chao, Lu Xuechang, Lou Ye, Wang Xiaoshuai, and Jia Zhangke. Also included in the book are introductions to representative works by these filmmakers, their directorial notes, and interviews with them (see Yingjin Zhang's chapter). Particularly noteworthy is the section outlining the major developments of underground film as well as its genealogy. The book's wide coverage has yet to be surpassed.[5]

Other leading film scholars have also expressed their views on the subject. For instance, Han Xiaolei, a BFA professor, published an essay on underground film in 1995, one of the most substantial discussions at the time.[6] The essays by Huang Shixian are among the most influential and best researched on this subject. In addition, Zheng Dongtian, himself an accomplished film director, has also written several excellent essays on the topic; and Zhang Xianmin has touched on the relationship between underground film and government censors. Apart from these critics affiliated with the BFA, Yin Hong, a professor at Qinghua University, also published two influential essays on underground film.[7]

Beyond the work of individual scholars, three major symposia have been devoted to a discussion of underground film in the past decade. The first, occasioned by a celebration of the career success of the BFA's new graduates of the 1989 and 1991 directing classes, took place in May 1995. On the surface, there was nothing out of the ordinary about the BFA's sponsorship of a conference that honored its graduates by examining films approved by government censors. However, under this legitimate cover the conference was actually devoted to discussing underground films. In retrospect, this symposium was a deliberate attempt to bring scholarly attention to films produced outside the established venues of film production and distribution. The proceedings of this symposium were later published in the BFA's journal. Such well-known faculty members as Xie Fei, Zheng Dongtian, Ni Zhen, Zhong Dafeng, Han Xiaolei, Wang Zhimin, and Huang Shixian all contributed articles to this special issue.[8]

The second symposium, jointly sponsored by the China Filmmakers' Association, the China Film Corporation, and the Beijing Film Studio, with the leading academic journal, *Dianying yishu* (Film Art), in charge of the organizational details, was held in November 1999 under the title "A Symposium on Films by Young Filmmakers" (Qingnian zuopin yantao hui). Some well-known underground film personalities, such as Wang Xiaoshuai, were included in the symposium. Inviting them to engage in conversations with government cultural officials, established film studio managers, and film scholars made this a watershed event.

One of the key issues the symposium organizers addressed was how to respond to the emergence of underground film. In her opening speech, Zhao

Shi, an official from the Mass Media Bureau of the central government, gave a clear signal that the government wished to co-opt the underground film movement.[9] A participant at the symposium, Huang Shixian, later observed that the 1999 symposium in Beijing had occasioned a "mutual understanding" between government officials and underground filmmakers.[10] Huang's exceedingly optimistic assessment of the relationship aside, underground film did begin to surface without much official objection after the symposium. Some of the proceedings from the conference were published in the January 2000 issue of *Dianying yishu*. Since then, there have been noticeable increases in scholarly discussions of the subject in reputable journals and academic publications.

The third symposium was held in July 2002 in Shanghai, jointly sponsored by Shanghai University and the Shanghai Film Corporation. The theme of the symposium was "Dialogue: The Moving Images of China's Newborn Generation" (Duihua: Zhongguo xinshengdai yingxiang). In addition to including some leading film scholars, the symposium also invited prominent figures in the underground film movement to engage in dialogue with mainstream filmmakers. Jia Zhangke, Wang Xiaoshuai, Zhang Yang, Wang Guangli, Li Xin, and Li Hong were all present at the symposium. Comparatively speaking, the Shanghai symposium may not have received as much media attention as the event in Beijing two years earlier, but it was more substantial in terms of the questions addressed and the range of issues discussed. The proceedings of this conference were later published in an edited volume by Xuelin Press, *Duoyuan yujing zhong de xinshengdai dianying* (Newborn Generation Films in Multiple Contexts).[11]

LABELS AND IDENTITIES

What label is most appropriate for underground filmmakers? Scholars in China have been hotly debating this issue. Needless to say, different labels reflect different assessments of the political orientation, artistic achievements, and intellectual genealogy of underground film. In one of the earlier reports on the underground film movement, Zheng Xianghong referred to the individuals behind the movement as "independent filmmakers" (*duli yingren*) and gave them high marks for exploring new approaches to filmmaking. At a time when the state had just cracked down on filmmakers who had defied official rules, Zheng's endorsement of independent films had obvious political meaning. While accepting Zheng's label, some critics understood the independent orientation of underground films in terms of developmental strategy, stressing the need for young filmmakers to take the risks associated with experimental filmmaking and to accumulate as much experience as possible so they will be better prepared to launch their careers in the future. Viewed from this perspective, the risqué nature of underground film has more to do with its precarious position in the marketplace, not its political subversiveness.[12]

One of the objectives of the 1999 symposium was to come up with a basic assessment of underground film. Many participants observed that most of the underground films were conceptually and thematically rooted in individualistic values. Technically, they suffered from poor craftsmanship; politically, they frequently veered away from the ideological line sanctioned by the state. The young filmmakers' preoccupation with the lives of marginalized people and their tendency to deal with politically sensitive subject matter made their films frequent subjects of controversy and targets of censorship. Even so, the participants in the symposium took the view that these films would be better labeled as "independent" rather than "underground."[13]

Some film scholars and critics did not like either "underground" or "independent" designations. Instead, they preferred such terms as "the sixth generation" or "the newborn generation," arguing that when compared to films produced by other generations, the underground films exhibit many unmistakable common characteristics. Their exploration of unconventional subject matter, preference for formulistic narrative structure, interest in social and political views not endorsed by the state, and obsession with the psychological depth of characters set them apart from mainstream culture in contemporary China.[14] In many ways, preoccupation with being different, innovative, and avant-garde is central to the self image of underground filmmakers. Hence, it is appropriate to view this group of filmmakers from the generational angle.[15]

However, the problem with this approach is that in stressing these collective commonalities, the filmmakers' individual styles and personal trademarks are either erased or ignored. For this reason, Han Xiaolei questioned the use of "generation" as a meaningful concept in discussions of underground film. Han and Zheng Dongtian both believed that the emergence of underground film signaled the arrival of a new kind of cinema in Chinese film history, one truly derived from individualized experience.[16]

Concurring with this view, several commentators coined the term "me-me-ism" (*wowo zhuyi*) to characterize the ideological orientation of underground film (see Paul Pickowicz's chapter). As Qu Chunjing explains, individual subjectivity has long been suppressed in Chinese history and its absence on the screen testifies to that suppression. Seen from this perspective, the cultural significance of underground film lies in the fact that it has resurrected individual subjectivity from the dustbin of history. In so doing, it rejects the fifth generation's embrace of the mainstream value of privileging meta-history at the expense of the individual subjectivity.[17] In this sense, me-me-ism should not be understood as synonymous with egocentrism, but as a defiance of the hegemony of collectivism.[18]

The use of different labels highlights the conflicting views and assessments of underground films. Such supporters of underground film as Han Xiaolei defend the work on the grounds that it is not antiestablishment and caution government officials not to be easily persuaded by Western media, which tend to misinterpret the movement as politically subversive. Han argues that such an interpretation serves the ideological agenda of the West and does not reflect cultural reality in China. In his view, all that the underground filmmakers want is more artistic freedom. They should be allowed to experiment with unconventional approaches to filmmaking.[19]

Huang Shixian agrees and suggests that the main thrust of underground film is the humanistic search for the meaning of life, which is typical of young filmmakers and hardly revolutionary. Despite its apparent postmodern facade, underground film is not about deconstructing fundamental social and political values. In comparison with the fifth-generation filmmakers who were obsessed with national and historical allegories, the underground filmmakers are more interested in the social realities of their immediate surroundings and the affirmation of the importance of humanity.[20]

One of the key questions in the discussion of underground film concerns its ideological orientation. Is it as politically oppositional and culturally subversive as some critics, especially those outside China, have claimed it to be? Does the critical acclaim underground filmmakers have won outside China mean that they have surrendered themselves to Western cultural hegemony while defying cultural and political authorities at home? In a nutshell, do their films smack of self-Orientalism?

Chinese film critics are fully aware that Chinese underground film is a part of a global trend that witnesses a shift toward independent filmmaking (see Chris Berry's chapter). In the Chinese case, the underground filmmakers' refusal to conform to the official ideological position and to serve the state, as well as their elitist view regarding popular culture, have greatly reduced the chance that their films will have a mass appeal. The experimental nature of their work makes it impossible for their films to be distributed in the mainstream market. Hence, unofficial screening is the only way in which these films can reach their domestic audience. It is in this context that they try to appeal to the international market. Indeed, some have succeeded in becoming the darlings of international film festivals.[21]

Dai Jinhua, a leading film scholar in China, insists that the "success" of the underground filmmakers abroad is, to some extent at least, occasioned by Western critics' misinterpretation of the cultural and political meanings of these films. She observes that when Wu Wenguang's *Bumming in Beijing* (1990) was screened at the Hong Kong International Film Festival in 1991, it immediately caught the attention of international film critics. At the same time, Zhang Yuan's *Mama* achieved similarly spectacular success in the West.

The two films went on to win more than a dozen awards at international film festivals despite their less than perfect production quality. In Dai's view, these films benefited from the international success of Zhang Yimou and other members of the fifth generation who had created an appetite in the West for Chinese films. Indeed, she thinks that Chinese underground cinema is welcomed in the West because it is an alternative to Zhang Yimou's films, which have become all too familiar.[22]

Although few scholars in China doubt that the underground filmmakers are talented, they do question whether their extremely high visibility abroad is for reasons other than their artistic creativity. These scholars take note of the fact that almost every underground film has received some form of international recognition. Instead of taking pride in the fact that Wang Xiaoshuai's *The Days* has been collected by the Museum of Modern Art in New York and listed by the BBC as one of the "Hundred Classics of World Cinema," they see these honors as unwarranted. In their view, Western critics, who are usually extremely "stingy" in offering endorsements to third-world cinema, seem to cut slack for Chinese underground filmmakers.[23]

In 1993 the Rotterdam International Film Festival organizers invited Huang Jianxin, a member of the fifth generation, to participate in the gala. Initially, the Chinese government approved Huang's trip to Holland, but shortly before the festival's opening, changed its mind. Consequently, Huang was unable to go to Rotterdam. Surprisingly, the organizers of the film festival did not seem to be disappointed at all upon hearing the news. They did not even bother to lodge a protest with the Chinese government, as they had often done in the past on similar occasions. The reason they could shrug off the bad news was that they had secured the entries of several Chinese underground films to which they had now turned their attention. These films included *Beijing Bastards* and Ning Dai's *Shutting Down* (1993), which in the eyes of many Chinese critics are not well crafted, despite their novelty. In the case of *Shutting Down*, it was a documentary made with a home video camera and its production quality fell far below normal professional standards. Yet, it was considered "one of the most important Chinese films" at Rotterdam. This and other cases in which European and American film critics' "unusual" generosity in giving the most coveted awards and honors to China's sixth-generation filmmakers caused film critics in China to question the political motivations of Westerners. European critics did not seem to have been as generous with filmmakers from other third-world countries who operate outside the Hollywood mode of filmmaking.[24]

Some critics in China argue that the insistence on the "underground" label in Western discourse about newborn generation film betrays an ideological agenda. The glaring inattention in the Western press to the artistic qualities of the films in question seems to confirm that many people in the West are preoccupied with the supposed political significance of these films. As Zhang Yang commented at the symposium held in Shanghai in 2002,

> I find the discussion of (underground) film in the media ludicrous and extremely biased. . . . It is as if the significance of independent filmmaking is predicated on rebelliousness alone. No one seems to really care whether the film in question is well made and everyone is preoccupied with its ideological position. . . . I don't think this is right. The criterion should be whether the film is a good piece of work or not.[25]

Chinese film critics also pay attention to the political implications of underground film, but in contrast to the emphasis of Western critics on its "oppositional" thrust, they are much more interested in its other revolutionary aspects, including its attempt to break away from didacticism in filmmaking, its challenge to the outdated film production and distribution system, and its experiment with new approaches to filmmaking. They find it peculiar that these dimensions are rarely given sufficient attention in the West and generally think that the sixth-generation filmmakers fulfill a need in the West to identify the Other. Earlier, Zhang Yimou stimulated Western interest in the "Oriental gaze." Looking at the situation from this perspective, they predict that Chinese independent filmmakers face two challenges simultaneously: on the one hand, they have to resist the tyranny of mainstream culture; on the other, they have to resist the distortion and misinterpretation of their work by Western cultural imperialists.[26]

SIGNIFICANCE AND LIMITATIONS

Chinese film scholars and critics generally welcome underground film. While scholars like Huang Shixian stress its humanistic thrust, Dai Jinhua emphasizes its "enlightenment" value, arguing that despite the seeming postmodern posture, many underground films are about constructing or promoting certain moral and ethical codes of conduct compatible with modern society. In this regard, they are essentially at odds with the cynicism and deconstructive thrust embedded in postmodernism. Dai uses Wu Wenguang's *Bumming in Beijing* as an example to illustrate her point and believes that the central theme of this film is about individuals awakened to their own subjectivity. Functionally, films such as this promote independent thinking and individual autonomy, both of which have been suppressed in China for historical and political reasons, and are now very much in need of cultivation (see Matthew Johnson's chapter).

Dai's view is supported by some of the underground filmmakers themselves. For instance, Zhang Yuan explains that his *Beijing Bastards* is about a new generation of Chinese struggling to find their individual places in society through their own search for meaning and explorations of life. Zhang further points out that underground film is simultaneously motivated by two impulses—passion and objectivity. That is to say, its characters all passionately embrace individual autonomy and refuse to function as historical and national allegories, and the representation of social reality contained in such films is guided by a strong sense of objectivity and detachment. As a result, many underground films have a strong "on the spot" feel and the narrators often function as witnesses to the events portrayed on screen. This passionate pursuit of objectivity has produced a cinematic style that seems aloof—indeed, almost callously indifferent—to the filmic objects. The camera is also often positioned to function as a witness to events and thus accentuates a sense of immediacy and objectivity. Common among all underground film is an aesthetic quality that privileges emotional intensity and the macabre. However, many critics also make the observation that the excessive dose of adolescent narcissism in most underground films has seriously compromised their artistic appeal.[27]

Cui Zi'en, an activist in the underground film movement himself, does not think the preoccupation with individualism is necessarily what makes underground film stand out. Instead, he suggests that its rejection of the theatrical is the most revolutionary contribution to Chinese filmmaking, which in Cui's view, has been historically grounded in theatricality. The audio-visual components of cinema have often been neglected. Now, the underground filmmakers' weak ties to the native filmmaking tradition allow them to break away from that convention. In the meantime, their familiarity with modern Western aesthetics gives their work a solid contemporary feel and a "here and now" quality. Needless to say, Cui's comments betray his preference for novel themes, unconventional characters, cleverly crafted stories, and innovative approaches to filmmaking. Not surprisingly, he sees the unpopularity of underground film in China as proof that it is ahead of its time.[28]

Other critics share Cui's view that the underground filmmakers are path blazers who explore and experiment with new ways of making films. In other words, even if they do not like everything about underground film, they see its emergence as a harbinger of a future in which underground filmmakers will play the leading roles. For those critics, the trials and failures associated with underground film are a necessary part of a process that will lead to final triumph: its gradual acceptance by the state is an indication of its more promising future.[29]

Not everyone holds this rather rosy view of underground film. Film critic Ma Ning, for instance, points out that the humanistic values so prevalent in underground films do not constitute a serious challenge to mainstream ideology. In fact, underground film is no more politically subversive and artistically novel than many films approved by government censors and distributed in the mainstream market.[30] Another critic, Zhang Fu, argues that compared to the earlier generations, the underground filmmakers lack a sense of artistic consciousness. They may not like the way things are, but have no idea how to improve things either. They may be more defiant and oppositional than the previous generations, but have yet to demonstrate any intellectual depth of their own. In the short term, their eagerness to be technically innovative and politically subversive may help put them in the spotlight, but in the long run, they will have to go beyond shock value and become well rounded.[31]

To many critics of underground film, the artistic vision demonstrated in these films is rather narrow and limited. Zhang Yuan's *Beijing Bastards* is viewed as nothing more than a purposeless search, He Jianjun's *Red Beads* (1993) as largely a monologue, and Hu Xueyang's *The Drowned Youth* (1994) as close to a tearjerker. Meanwhile, Wang Xiaoshuai's *The Days*, Guan Hu's *Dirt* (1994), and Lou Ye's *Weekend Lovers* (1994) all reveal a desire to move from the margin to center stage. The use of the past tense in the voice-over, an attempt to reflect on the past from the perspective of the present, testifies to that desire. These critics also fault underground film for its sense of detachment from the events and characters on the screen as well as the fractured manner in which underground filmmakers deal with the temporal dimension. To them, these strategies betray the directors' collective psychological hangover from adolescent obsession with growing up.[32]

Ying Xiong, another BFA professor, is skeptical about the underground filmmakers' marginal position and believes that this position is partly a strategy used by the filmmakers to gain publicity and increase their professional profile before joining the mainstream film industry. For Ying, the question is not about whether they will move on to the center stage from the margin, but whether they will be competent enough to meet the challenge of mainstream film production and distribution. Ying thinks that the underground filmmakers' limited experience in making documentaries and feature films has not given them enough preparation to succeed in the real world. To buttress his point, Ying points to the gap between underground filmmakers' preoccupation with urban youth culture and their insufficient technical ability to deal with such subject matter. His central message to the underground filmmakers is that they should master the cinematic techniques used in mainstream filmmaking and apply them skillfully in presenting issues pertaining to youth culture. The example Ying has in mind is Mike Newell's *Four Weddings and a Funeral* (1994), which uses conventional cinematic techniques to communicate unconventional ideas.

Apparently, Ying takes the view that underground filmmakers have much to learn and ample room to improve in the area of conventional cinematic techniques. In his view, even if they are only interested in making experimental films, they will have to develop a distinctive cinematic style. Directors like

A suffering patient in a mental hospital in He Jianjun's Red
Beads *(1993)*

Wong Kar-Wai (Wang Jiawei) have done this by producing such masterpieces
as *Ashes of Time* (1994) and *Chungking Express* (1994), which are distinguished
by their good use of innovative filmmaking techniques and unique cinematic
style. In other words, viewed as a group, the Chinese underground filmmakers
are still somewhat amateurish both cinematically and technically. If they want
to be taken more seriously, they will have to be more flexible with regard to
mass culture and popular taste. In order for them to take the center stage and to
be accepted by the public, it is not enough for them to concentrate on novelty
alone. They also need to engage with mainstream culture in some fashion.[33]

Ying's view was echoed at the Shanghai symposium on the newborn generation. As one participant quipped, the underground film directors are totally
clueless. Despite their intention to engage in constructive social critique and
their effort to promote enlightenment through film, they have not found the

The crew at work in the street shooting Lou Ye's Weekend Lovers *(1994)*

appropriate venues to achieve their noble goals. Their excessive reliance on romantic love is both instinctive and driven by necessity. Their foundation is shaky in both traditional and modern learning. Hence, they are incapable of making films like Zhang Yimou's *The Road Home* (1999), which requires a strong identification with traditional values, or Zhang Yang's *Shower* (1999), which dwells on a nostalgic sentiment. The primary subject matter on which many underground films have focused is urban life, which is treated in such an abstract fashion that few viewers can relate to what is on the screen. Meanwhile, the lack of moral conviction among the underground filmmakers has produced a sense of moral ambiguity in their films. At the technical level, few of their films can sustain a prolonged dramatic tension and consequently, the narrative is fragmented and lacks cohesion.[34]

In contrast to the harsh remarks by these critics, Yin Hong endorses underground films because they are honest and innocent. In his view, most mainstream films are contrived, hypocritical, and profit driven and they cater to popular taste. By contrast, underground film is idealistic and brings some fresh air to the Chinese film industry. They have not been widely accepted yet, but that is precisely because of their avant-garde nature. As the product of global cultural trends and aesthetic developments, Chinese underground film explores humanity from a global perspective and attempts to find a more meaningful way to interact with the world. Yin specifically credits underground film for revolutionizing cinematic language through its use of music and tracking shots, which turn the enclosed spatial structure into an open temporal structure. In so doing, underground filmmakers not only embrace new trends in world cinematic aesthetics, but also offer a new way of articulating human experiences in the contemporary world.[35]

Others are not as sanguine. Zhong Dafeng, a BFA professor, has argued that the gap between underground films and popular taste is so huge that they are not likely to merge with mainstream filmmaking anytime soon. Furthermore, because the government's cultural officials generally do not like underground films, publicity and promotion for such films are consequently limited. He points out that the different assessments of underground film are derived from two fundamentally different expectations on what film is about. People who see film as a new medium for artistic expression tend to be more receptive to underground film, whereas people who view film's function as mass entertainment tend to fault underground film for its alleged elitism.[36]

CONCLUSION

As an ongoing movement, Chinese underground filmmaking defies any attempts on the part of Chinese scholars to reach a definitive conclusion at this point. Indeed, since 2003, several exploratory volumes on underground film have appeared in China.[37] In addition, a number of college textbooks have devoted considerable space to the subject.[38] These developments suggest a growing acceptance of underground film by the official establishment as well as an increase in scholarly attention. In some ways, the growing interest in the phenomenon is itself a testimony of the historical significance of underground filmmaking.

It is interesting to note, however, that as underground film gradually gains legitimacy in China, many underground filmmakers have "surfaced" or gone "aboveground" to engage in mainstream media production. Following his first officially approved film, *Seventeen Years* (1998), Zhang Yuan directed *Green Tea* (2003), staring two major stars, Jiang Wen and Zhao Wei. The film was distributed nationwide and was well received by critics. A year before, Zhang directed a filmed stage play, *Sister Jiang, a Revolutionary Martyr* (2002), which is based on a well-publicized story of an underground Communist who was executed by the Nationalists in 1949. Guan Hu, too, became very involved in television production, directing three popular multiepisode television series: *Black Hole* (Heidong, 2002), *The Winter* (Dongzhi, 2004), and *Migrant Workers* (Shengcun mingong, 2005). In the meanwhile, Jia Zhangke's new film, *The World* (2004), was eagerly taken up by mainstream distributors for wide screening in commercial theaters. This latest development seems to validate the perception held by many critics that for many underground filmmakers, making unconventional, illegitimate, small-budget art films is not fundamentally an "art for art's sake" endeavor, but rather a practical strategy to enter the extremely competitive mainstream film and television industries. Once that objective is achieved, they may quickly—with or without hesitation—abandon underground filmmaking. Whether this view represents a fair evaluation in the long run remains to be seen.

NOTES

1. See Fenghuang weishi (Phoenix Satellite TV), ed., *DV xin shidai 1* [DV New Generation 1] (Beijing: Zhongguo qingnian chubanshe, 2003), 5–8.
2. Han Xiaolei, "Guanyu xinyidai daoyan qun" [About the Newborn Generation of Film Directors], *Beijing dianying xueyuan xuebao*, 1995, no. 1:103–11.
3. Zheng Xianghong, "Duli yingren zai xingdong: suowei Beijing dixia dianying zhenxiang" [Independent Filmmakers in Action: The Truth about Underground Film in Beijing], *Dianying gushi*, 1993, no. 5:4–7, and "Zhang Yuan fangtan lu" [An Interview with Zhang Yuan], *Dianying gushi*, 1993, no. 5:8–9.
4. Cui Zi'en, "Dianying minjian sheng" [Unofficial Voices from Film], *Yinyue yu biaoyan*, 2001, no. 3:32–38, and "Yese liaoren: Zhongguo duli dianying de xiao quan-

jing he da texie" [Tantalizing Night: Independent Film in China in a Small Panorama and a Big Close-Up], *Furong*, 2002, no. 2:70–80.

5. Cheng Qingson and Huang Ou, *Wode sheyingji bu sahuang: xianfeng dianying ren dang'an—shengyu 1961–1970* [My Camera Doesn't Lie: Documents on Avant-garde Filmmakers Born between 1961 and 1970] (Beijing: Zhongguo youyi chuban gongsi, 2002).

6. Han Xiaolei, "Dui diwudai de wenhua tuwei: houwudai de geren dianying xianxiang" [A Cultural Breakaway from the Fifth Generation: The Phenomenon of Personal Film in the Post–Fifth Generation], *Dianying yishu*, 1995, no. 2:58–63.

7. For example, see Huang Shixian, "Qingchun dubai: qianweixing yu dazhong-xing—Zhongguo dianying xinshengdai jiqi xinzuo *Chaoji chengshi* sumiao" [Mono-logues of the Youth: Avant-gardism and Mass Appeal—A Sketch of the Newborn Generation Film *Super City*], *Dianying shuangzhoukan*, 1998, no. 7:70–72; "Diliudai bei mingming" [Naming the Sixth Generation], *Dianying pingjie*, 2000, no. 3:15–19; and "Diliudai: laizi bianyuan de chaoxun" [The Sixth Generation: The Tidal Wave from the Margin], in *Duoyuan yujing zhong de xinshengdai dianying: Zhongguo xinshengdai dianying* [Newborn Generation Films in Multiple Contexts: Essays on Chinese Newborn Generation Film], ed. Chen Xihe and Shi Chuan, 23–39 (Shang-hai: Xuelin chubanshe, 2003); Zheng Dongtian, "Diliudai dianying de wenhua yiyi" [The Cultural Significance of the Sixth Generation Film], *Dianying yishu*, 2003, no. 1:42–43; Zhang Xianmin, "Meiyou gongkai de guangying: dalu 1990 nian hou de jin-pian shi" [The Unexposed Films: A History of Banned Films in Mainland China after 1990], *Fenghuang zhoukan* 34 (2002); Yin Hong, "Diwudai yu xinshengdai dianying shidai de jiaocha yu guodu" [The Cross-Over between and Transition from the Fifth Generation to the Newborn Generation Film], *Dianying yishu*, 1998, no. 1:23–27, and "Zai jiafeng zhong zhangda: Zhongguo dalu xinsheng dai de dianying shijie" [Grow-ing Up between the Fissures: The Film World of the Newborn Generation], *Ershiyi shiji* 49 (Oct. 1998): 88–93.

8. See the section devoted to newborn generation films in *Beijing dianying xueyuan yuanbao* 1995, no. 2:100–203.

9. Zhao Shi, "He qingnian pengyou tanxin" [A Heart-to-Heart Talk with Young Friends], *Dianying yishu*, 2000, no. 1:4–7.

10. Huang Shixian, "Diliudai."

11. See Chen Xihe and Shi Chaun, ed., *Duoyuan yujing zhong de xinshengdai dianying*.

12. Cited in Zheng Xianghong, "Duli yingren zai xingdong."

13. For a more detailed report about the symposium, see *Dianying yishu* 2000, no. 1:9–10.

14. Pan Ruojian and Zhuang Yuxin, "Guanyu xinshengdai taolun jiyao" [A Review of the Discussion about the Newborn Generation of Filmmakers], *Beijing dianying xueyuan xuebao*, 1995, no. 1:168–69.

15. Shi Chuan, "Daiqun mingming yu daiqun yuma" [The Labels and Linguistic Codes Associated with Generations], in Chen Xihe and Shi Chuan, *Duoyuan yujing zhong de xinshengdai dianying*, 234–42.

16. Han Xiaolei, "Guanyu xin yi dai daoyan qun," 108.

17. Qu Chunjing, "Dianying wenxian jiazhi yu yishu pinwei: tan xinshengdai dianying de chengbai" [Film's Documentary and Artistic Values: Newborn Generation Films' Success and Failure], in Chen Xihe and Shi Chuan, *Duoyuan yujing zhong de xinshengdai dianying*, 192.

18. Liu Guangyu, "Ziyou de shuxie yu chenzhong de yingxiang: Zhongguo dianying diliudai de jingshen sumiao" [Free Writing and Loaded Images: A Sketch of the Chinese Sixth Generation Filmmakers], in Chen Xihe and Shi Chuan, *Duoyuan yujing zhong de xinshengdai dianying*, 259–61.

19. Han Xiaolei, "Guanyu xin yi dai daoyan qun," 108.

20. Huang Shixian, "Diliudai," 25.

21. Jin Danyuan and Ding Ning, "Zai hou yujing zhong qidai tupo: lun Zhongguo xinyidai daoyan de duochong xuanze" [Anticipating a Breakthrough in the Postcontext: Multiple Choices of the New-Generation Directors], in Chen Xihe and Shi Chuan, *Duoyuan yujing zhong de xinshengdai dianying*, 52, 59.

22. Dai Jinhua, *Wuzhong fengjing* [A Scene in the Fog] (Beijing: Beijing daxue chubanshe, 2000), 380–416.

23. Dai, *Wuzhong fengjing*, 380–416.

24. Dai, *Wuzhong fengjing*, 380–416.

25. Chen Xihe and Shi Chuan, *Duoyuan yujing zhong de xinshengdai dianying*, 390.

26. Dai, *Wuzhong fengjing*, 380–416.

27. Dai, *Wuzhong fengjing*, 380–416.

28. Cui Zi'en, "Yese liaoren," 70–71.

29. Huang Shixian, "Diliudai."

30. Ma Ning, "Zhongguo dianying keneng cunzai de kunhuo" [Some Possible Confusion for Chinese Film], *Dianying yishu*, 2002, no. 1:64.

31. Zhang Fu, "Yige fengge zhuyi de shidai: 90 niandai Zhongguo dianying de tuwei biaoyan" [An Era of Stylism: Breakthrough Performances of Chinese Films in the 1990s], *Beijing dianying xueyuan xuebao*, 1995, no. 1:118–20.

32. Zhang Fu, "Yige fengge zhuyi de shidai."

33. Ying Xiong, "Tianjiang daren: diliudai de jiyu yu wenti" [An Immense Responsibility: Opportunities and Problems Faced by the Sixth Generation], *Beijing dianying xueyuan xuebao*, 1995, no. 1:126–27.

34. Shen Liang, "Keai de chuantong: lun diliudai dianying zhong de baoshou qingxiang" [A Lovely Tradition: The Conservative Tendency in Sixth Generation Films], in Chen Xihe and Shi Chuan, *Duoyuan yujing zhong de xinshengdai dianying*, 243–54.

35. See Chen Xihe and Shi Chuan, *Duoyuan yujing zhong de xinshengdai dianying*, 103.

36. Zhong Dafeng, "Tizhi nei de caihua" [The Talents within the System], *Dianying yishu*, 2000, no. 1:17.

37. For example, see three books published in 2004: Cheng Qingsong, *Kandejian de yingxiang* [Films Permitted for Watching] (Shanghai: Sanlian shudian, 2004); Zhang Xianming, *Kanbujian de yingxiang* [Films Banned from Watching] (Shanghai: Sanlian shudian, 2004); Mei Bing and Zhu Jingjiang, *Zhongguo duli jilupian dang'an*

[Records of China's Independent Documentary Cinema] (Xi'an: Shaanxi shifan daxue chubanshe, 2004).

38. For instance, see Chen Xuguang, *Zhongguo dangdai yingshi wenhua yanjiu* [A Study of Film and Television Culture in Contemporary China] (Beijing: Beijing daxue chubanshe, 2004); Zhou Xing, *Zhongguo dianying yishu shi* [A History of Chinese Film Art] (Beijing: Beijing daxue chubanshe, 2005); Wu Xiaoli and Xu Shengmin, *Jiushi niandai Zhongguo dianying lun* [Chinese Films in the 1990s] (Beijing: Wenhua yishu chubanshe, 2005).

8

Film Clubs in Beijing: The Cultural Consumption of Chinese Independent Films

Seio Nakajima

Concomitant with the rise of the so-called urban generation of Chinese film-makers, academic studies on this group of filmmakers and their works have emerged since the 1990s. However, most of the existing research focuses on analysis of film texts, while detailed discussions of the social and cultural context of production, distribution, and exhibition of those films have yet to be developed.[1] In this chapter, I attempt to contribute to filling this gap in the study of Chinese independent film by foregrounding one concrete aspect of film consumption—that is, film clubs that emerged in the last decade in Beijing.

This chapter is based on my ethnographic participant observation of film clubs in Beijing from February 2003 to August 2004. I also supplement my observation of club activities by interviewing organizers and participants. Given the fact that most Chinese independent films either are not distributed domestically or are given very limited distribution, the film clubs provide an important public space where exhibition and consumption of those films take place. The study of film clubs gives us a lens through which we can observe how Chinese audiences *actually* watch independent films, and in what kind of situations. Thus, the first task of this chapter is to clearly describe the charac-teristics of film clubs in Beijing and introduce this little-known phenomenon of an alternative film culture in China.

Theoretically, I tackle two interrelated questions suggested by Pierre Bourdieu's theory of "the field of cultural production." The first question is: how can we adequately combine an analysis of the social context of produc-tion, distribution, and exhibition, with the study of film texts? The second question is: whether and how we can extend Bourdieu's analysis of the field of cultural production to that of a *field of cultural consumption*. I will address both questions by examining one specific aspect of social context: film consumption in Beijing film clubs.

FROM THE FIELD OF CULTURAL PRODUCTION
TO THE FIELD OF CULTURAL CONSUMPTION

Bourdieu's approach to the field of cultural production attempts to transcend the antinomy of two futile conceptions in accounting for the process of cultural production—the antinomy between "internal reading" and "external reading."[2] According to the first, a text has to be read "formally," that is, independent of the social and historical contexts surrounding the production of the text (e.g., where it was written, when it was produced, who wrote the text). The external reading attempts to relate a text to its socioeconomic conditions of production and producers. As a sociologist, Bourdieu does not deny the importance of social contexts in which cultural works are produced. What he strongly rejects is "reflection theory," an approach that "relates them [cultural works] directly to the social characteristics of the authors, or of the group to whom they were addressed or were assumed to be addressed, and regards them as expressing those social characteristics."[3] He rejects this sort of external analysis as a fallacy of "short circuit."[4]

But how can we go beyond the apparent *aporia* between internal and external analysis? The answer exists in the concept of field. Bourdieu differentiates society into a number of relatively autonomous "fields" (e.g., literary, religious, economic, scientific).[5] Each field is autonomous to the extent that its logic or "rules of the game" are *specific and irreducible* to those that regulate other fields."[6] At the same time, all fields contain similar structural oppositions between the dominant and the dominated, or the powerful and the powerless, and decide which rules prevail in a certain field. This structural opposition is maintained according to the specific mechanism of legitimation or "criteria of reward" for different kinds of "capital" (e.g., economic, cultural, social, political) as well as economy of exchange (i.e., "conversion rate") regulating those different forms of capital.[7] In addition, each field (e.g., literature, music, paintings) is encompassed by what Bourdieu calls a "field of power," which expresses the power relations among different fields. Within the field of power, the literary field or the field of cultural production in general is situated in the *dominated* position in relation to those fields such as the economic and political fields, which are situated in the *dominant* pole in the overall field of power. In accordance with the power relations among the fields, each field contains within itself a "heteronomous pole," a part of the field influenced by the logic of the field outside itself, and an "autonomous pole," a part of the field governed by the logic unique to the field in question.[8] For example, in the literary field, the autonomous pole within the field (e.g., poetry) may insist on the logic of "art for art's sake" indifferent to the logic of economic success and reward, which is the logic existing in the economic field. On the other hand, the heteronomous pole within the literary field (e.g., popular novel) may well pursue the rules of the game of the economic field.

One of Bourdieu's main hypotheses about the field of cultural production is that there exists a "homology" or correspondence between the space of producers and the space of products. According to Bourdieu,

> The science of the work of art thus takes as its very own object the *relationship between two structures*, the structure of objective relations between positions in the field of production (and among the producers who occupy them), and the structure of objective relations among the position-takings in the space of works. Equipped with the hypothesis of a homology between the two structures, research—by setting up a to-and-fro between the two spaces and between identical data offered there under different guises—may accumulate the information which gives us *at one and the same time* works read in their interrelations, and the properties of agents, or their positions, also apprehended in their objective relations.[9]

In addition, Bourdieu introduces the concepts of "habitus" and "trajectory" by making reference to the notion of field in physics.[10] In the case of the "field of force," molecules entering the field can be defined by the characteristics of the molecules (e.g., types and sizes) and the inertia of those molecules. In the field of cultural production, the actors entering the field can be characterized by their habitus (historically and socially constructed dispositions) and their trajectory (where they come from, where they are heading) within the field.

Bourdieu mobilizes these concepts to analyze the field of cultural production, rather than cultural consumption. This is because, for him, "in a field whose autonomy is developed, distinction between issues of production and consumption becomes blurred" due to the fact that consumers of cultural products are often themselves producers of those products.[11] However, as I try to show in this chapter, even in the arguably most autonomous sector in the field of cultural production of Chinese films (i.e., independent films), producers and consumers do not always coincide. It is true that some film club organizers and members are film directors and producers, but the majority of participants in club activities are not filmmakers themselves. This is why I argue that an investigation of the field of *cultural consumption* is worth pursuing in its own right. In addition, I will show that Bourdieu's insights into cultural production can be applied effectively to an analysis of consumption in a cultural field.

SPACE OF CULTURAL CONSUMERS:
CASE STUDIES OF FOUR FILM CLUBS

In order to highlight the differences among film clubs, I chose four film clubs whose significance in the field of cultural consumption in Beijing can be conceptually positioned in a three-dimensional space (see figure 8.1). There are three axes in the figure, and each has two levels, high and low. The vertical axis represents the amount of cultural capital possessed by the organizer(s) and members of film clubs—the amount measured by their knowledge of film, particularly Chinese independent films, and the degree of the club's emphasis on cultural capital. One horizontal axis represents the amount of economic capital as well as the degree of emphasis on the importance of economic capital. Economic capital here refers to relatively tangible financial and material objects, such as money and physical possessions. Another horizontal axis represents political capital accented by the film clubs. For Bourdieu, "political capital" usually represents such things as political posts in the state bureaucracy, and connections to or patronage by powerful figures. However, I argue that the term can be effectively extended in contemporary Chinese society to include the ability, willingness, and resources necessary to engage in political debates, sometimes in defiance of such dominant players as the film bureaucracy. To protect the privacy and safety of the people interviewed, I use pseudonyms for all film clubs in this chapter.

The first film club, the Film Movement Society, is located in a position of high cultural capital, low economic capital, and high political capital. In contrast to other film clubs that appeared subsequently in Beijing, this club is distinguished by its willingness to engage in political debates in its activities. Thus, I call this club a *politically oriented film club*. The second club, Culture Salon, is located in a position of low cultural capital, high economic capital, and low political capital. Their main emphasis is on economic capital, and therefore I call this club a *commercially oriented film club*. The third club, Formula 3, is located in a position of high cultural capital, low economic capital, and low political capital. I call it an *"art for art's sake" film club* because it emphasizes cultural activity more than economic activity, explicitly favoring more autonomous or avant-garde works within the already autonomous field of Chinese independent film. The fourth club, Studio Z, positions itself at high cultural capital, high economic capital, and low political capital. Its activities combine elements of art and commerce, and I call it an *artistic, commercial film club*. Now that I have provided the overall conceptual space in which Beijing film clubs can be schematically positioned, I will introduce these four cases in detail (see table 8.1).

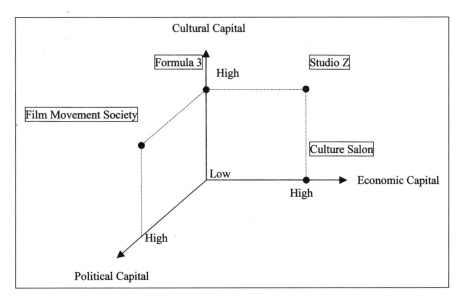

Figure 8.1. Schematic presentation of the space of Beijing film clubs

The Film Movement Society: A Politically Oriented Film Club

A politically oriented film club, the Film Movement Society was established as a "film viewing social organization" (*guanying shetuan*) by a group of college students in the spring of 2000. Its core organizers included students from the Directing Department of the Beijing Film Academy (BFA) as well as students from the Department of Art at Beijing Normal University. Given the organizers' backgrounds, the club places strong emphasis on *cultural capital*, and it did not register with the government. Its main venue was a bar located near the BFA in the neighborhood called Huangtingzi in the Haidian District. Not a club member, the owner provided the bar as a main venue for screening and discussion. The club did not have a formal membership system, nor did it require fees to attend. As one organizer recalls, "It was really an open entity. Anyone could join screenings and discussions. . . . People interested in film can participate whenever they want to."

Unlike some film clubs that organize both film and nonfilm activities, the Film Movement Society devoted most of its attention to film appreciation and promotion, and its core activities were film screenings and discussions. It programmed two kinds of screenings. The first was the exhibition of films by "classic masters" (*jingdian dashi*), including Michelangelo Antonioni,

Table 8.1. Summary of the Four Film Clubs

Name	Type	Established	Registration	Characteristics of Organizer(s)	Main Venue(s)	Membership System/Fees	Film-Related Activities	Non-Film-Related Activities	Characteristics of Participants	Participants
The Film Movement Society	Politically oriented	Spring 2000	None	Students at the Beijing Film Academy and Beijing Normal University	Bar located near Beijing Film Academy; later at different university campuses	None/None	1) Screenings and discussions of films by "classic masters"; 2) screenings and discussions of Chinese independent films; 3) organization of a film festival	None	Students and people from the media, younger crowd, 18–25 years old	Minimum 30, often up to 70–100
Culture Salon	Commercially oriented	Early summer 2003	Registered as a cultural communication company with Chaoyang Bureau of Industry and Commerce	A couple with college degrees in international trade and design	Bar owned and managed by a couple	None/30 yuan per activity	Screenings and discussions of Chinese independent films with English subtitles	1) English conversation; 2) "Cultural Exchange Weeks" with foreign embassies; 3) other cultural activities such as lecture on "coffee culture"	Foreign "expatriates," Chinese businesspeople, relatively older people, 25–40 years old	20–30 seated, up to 60 with some standing

Name	Type	Established	Registration	Characteristics of Organizer(s)	Main Venue(s)	Membership System/Fees	Film-Related Activities	Non-Film-Related Activities	Characteristics of Participants	Participants
Formula 3	Art for art's sake	Fall 2003	None	Writer	Bar owned and managed by the organizer of film club	None/None	Screenings of Chinese independent films, esp. experimental works, or those bordering on film and other art media	A variety of activities in art: music, dance, performance art, literature, poetry, etc.	Artists, small circle of people in the Beijing independent film world, students at the Central Academy of Fine Arts, age varies from 18 to 50	10–15 average, max. 20–30

Table 8.1. Continued

Name	Type	Established	Registration	Characteristics of Organizer(s)	Main Venue(s)	Membership System/Fees	Film-Related Activities	Non-Film-Related Activities	Characteristics of Participants	Participants
Studio Z	Combination of art and commerce	Summer 2002	None	Graduates of Beijing University; the main organizer has a degree in finance	Public library; exhibition hall at a bookstore in Wangfujing; university campuses	Normal membership= 200 yuan per year; VIP membership= 1,500 yuan per year; one-timer fee=5–20 yuan per activity	1) Screenings and discussions of Chinese independent films; 2) screenings of blockbuster imports; 3) screenings of older domestic films; 4) screenings of films with limited domestic circulation; 5) organization of "film exhibitions"; 6) lectures related to filmmaking; 7) academic lectures	None	Students and recent graduates, young independent filmmakers in Beijing, 18–30 years old	20–30 for small events, 100–800 for large events or entertainment fare

Ingmar Bergman, Luis Bunuel, Federico Fellini, Jean-Luc Godard, Andrei Tarkovsky (*Violin and Roller*, 1960), and French New Wave auteurs, as well as Taiwan director Edward Yang (Yang Dechang, *A Brighter Summer Day*, 1991) and a few Japanese directors. The club also showed a series of Dogma 95 films, including those by Lars von Trier.[12] The "classic masters" series usually occurred on Friday, and because the club could not invite directors for discussion, sometimes it invited BFA graduate students and professors to lecture on relevant subjects.

The second type of activity was the screening of Chinese independent films, both fiction and documentary. The club usually programmed this screening on weekend afternoons so that more people could attend. The screening was often followed by questions and answers involving directors and other film workers.

The majority of participants were college students and recent graduates, most affiliated with the BFA. A regular pool of participants also came from the media, and their presence allowed the club to extend beyond college students and to exert a certain social impact. One former participant reminisced, "The crowd was definitely younger, with the majority of the participants between ages eighteen to twenty-five." The club was popular among people interested in Chinese independent films. In one estimate, the numbers were "never below thirty. A minimum forty to sixty people attended, and regularly the number reached seventy-five to one hundred. Often, there were not enough seats, so it was common to see people standing in the back, enthusiastically watching the film and participating in the discussion."

While continuing with screenings in the bar, the club extended activities to university campuses, such as Beijing University, Beijing Normal University, and Qinghua University. It showed films in multimedia classrooms as well as in school libraries. Because VCDs or DVDs were not yet widespread, the screening was often done by projecting VHS tapes on a screen. The screen in the bar was about the size of 2 by 1.5 meters.

Although the "Film Movement Society" is a pseudonym used in this chapter to maintain anonymity, the club's Chinese name includes the character for "society" and a term whose meaning is similar to "movement." The naming itself indicates the club's leaning toward sociopolitical issues. As one organizer told me:

> We really had a clear sense of social responsibility. As the terms "movement" and "society" tell you, we didn't want just to watch films for the sake of watching. The film was not just art. We had cultural ideals, and we wanted our club to have social implications and social impact beyond the film world. We wanted to change something in society, and that was really the main purpose of our activity. In order to accomplish this goal, we need to understand not only films but also society, the social, cultural reality of China.

One participant recalled, "They had a very high-profile political orientation. Often the discussion was heated and touched on big issues like the future of Chinese society and politics as well as the role of film in that future." Another participant remarked on the role of the state in filmmaking, and his remark was quite political in nature:

> This country is like one where there's a rule that every household must eat potato for lunch and cabbage for dinner. It's like a country where this habit of eating potato and cabbage continues for a whole year according to an officially drafted plan. Under this specific situation, independence doesn't necessarily mean expressing something essentially independent in terms of filmmaking style or film contents. Just deciding to do things differently, say, eating cabbage for lunch and potato for dinner, could already mean independence. In China today, being independent doesn't have concrete or essential meaning without the existence of those state regulations. Films become independent when put in relation to the political pressure in contemporary Chinese society. So, I don't necessarily think independent films should be something "avant-garde" or cutting-edge in terms of film styles. In other words, independence means searching for an alternative to the ways dictated by the state. Although some people say that the government and the Film Bureau have recently become more helpful to Chinese filmmakers, I think everything the government does is working in the negative. In China today, I think the more government becomes involved in filmmaking, the more the situation becomes a mess.

Another example of the club's political leaning can be gleaned from a film series it organized in the fall of 2002. Under a monthly theme of "foreign political films," it screened four films that supposedly deal with political issues from different angles. These were Sergei Eisenstein and Grigori Aleksandrov's *The Battleship Potemkin* (1925), Costa-Gavras's *Z* (1969), Emir Kusturika's *Underground* (1995), and Danis Tanovic's *No Man's Land* (2001).

One organizer compared the Film Movement Society with other film clubs in Beijing:

> There are now more film clubs in Beijing, like Studio Z, Film Club 8, Formula 3, and Penthouse. But they don't have anything constructive; their activities don't change anything, don't add anything to society, and they don't have any creativity. Of course I admit they have important meaning because they continue to exist and show films to people. That's important. But still, they don't have constructive meaning beyond that. I think this is the biggest limitation of film clubs in Beijing today. We had a sense of self-determination (*zijuexing*), and we had concerns and relations with the whole society.

The organizer also commented on the significance of educational background:

> I don't want to say that the people who organized film clubs later differ in social status (*shenfen*). I don't have any intention of looking down on them. But many

of them have an economic background. You know, the organizer of Studio Z studied international finance in college. His thinking is "industrialization" (*chanyehua*), which may not be a good word, but they want to make money by showing films. I don't think doing it that way is a bad thing. But their thinking is mixed (*hunza*). They just have fun, but later nothing remains.

Clearly, the criticism here is directed at the *habitus* of one organizer of Studio Z, in that its activity is assumed to be merely a means of earning money. Another point of the criticism is the *trajectory* of the Studio Z organizer, whose college education in international finance is seen to have somehow reduced the credibility of his operation in the field of cultural consumption.

It is evident that the Film Movement Society was a pioneer in unofficial film screenings in Beijing and its activities were quite influential. Indeed, almost all the people I met in Beijing film clubs mentioned the Film Movement Society. However, due to its political orientation, the club had encountered "political trouble" with the government.[13] Besides, the core group of their members also differed in opinions on how to carry on club activities. This was one of the reasons why the club suspended its activities in the second half of 2002. By the year's end, after about two years of operation, the club was disbanded.

The political orientation of the Film Movement Society was recognized by other film clubs. For example, the main organizer of Studio Z told me:

> You know, the Film Movement Society was quite active in 2000 and 2001, but it had some trouble. The name itself was problematic for some people, for the term "society" (*she*) is controversial. It reminds people of an entity oppositional to the state or dangerous to society. So the government had problems with that name. The club aspired to be a "social organization," but to be recognized as a legal social organization, you have to register with the Ministry of Civil Affairs (*Minzhengbu*), and the process I heard is very complicated. But as you can tell, the Film Movement Society was not registered with any government offices, and that made it an illegal organization. They were other reasons for ending their activity, including different opinions on the part of organizers, but one of the most important reasons for their demise was surely their explicit political orientation.

If personal judgment is insufficient as evidence, a document published by the Film Movement Society may further reveal its political orientation. Like the "Vow of Chastity" issued by Dogma 95, the club's "Rules of Activity" (*huodong zhangcheng*) contain this clause: "Cultural colonization is taking place quietly in conjunction with the global spread of American political and economic hegemony. With their audio-visual temptation, Hollywood films work like specters, providing satisfaction while depriving the audience of the right to think." Albeit its target is not exactly the Chinese government, this statement demonstrates the importance of political capital (e.g., "talking politics") in the operation of this club.

I should clarify that by "political" I mean the willingness and ability to engage in political discussion. This ability seems to be rare in most film clubs that have emerged subsequently in Beijing. The organizers of the other three clubs discussed in this chapter, for example, have all distanced themselves from politics, and this fact makes the Film Movement Society unique in the field of cultural consumption. Thus, I call it a politically oriented film club and position it "high" on the axis of political capital.

Apart from politics, the Film Movement Society also emphasized film knowledge, and this is why I assess the club "high" in cultural capital. In terms of economic capital, I place this club "low" because the purpose of activity was not centered on making money. In spite of its location inside a bar, the management and ownership of the bar and the club were completely separate. One organizer told me that, basically, their activity did not include economic transactions, and they did not give honoraria to directors invited for discussions.

To document fully the process of conversion of different types of capital requires a diachronic analysis longer than is possible in this chapter. However, even within the relatively short time span of this research, there were interesting signs of such conversion. In the case of the Film Movement Society, its political capital seemed to have worked as a kind of *symbolic capital* to enhance the legitimacy of cultural capital it possessed. For example, it had planned to screen Jia Zhangke's *Platform* (2000) as the concluding feature at a film festival it organized (see appendix 8.1). But because the film was "banned" in China, the group had trouble with the government and had to show it in a drive-in theater in the suburbs rather than in the BFA main theater, where the festival was held. This "political trouble," I argue, functioned as a kind of symbolic capital to enhance the legitimacy of the festival—a festival whose cultural capital was foregrounded in the organizers' knowledge of Chinese independent films and their ability to appreciate them properly. A number of organizers and participants recalled this event as a high point in the development of Chinese independent film because they were setting a historical precedent by gathering in mass and appreciating the "banned film" in defiance of state censorship (see Paul Pickowicz's and Yingjin Zhang's chapters).

Culture Salon: A Commercially Oriented Film Club

A commercially oriented film club, Culture Salon was established by a couple in the early summer of 2003 in the thick of the SARS epidemic. The woman holds a degree in international trade, and the man in design, thus marking their "trajectory" as from outside the film world. The woman admits that she is not very "artistic" because she worked in an advertising company for six years and all she knew then was how to make money. However, as her partner, who worked in a design firm, began to concentrate on painting, she became interested in the arts and started activities related to art and culture, including film screenings.

Culture Salon was originally based in a bar located in Sanlitun, the busiest bar-hopping area in Beijing frequented by foreign expatriates. Although the club moved to the "Dashanzi art district" in September 2004, my description centers on their prerelocation activities so as to cover roughly the same period as other film clubs under discussion.[14] The bar is registered as a "cultural communication company" with the Chaoyang Division of the Beijing Municipal Bureau of Industry and Commerce and is therefore a legal entity. The bar does not have a membership system, but instead charges 30 yuan for film attendance and offers a complimentary drink. As the owners acknowledge, the money generated by the club is a vital source of their income.

To enhance its economic capital, the club offers a variety of activities, including a salon for practicing spoken English, as well as a series called "Cultural Exchange Week," in which the club cooperates with foreign embassies (e.g., India, Spain, and Mexico) and introduces their cultures. For film screenings, the club often invites directors and other film workers involved for on-site discussion. A major part of the screenings is devoted to Chinese independent feature-length films, documentary and fiction alike (see appendix 8.2).

One notable characteristic of the club is the direct connection between its cultural activities and the economic function of the bar. Another characteristic is that its ticket-paying participants include many expatriates in Beijing. In fact, the female owner speaks English fluently and has the ability to communicate with people from different cultural backgrounds. Not surprisingly, all films screened in the club carry English subtitles, a decision specifically targeting a foreign audience.

Compared with other clubs, student participation in Cultural Salon is rather low, due in part to its rather high admission (30 yuan) and in part to its location far from major college campuses. Thus, excluding foreigners, most Chinese participants are businesspeople who frequent bars in the "fashionable" Sanlitun area. Understandably, the average age of the participants is higher than those clubs frequented by students. Indeed, one owner expressed contempt for these students:

> First, I thought I would welcome college students who like to watch films. In fact, at the beginning I tried to show films without charging a fee. But I soon realized that college students just come to watch films without consuming anything from the bar. Sometimes, they even bring in their own drinks. It's okay for them to come, but I don't want to alienate other important groups of people who are willing to pay money and watch films. So I started to charge 30 yuan each time. Indeed this kept away many "free-riding" students, and things began to go well after that.

The number of participants varies from activity to activity, but film screenings usually attract twenty to thirty people due to the bar's limited space. The largest number I saw in the bar reached around sixty. The bar in its original location had a screening room on the second floor, where there were several tables for drinks and light snacks. If packed, the space could hold up to thirty to forty people with seating, but more people could stand in the back of the room. The screen was about 2.5 by 2 meters, and a projector was connected to the VCR, DVD player, DV camera, and so on.

The club sees film activities as a significant part of its identity. As the male owner assured me, the reason for opening the bar was to provide a space where people could gather and discuss cultural issues, hence the club's name. However, it is also a commercial bar in the sense that earning money to keep the bar going is equally important. As the female owner says, in the future they may raise the admission fee to 50 or even 80 yuan in order to maintain the "quality" of its activity and audience.

To distinguish their taste, the female owner stresses that their choices are "healthier" than some other clubs:

> I don't choose to show things that are "negative" (*xiaoji*) or not very healthy because if I show those things, people will come to my bar just to satisfy their "curiosity" (*lieqi*). For example, although I don't have anything against gay and lesbian films—indeed we showed Li Yu's *Fish and Elephant* (2000) and Zhang Yuan's *East Palace, West Palace* (1996)—I didn't want to emphasize them as just gay and lesbian films. Some other clubs in Beijing try to be sensational and make those films their selling point. I don't want to do that. I only want to show healthy things, not radical stuff. We are also different from film clubs such as Formula 3. Although they also have a bar, they are run by a small circle of people in the film world. I want to bring in people from different backgrounds, including foreigners. I don't want to alienate foreigners who pay money to come here by admitting too many Chinese people, especially students, who take advantage of our activity.

It is easy to imagine the view from the other side, as many people in Beijing have considered Culture Salon a commercial operation. For example, one organizer of the Film Movement Society asserts, "I've never been to Culture Salon, but I've heard they're mixing commercial and cultural purposes."

In brief, although Culture Salon has featured Chinese independent films like other clubs, its commercial profile looms large because its cultural activities are seen as subordinate to the bar's commercial operation. Besides, the owners come from outside the film world and their knowledge of film is limited. In fact, they commissioned a former organizer of Studio Z to curate film activities. Understandably, the club does not emphasize politics, and it intentionally avoids screening films judged to be "unhealthy."

As for the economy of exchange of different types of capital, this club shows a clear case of conversion of economic capital to cultural capital. This strategy of conversion seems to work so well that, as the club has accumulated more cultural capital related to Chinese independent film after its relocation in the Dashanzi art district, its film-related activities have been recognized as some of the most dynamic among Beijing clubs. For example, a retrospective of Ning Ying's works organized by the club in October 2004 attracted more than two hundred people. This process of conversion suggests that the club is moving from the position characterized by high economic capital, low political capital, and "low" cultural capital to a position of "high" cultural capital.

Formula 3: An "Art for Art's Sake" Film Club

An "art for art's sake" film club, Formula 3 was established in the fall of 2003 by the former owner of a restaurant located near Beijing University. He never had formal education in literature but has been writing short stories and considers himself a writer. The club is located in a bar called Formula 3, which serves light meals in addition to drinks, and is registered as a "Western-style restaurant" (*xican ting*) with the Chaoyang Division of the Beijing Municipal Bureau of Industry and Commerce. Nonetheless, the club's cultural arm has never registered with any government offices. Although I call it a film club, it does not have a strict membership system, nor does it require participants to pay for film screenings, although they often order items from the bar.

One characteristic that distinguishes this club from others is its presentation of a wide range of art-related activities in addition to film screenings. These activities cover music, drama, contemporary dance, poetry reading, performance art, and discussion of literature and music (including hip-hop). Another characteristic is that the participants seem to be people who know each other well. Many participants are themselves involved in arts, such as drawing, photography, graphic design, music, literature, and dance. Because the bar is located near the Central Academy of Fine Arts, many participants are students from the academy.

The number of participants varies according to activities, but since the club's activity often falls within the margin of the world of arts and film, attendees rarely exceeded twenty. The bar has a separate screening room with a screen measuring 2 by 1.5 meters, and a projector connected to the VCR and DVD players, DV camera, and so on. The club does not have a regular film schedule, but it usually organizes individual series based on certain themes such as "New Visual Works by Chinese Women." A series normally lasts for a few days, with a few hours of screenings and discussions scheduled each night.

The owner sees his club as unique because it focuses not only on film but also the arts adjacent to or even outside the film world. Even when concentrating on film, it shows more experimental films or films difficult to see elsewhere. As people from other film clubs characterize it, Formula 3 is more interested in serving people of its own circle rather than opening up to the public.

Although the club is attached to a commercial bar, its emphasis is to schedule films marginal to the already marginal world of Chinese independent films. To use Bourdieu's terms, the club is located in the autonomous pole of the relatively autonomous field of Chinese independent film. As many participants are his personal friends, the owner often treats them to drinks and food, so the activity usually does not help the bar financially. In fact, the owner has considered selling the bar.

Contrary to the Film Movement Society, Formula 3 firmly avoids political issues. In several discussions I attended, the questions often included "What is your theory of art?" and "How do you define beauty?" One frequent participant told me, "As far as I remember, nothing related to politics was discussed in their activities." On the other hand, unlike Cultural Salon, Formula 3 does not do well in the conversion of different types of capital. The organizer has converted economic capital to cultural capital by opening a bar, but he seems to be losing economic capital while accumulating cultural capital, and this loss has threatened the existence of this "art for art's sake" film club.

Studio Z: An Artistic, Commercial Film Club

An artistic, commercial film club, Studio Z was established in the summer of 2002 by a group of recent graduates of Beijing University. One of its principal organizers earned a finance degree and tried different businesses related to arts and culture. First, in 2000 he launched a website posting cultural information. Then, with some friends, he opened a small shop selling CDs (e.g., college-chart music) and VCDs (e.g., Hollywood and Hong Kong entertainment fare). He was still a senior at Beijing University when he experimented with these small-scale commercial activities. However, as more elaborate pirated copies began to circulate in Beijing, the shop did not do well, and he closed it in one year. In his recollection, "I just started those things as a hobby. I was more interested in web design and the Internet than in films themselves. . . . It didn't have to be film, but it just happened that way."

After his original partners left by the end of 2001, this organizer worked alone and began preparing for his next stage. He once thought of starting an online film and music store but gave up mainly because of piracy issues and the underdeveloped system of e-commerce in China at that time. Instead, he started to concentrate on film club activities. The first Studio Z event he organized was a screening of Wang Xiaoshuai's *Beijing Bicycle* (2000) and a follow-up discussion with the film's director of photography. As of December 2003, when I interviewed him, the club had not registered with the government, although he planned to register with the Beijing Municipal Bureau of Industry and Commerce by setting up a culture company.

In contrast to other film clubs, Studio Z does not have a regular venue for hosting activities. Its first event took place in the National Library in the Haidian District, but its subsequent screenings were moved between a bookstore in Wangfujing and different college campuses (see appendix 8.4). Among the four film clubs, Studio Z is the only one operating on a strict membership system. A regular member pays 200 yuan per year to enjoy the benefits of video screenings, newsletters, and five free VCDs. A VIP or gold member pays 1,500 yuan per year and gets additional privileges such as free 35mm film screenings. The organizer estimated around two hundred regular members and a few VIP members by 2003. Nonmembers can still participate but have to pay 5 to 10 yuan for each regular screening and 20 yuan for special occasions (e.g., blockbuster films).

Almost all Studio Z activities are related to film, and the club screens the largest variety of films and has the highest frequency of screenings among all film clubs. In a series called "Conversations with Film Directors," the club usually shows Chinese independent films and invites directors or other film workers involved for postscreening discussions. It has exhibited a series of blockbuster films, such as the Wachowski Brothers' *The Matrix Revolutions* (2003) and Wai Keung Lau and Siu Fai Mak's *Infernal Affairs, III* (2003). This exhibition series is usually hosted in the BFA main theater, which seats up to eight hundred people. The club also features domestic films that are relatively old or are difficult to see as 35mm projections, including Jiang Wen's *In the Heat of the Sun* (1994), as well as Chinese films with limited domestic circulation, for instance Huo Jianqi's *Postman in the Mountains* (1998) and *Nuan* (2003). More significantly, the club organizes "film exhibitions" (*yingzhan*) and "film exchange weeks" (*dianying jiaoliu zhou*), featuring documentary films and young directors' works. The club sometimes cooperates with other organizations, such as campus film associations, when launching such special events. In addition, the club sponsors lectures on filmmaking, with topics ranging from "How to Become a Film Producer" to "Lighting in DV Filmmaking," as well as academic talks by film scholars and critics. Finally, the club has begun to produce films, and a couple of its productions have been featured in international film festivals, which illustrates their relatively high quality.

Given the variety of its activities, Studio Z has to rely on different venues and equipment. For small campus screenings, it uses a screen and a video projector connected to VCR, DVD/VCD, or DV. For large screenings like Gore Verbinski's *Pirates of the Caribbean* (2003), it rents the BFA main film theater equipped with 35mm projection. Predictably, the majority of Studio Z's audiences are college students, although the club also attracts recent graduates and older people involved in filmmaking. The numbers of participants vary

Romance between two high school students in Wang Xiaoshuai's Beijing Bicycle *(2000)*

significantly according to activities. For small screenings, it is twenty to thirty people, but for blockbuster films, several hundred may show up.

One salient characteristic of Studio Z is its remarkable balance between both economic and cultural aspects. Since its club activity constitutes a means of generating money, it features commercial titles to supplement independent films. As the core organizer admits, "We are not a social organization. We exist as a commercial entity." For this reason, other film clubs regard it as a club combining art and commerce. One organizer of the Film Movement Society remarks, "I'm not saying it's bad, but you know Studio Z's activity is a way to earn money." Studio Z is also judged to provoke "too much sensation," as the owner of Culture Salon remarks: "They sometimes want to show sensational things to attract attention. They show gay and lesbian films to get a kind of unhealthy attraction." In short, Studio Z occupies an *ambivalent* position: some see it as depending too much on commercialism, while others see it as privileging underground avant-gardism.

Studio Z is thus stretched between the commercial and artistic poles in the field of cultural consumption. Its emphasis on economic capital helps it generate a fair amount of profit,[15] but it simultaneously promotes "film as art" through a variety of programs, especially those on Chinese independent film.

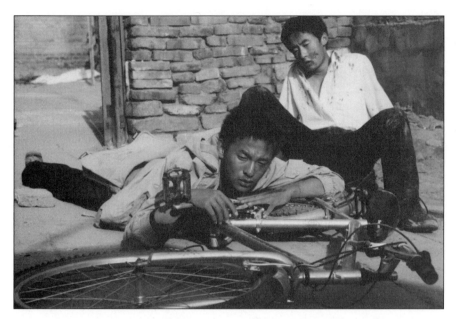

The aftermath of a bloody fight in Wang Xiaoshuai's Beijing Bicycle *(2000)*

As for politics, the Studio Z organizer has avoided any direct engagement: "We are not a social organization. We exist as an economic entity. . . . I'm not interested in politics. I just want to promote film."

Admittedly, balancing elements of art and commerce is an inherently difficult act because an economic orientation is rather suspect in the relatively autonomous field of art. The organizer of Studio Z is aware of the ambivalence of his club:

> I thought I would not want to make my film club too much of a commercial entity. But then for a variety of expected and unexpected reasons, it has become really commercialized (*shangyehua*). But I still like organizing activities, so I will continue with the club. But at the same time, I want to do something that can directly impact society or solve social problems. This is the reason why I have started an NGO helping elementary school education in remote villages of Sichuan.

In terms of conversion of various types of capital, Studio Z is unique in its balance between focusing on autonomous, independent Chinese films and highly commercial films. However, the club has not found a stable position between art and commerce. Thus, it can be characterized by its simultaneous accumulation of both economic and cultural capital without a patent mechanism of conversion of one to the other.

THE CULTURAL GEOGRAPHY OF FILM CLUBS IN BEIJING

This section briefly discusses the physical locations of film clubs in Beijing (see figure 8.2). Without engaging in a reading that is exclusively deterministic, I suggest that the striking correspondence between the location and the character of film clubs demonstrated below is not merely a random phenomenon.[16]

First, the Film Movement Society was located in a bar close to the BFA. Because the BFA is the national center for film education, film officials and film faculty often meet to discuss issues of film policy. In fact, the state film bureaucracy has commissioned BFA faculty to conduct research projects, and one such result is the "Notice on DV Film Management," published as an official document by the State Administration of Radio, Film and Television (SARFT) on May 24, 2004. Moreover, the BFA is also one of very few places where state officials and independent filmmakers have met face to face. In 2003, the Film Bureau telephoned Wang Xiaoshuai and proposed a roundtable discussion between independent directors and state film officials. Wang notified other independent directors and critics, and a roundtable was held on November 13 at the BFA and attended by He Jianjun, Ju Anqi, Jia Zhangke, Lou Ye, Wang Xiaoshuai, Zhang Xianming, and Zhang Yaxuan, all of whom signed a petition to the government asking for changes in film policies and regulations.[17]

Of course, the Film Movement Society's decision to operate near the BFA might have been influenced by other factors, such as the fact that the owner of a nearby bar was willing to provide space for their activities. In any case, the physical proximity of the BFA made it much easier for students and professors to attend the club's events. The geographical location of this politically oriented film club facilitated its combination of culture and politics—a distinctive feature more a result of social-contextual factors than a random personal choice.

Second, Culture Salon chose to open in Sanlitun, an area of fashionable expatriate nightlife. The Dashanzi art district, where it was relocated in 2004, is now famous for its renovated venues featuring bars, cafés, and art galleries. The district was originally a low-rent community attractive to artists who lived and worked in the vast empty space left by the closure of the former state-owned Factory 798. However, with the recent influx of foreign capital (e.g., French, Japanese, and Korean), the rents in Dashanzi skyrocketed (doubling in one year from 2004 to 2005), and the district has become one of the most expensive commercial areas in the city.[18] Obviously, the choices of Sanlitun and Dashanzi reveal Culture Salon's commercial orientation.

Third, Formula 3, characterized by its "art for art's sake" tendency, is located in Wangjing, an area of newly developed high-rise residences close to both the Central Academy of Fine Arts and the low-rent Huajiadi neighborhood preferred by independent artists and filmmakers. It may be a pure coincidence, but the club is physically located in an *underground* bar below an

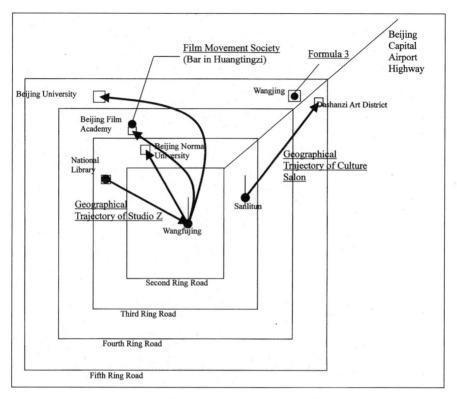

Figure 8.2.   Cultural geography of Beijing film clubs

apartment complex, accessed through a heavy wooden door and a long dark hallway. The bar's physical appearance fits perfectly the image of the club as the most "avant-garde" among all film clubs in Beijing.

Finally, Studio Z is unique in that it does not have a regular venue of its own. Its physical movement from the National Library (an official establishment) to a bookstore in Wangfujing (a tourist-friendly downtown shopping area) and to various college campuses (educational sites) visually illustrates the club's delicate balancing acts of combining art and commerce and negotiating between mainstream (both political and commercial) and underground.

THE SPACE OF TEXT

Although all four film clubs have extensively featured Chinese independent films, each of them displays a different emphasis within the overall intertextual space of contemporary Chinese film culture.

First of all, let us examine the Film Movement Society, which organized two kinds of screenings, one by "classical masters," and the other by Chinese independents (see appendix 8.1). Films shown in the latter category included Wang Xiaoshuai's *The Days* (1993) and *So Close to Paradise* (1998), He Jianjun's *Postman* (1995), Zhang Ming's *Rainclouds over Wushan* (1996), Lou Ye's *Suzhou River* (2000), as well as Zhang Yuan's earlier films. Among documentary films (see Matthew Johnson's, Valerie Jaffee's, and Chris Berry's chapters) were Wu Wenguang's *Jiang Hu* (1999), Yang Tianyi's *Old Men* (1999), Zhu Chuanming's *Beijing Cotton-Fluffing Artisan* (1999), Du Haibin's *Along the Railroad* (2000), and Ju Anqi's *There's a Strong Wind in Beijing* (2000). In addition, some student works, such as Yang Chao's thirty-minute *Runaway* (2001), were presented.

As one organizer opines, the climax of the club was "The First Independent Film Festival" it cosponsored (see appendix 8.1).[19] The festival was divided into several sections and combined competitions and forums on DV films as well as a special focus on Jia Zhangke. The competitions were held in three categories: experimental shorts, dramatic shorts, and documentary films. Although student works were mixed with more established professional productions, the variety itself conveyed the dynamic of the film club in its heyday.

The festival's film selection did not foreground an explicitly political orientation, but programming so many types of independent films was revolutionary in itself because independent filmmaking was considered illegal by the state. In addition, the festival's competition highlighted a set of criteria of filmmaking and film appreciation different from the official ones. Furthermore, two sensitive terms—"independent" (*duli*) and "festival" (*jie*)—in the festival's name suggested a political stance. As one frequent film club participant explains, "I also tried to organize a film screening activity using the word 'independent,' but I decided not to use the word because many people told me that word might get our activity into trouble." Another person who has organized a series of film events in Beijing comments: "The word 'festival' is only allowed for a government-sponsored event, like the Shanghai International Film Festival or the Changchun Film Festival. When we organize a de facto festival, we use the term 'film exhibition' (*yingzhan*) to avoid political trouble."

Although individual films taken out of context may not suggest any explicitly political orientation, the list of films as a whole, as well as the context of film screening (e.g., its insistence on the name "festival" and its open competitions), indicates the political orientation of the Film Movement Society.

Next, let us examine Culture Salon, which programmed a series of Chinese films from November 2003 to December 2004 (see appendix 8.2). The series included both important independent fiction films as well as documentary films, and deserves further elaboration. First, these titles do not include Chinese experimental films, which might appear too "exotic" (*lieqi*) in the owners' judgment.

実验电影俱乐部
Film Link

目标Concept
本着对文化的敬仰和对所有为之努力的人们的支持
为了所有热爱电影的人们。
This is forum for movie-lovers to discuss films with
local film-makers and people in the industry

周期:每月两次
Twice A Month

影展影片之五 5ᵗʰSession
《邮差》1995,中国
POSTMAN (P.R.C.,1995)
《邮差》1996, 韩国
IL Postino(Italy, 1996)
讨论 Talk with Director:何建军 **He Jianjun**

投递?
Diliver?

地点：藏酷（新媒体艺术中心）
Address:**The Loft(New Media Art Centre)**
时间：2001年4月15日 星期日下午3:00点
Time:**Sunday April 15ˢᵗ, 2001 @ 3:00p.m.**

门票：10元
Entry:10yuan
年费：200元
Yearly Membership:200yuan
策划人：李振华
Curator:Li Zhenhua

信息查询：1330 1070 144/movie2000@sina.com

主办: 芥子园
特殊媒体协办: 随意卡广告网 easycard.com.cn
赞助支持: 壹默视觉制作 IMAGE ELEMENT

随·意·卡 www.easycard.com.cn.查询:(010)-64943217 免费广告朋信片.© Image Element.E03.01

The back of a Beijing film club postcard advertising He Jianjun's
Postman *(1995)*

Second, some representative films from the "urban generation" are missing, for example those by Zhang Ming and Lou Ye. One explanation is that, as a rule, the club never shows a film without the permission of the director or producer, which has apparently limited its choices. Finally, it only presents films with English subtitles, presumably not to "alienate" its English-speaking audience. Although on the surface its list of films differs little from those of other film clubs, Cultural Salon demonstrates its preference for certain independent films and its distinctive concerns with legal and linguistic issues (subtitles). Such preference and concerns are linked to its commercial orientation.

Let us examine the Chinese films screened by Formula 3 from September 2003 to January 2005 (see appendix 8.3). Again, while overlapping with other film clubs (e.g., Ning Ying's *For Fun*, 1992), its list clearly points toward rarer, more experimental works (e.g., the "Classic Chinese films from old Shanghai prior to 1949") as well as films bordering on other artistic media (e.g., when the club invited the drum music performance group depicted in Wei Ating's documentary *Five-Tune Big Drums* [2004] to perform live at the film's premiere). Its activities often combine different art forms. Evidently, the films it chose correspond to the club's social-geographic location and its emphasis on "art for art's sake."

Finally, let us examine Studio Z's programs from July 2002 to December 2003 (see appendix 8.4), which are most comprehensive among all Beijing clubs (except for experimental works) and demonstrate outstanding characteristics. For one thing, it showed a fifth-generation classic, Chen Kaige's *Yellow Earth* (1984), as well as films that, in the organizer's view, "people heard about but were not widely exhibited in China" (e.g., Huo Jianqi's works), and these films were shown in 35mm format. Also shown in 35mm were imported blockbusters from Hollywood and Hong Kong, sometimes even during these films' first run in Beijing theaters.[20] Again, the combination of commercial films and independent works in the same program accents the club's distinction as an artistic, commercial entity.

TOWARD A SOCIOLOGY OF FILM CONSUMPTION

Among the three tasks I set at the beginning of this chapter, the first is to clearly describe the characteristics of film clubs in Beijing. Although I could not discuss all film clubs in the city, by highlighting significant differences in four representative clubs, I have demonstrated the variety and heterogeneity of film clubs using the rich data I gathered through my fieldwork in ethnographic participant observation.

I addressed two interrelated questions inspired by Bourdieu's work. First, how can we adequately combine an analysis of social context of production, distribution, and exhibition, with the study of film texts? By discussing both the social context of consumption and the films consumed, it becomes clear that focusing only on one or the other would miss the overall structure and dynamics of the field of cultural consumption of Chinese independent films. Although several films have screened in all four clubs, the social context of screening, such as whether they were entered in competitions or whether they carried English subtitles, has significantly influenced how the field of consumption as a whole was structured. In other words, there exists a "homology" or correspondence between the *space of context* and the *space of text*.

Moreover, by detailing the social, cultural context of consumption as well as different combinations of films screened, I have identified the historical and institutional conditions in which this homology takes place.

The second question inspired by Bourdieu was: can we extend an analysis of cultural production to that of cultural consumption? My answer is positive, and I have tried to prove it in several ways. First, the fact that the four film clubs were aware of each other and tried to construct an identity vis-à-vis others suggests that a relatively autonomous field of cultural consumption of Chinese independent films exists in Beijing and has developed its specific logic and rules. Second, the notion of homology proves quite useful in delineating the overall contours of the field of cultural consumption in film clubs. Third, different forms of capital (e.g., cultural, economic, and political) are assigned different importance in different film clubs, and I have shown that various mechanisms of conversion of different types of capital existed in the four film clubs. Fourth, the concepts of habitus and trajectory prove meaningful in explaining how the individual backgrounds of their owners have shaped the distinctive characteristics of the film clubs in Beijing.

Two other points are worth elaborating further. One, the overall "field of power" (i.e., politics and economy) in contemporary Chinese society has exerted a deep impact on the structure and dynamics of the field of cultural consumption. The fact that the Film Movement Society ceased to exist is partly a result of the power of the film bureaucracy as well as numerous administrative divisions of public security, which could always put pressure on film club activities when groups engage "too much" in politics. Also, the fact that Formula 3, the club characterized by autonomy from the logic of commerce, is on the verge of closing shows us the difficulty of maintaining the autonomous logic of "art for art's sake" in the increasingly "marketized" field of consumption. Put differently, even in the relatively autonomous field of cultural consumption of Chinese independent films, the overall field of power in Chinese society divides the field into a dominant pole (with which the commercially oriented Culture Salon identifies itself and therefore is able to accumulate economic capital) and a dominated pole (to which Formula 3 chooses to belong).

The second point is that, even in the autonomous field of independent films, producers and consumers do not always coincide. As implied in Bourdieu's theory of cultural production, some film club organizers and members are film directors and producers, but the majority of the participants in film club activities are not filmmakers themselves. This significant difference from Bourdieu's model of cultural production indicates a unique feature of the field of cultural consumption.[21]

In conclusion, I would like to quote remarks by two scholars on the relevance of sociology to film studies. "Most versions of film studies have not yet embraced the idea of analysing consumption," Graeme Turner observes, and "this is nominated as an area urgently in need of development."[22] In a similar vein, Andrew Tudor deplores that "it is both surprising and disappointing to discover how little the discipline [of sociology] has contributed to our understanding of film."[23] Although space limitations have prevented me from dealing more substantially with the actual processes of film reception and appreciation by the participants of film clubs, this chapter is my initial attempt to move toward a sociology of film consumption.

NOTES

1. For pioneering work in this direction, see Mayfair Mei-Hui Yang, "Film Discussion Groups in China: State Discourse or a Plebeian Public Sphere?" *Visual Anthropology Review* 10, no. 1 (1994): 112–25.

2. Pierre Bourdieu, *The Rules of Art: Genesis and Structure of the Literary Field* (Stanford, Calif.: Stanford University Press, 1996), 193.

3. Pierre Bourdieu, *The Rules of Art*, 202.

4. Bourdieu, *The Field of Cultural Production: Essays on Art and Literature*, ed. and intro. Randal Johnson (New York: Columbia University Press, 1993), 181, 188; "Bungakuba no seisei to kozo" [Genesis and Structure of the Literary Field], *Bungaku* 5, no. 1 (1994): 56.

5. Pierre Bourdieu and Loic J. D. Wacquant, *An Invitation to Reflexive Sociology* (Chicago: University of Chicago Press, 1992), 16–17, 97–98.

6. Bourdieu and Wacquant, *An Invitation to Reflexive Sociology*, 97.

7. Diana Crane, "Reward Systems in Art, Science, and Religion," in *The Production of Culture*, ed. Richard A. Peterson, 57–72 (Beverly Hills, Calif.: Sage, 1976).

8. Bourdieu, *The Field of Cultural Production*, 38; *The Rules of Art*, 216–18.

9. Bourdieu, *The Rules of Art*, 233–34.

10. Bourdieu, "Bungakuba no seisei to kozo," 59.

11. Bourdieu, "Bungakuba no seisei to kozo," 60.

12. The information in this section is drawn from my interviews with the organizers and participants as well as my reading of the club's pamphlets and newsletters. In addition, a documentary by American director Angus McNelis, *Shades of Gray: A Visual Essay* (2001), includes a rare portrait of the atmosphere of the club in its heyday.

13. In China, "political trouble" means a number of different things. While no interviewee pinpoints the exact trouble the Film Movement Society encountered, I suspect that its closure might have resulted from combined pressures from state authorities, such as SARFT and the Beijing Bureau of Culture, in addition to the organizers' self-censorship. The rumor has it that one supportive professor had to submit a "letter of apology" to his institution, but local bars and cafés have routinely been advised by authorities of various kinds not to engage in any "inappropriate" or "illegal" activities.

14. One exception is my inclusion in appendix 8.2 of some films shown after the club's relocation.

15. My interview with the organizer of Studio Z shows the following costs of showing a 35mm film. The rent for the BFA main theater is 2,500 yuan, which allows enough time for two feature-length films. The charge for a 35mm film copy of a newly imported blockbuster during its first run in Beijing is 7,000 yuan. The rental costs drop to 3,000 or 4,000 yuan if the blockbuster film has been shown for one to three months. For a new domestic film still in its first run, the charge is 3,000 yuan. For old domestic films, the cost ranges from several hundred to 1,000 yuan. When *The Matrix Revolutions* and Huang Shuqing's *Forever Young* (1983) were shown consecutively, all eight hundred seats were sold out at 20 yuan per ticket. The income was 16,000 yuan. After subtracting the rental costs, the profit for the night was 5,500 yuan. Although the amount is meager by foreign standards, it is quite substantial when the average monthly income of a Beijing resident is 1,156.9 yuan (calculated from the annual income of 13,883 yuan in 2003 as reported by the Beijing Municipal Bureau of Statistics). Since their publicity expense is minimal, and personnel costs are close to nothing, 5,500 yuan for a night is quite a fortune for people in their late twenties.

16. This section is inspired by Bourdieu's analysis of Gustav Flaubert's novel, *Sentimental Education*; see Bourdieu, *The Rules of Art*, 40-43.

17. See *Nanfang dushi bao*, "Duli dianying qijunzi lianming shangshu dianying ju: zuotanhui neimu shoudu gongkai" [Seven Lords of Independent Film Signed a Petition to the Film Bureau: The Forum's Inside Information Made Public for the First Time], *Nanfang dushi bao*, Dec. 4, 2003.

18. See *Nanfang zhoumo*, "Dangdai yishu yu dazhong xiaofei de yanhuan" [Pleasurable Dialogue between Contemporary Art and Mass Consumption], *Nanfang zhoumo*, March 27, 2003, and "Gongchang he yishu" [Factory and Art], *Nanfang zhoumo*, March 27, 2003; Zhu Yan, *798: A Photographic Journal by Zhu Yan* (Beijing: Timezone 8, 2004).

19. In compiling appendixes 8.1–8.4, I have tried to make them as reliable as possible by comparing the data to other sources, including websites and published pamphlets and brochures, as well as interviews with the organizers and members of film clubs. I have excluded non-Chinese films from the lists, except when they are essential to the characteristics of a film club.

20. For example, when *The Matrix Revolutions* opened in Beijing on November 6, 2003, commercial theaters charged 50 to 80 yuan per ticket. This explains why Studio Z's double features for 20 yuan were extremely popular among students.

21. In a rare reference, Bourdieu suggests that the "significant part, if not all, of the things that occur in the field of film can be explained by considering the issue of consumption" ("Bungakuba no seisei to kozo," 60).

22. Graeme Turner, ed., *The Film Cultures Reader* (London: Routledge, 2002), 378–79.

23. Andrew Tudor, "Sociology and Film," in *The Oxford Guide to Film Studies*, ed. John Hill and Pamela Church Gibson, 190 (New York: Oxford University Press, 1998).

Films Screened at the First Independent Film Festival, Organized by the Film Movement Society

Note: For appendixes 8.1–8.4, only more or less known artists and titles are identified in English.

实验短片竞赛单元
COMPETITION IN EXPERIMENTAL SHORTS

《酱》（北京 · 富钰）4 min.
《链》（广州 · 曹斐）5 min.
《城市之光》 *City Lights*（上海 · 杨福东 Yang Fudong）6 min.
《四周》（沈阳 · 董为）20 min.
《生活很无趣，幸好有高跟鞋》（北京 · 胡吗个）8 min.
《痕迹》（北京 · 贾海清）3 min.
《拯救自己》（北京 · 曹淑华）2 min.
《你早，北京》（北京 · 赵亮）10 min.
《碰撞》（北京 · 乌尔善）5 min.
　　《on edge》（北京 · 孙略）4 min.
《多媒体情书》（北京 · 冯晓颖）8 min.
《脱口而出》（北京 · 乌尔善）6 min.
《遗嘱》（北京 · 王芬）7 min.
《后房，嘿！天亮了》 *Daybreak in the Back*（上海 · 杨福东Yang
　　Fudong）13 min.

剧情短片竞赛单元〈一〉
COMPETITION IN DRAMATIC SHORTS, I

《春暖花开》（北京 · 常征）38 min.
《我爱你》（北京 · 彭磊）3.5 min.

《附近的森林》（上海 · 丁正）50 min.
《夏日黄昏》（北京 · 杜杰）8 min.
《杀人叙事诗》（北京 · 宋明翰）38 min.
《Talk》（北京 · 孟军）9.5 min.
《犯罪分子》（北京 · 程耳）30 min.
《失去的一天》（北京 · 冯自立）7 min.
《霞飞路》（上海 · 程亮）32 min.
《奇迹》（北京 · 沈乔）10 min.

剧情短片竞赛单元〈二〉
COMPETITION IN DRAMATIC SHORTS, II

《孑孓》（武汉 · 方正）32 min.
《捉迷藏的规则》（北京 · 曲立男）6 min.
《低烧》（北京 · 喻蕾）22 min.
《清唱 · 静听》（北京 · 邵丹）18 min.
《沉没的午后》（沈阳 · 王林、付淞岩）40 min.
《失调257》（广州 · 曹斐）26 min.
《车四十四》*Bus 44*（北京 · 伍仕贤Dayyan Eng）11 min.
《啊 啊 啊》（北京 · 王芬）30 min.
《我的家》（北京 · 孟蕾）15 min.
《想去哪儿就去哪儿》（北京 · 吴楠）48 min.
《上班下班》（北京 · 孙明）10 min.

纪录片竞赛单元〈一〉
COMPETITION IN DOCUMENTARIES, I

《盒子》*The Box*（沈阳 · 英未未 Ying Weiwei）88 min.
《铁路沿线》*Along the Railroad*（北京 · 杜海滨 Du Haibin）98 min.

纪录片竞赛单元〈二〉
COMPETITION IN DOCUMENTARIES, II

《弟弟》（上海 · 周洪波）33 min.
《英和白》（武汉 · 张以庆）50 min.
《食指》（深圳 · 蒋志）40 min.
《自由边缘》（北京 · 孙志强）60 min.

《热带鱼》（北京 · 赵小宁） 30 min.

纪录片竞赛单元〈三〉
COMPETITION IN DOCUMENTARIES, III

《挣扎》（上海 · 舒浩崙） 50 min.
《群众演员》 *Extras*（北京 · 朱传明 Zhu Chuanming） 100 min.
《老田》（太原 · 常青） 90 min.

剧情短片/实验短片展映〈一〉
剧情短片/实验短片展映〈二〉
剧情短片/实验短片展映〈三〉

剧情短片展映片目（排序不分先后）
DRAMATIC SHORTS EXHIBITED (NOT RANKED IN ANY ORDER)

《纸》 *Paper* 丁建城 Ding Jiancheng, 70 min.
《熊》 陈峥 30 min.
《待避》 *Runaway* 杨超 Yang Chao, 30 min.
《女人樊梨花》 甘小二 38 min.
《三月某三天》 孙略 12 min.
《一个人的老吴》 刘涛 22 min.
《咖啡日记》 孙韬 19 min.
《夜像》 蔡笑扬 39 min.
《MASS》 *Mass* 崔子恩 Cui Zi'en, 7 min.
《李希的夏天》 李秀东 18 min.
《地铁》 刘铉 32 min.
《卖女孩的小火柴》 徐仙霞 16 min.
《行走的日子》 王东、毛晨雨 60 min.
《一个虚构真实者的真实虚构》 严尧 53 min.
《马小兵的中午觉》 缪佳欣 40 min.
《夜视镜》 来轶君 24 min.
《我的1999》 张民 15 min.
《女人不见了》 何亮 20 min.
《哗样年华》 徐鸢 5 min.
《公厕正反方》 *Public Toilet* 崔子恩 Cui Zi'en, 20 min.
《西天》 薛长青 20 min.
《存盘》 程亮 24 min.
《22元》 杜杰 5 min.

《王淑贞之生活》 *Life of Wang Shuzhen* 陆川 Lu Chuan, 20 min.
《太阳升起又落下》 张芳磊 8 min.
《看不见的城市》 张勇 35 min.
《盒子》 卢小宝 6 min.
《给爱情做场秀》 余静宜 50 min.
《沼泽湖》 张跃东 58 min.

实验短片展映片目（排序不分先后）
EXPERIMENTAL SHORTS EXHIBITED (NOT RANKED IN ANY ORDER)

《重复的故事》 漆锐
《行者1, 2, 3》 *Wanderer, I, II, III* 郑大圣 Zheng Dasheng
《滑动》 曹斐
《夜》 阎文亮
《非线圈》 李岱云
《5：6》 张亮
《我爱135》 王昊
《水》 张宁
《北京的风很大》 *There's a Strong Wind in Beijing* 雎安奇 Ju Anqi
《头发的故事》 孙略
《PROVERB》 周舟
《新生活》 石岗
《乒乓》 邱志杰
《小子别说太操》 赵亮
《魔术·灭点》 石岗

纪录片展映〈一〉
纪录片展映〈二〉
纪录片展映〈三〉

纪录片展映片目（排序不分先后）
DOCUMENTARIES EXHIBITED (NOT RANKED IN ANY ORDER)

《在上海》 *In Shanghai* 娄烨 Lou Ye
《一日机缘》 李松松
《高中》 赵原冰
《回到凤凰桥》 *Out of Phoenix Bridge* 李红 Li Hong
《生活在别处》 汪建伟
《北京弹匠》 *Beijing Cotton-Fluffing Artisan* 朱传明 Zhu Chuanming

《高楼下面》 *Under High-rise Buildings* 杜海滨 Du Haibin
《处境》 胡择
《夜莺不是唯一的歌喉》 唐丹鸿
《彼岸》 *The Other Bank* 蒋樾 Jiang Yue
《他乡之乡》 周洪波
《失踪》 薛长青
《八廓南街16号》 *No. 16 South Barkhor Street* 段锦川 Duan Jinchuan
《江湖》 *Jiang Hu: Life on the Road* 吴文光 Wu Wenguang
《家在北京》 *Housed in Beijing* 张献民 Zhang Xianmin
《九月的旅行》 陈青松
《中国行动》 *China Action* 温普林 Wen Pulin
《寻找》 鱼爱源
《新龙江颂》 沈晓闽
《Y2K千年虫》 缪佳欣

纪录片展映〈四〉
纪录片展映〈五〉

留学生作品展映
OVERSEAS STUDENTS EXHIBITION

闭幕片放映
CLOSING FEATURE

《站台》 *Platform* 贾樟柯 Jia Zhangke

Films Screened by Culture Salon

首届新锐纪录片展映月
THE FIRST NEW DOCUMENTARY MONTH

2003年
11月1日　《远山》，《平原上的山歌》，导演: 胡杰, 纪录片展映
11月8日　《这里是我朋友家》，导演: 周珏, 纪录片展映
11月22日　《张博士》, 59 min., 导演: 黄小娟
11月29日　《敬大爷和他的老主顾》 *Grandpa Jing and His Longtime Customers*, 导演: 施润玖 Shi Runjiu

首届新锐电影展映月
THE FIRST NEW FILM MONTH

2003年
12月6日　《沉默与美婷》 *Chen Mo and Meiting*, 导演: 刘浩 Liu Hao
12月14日　《王首先的夏天》 *High Sky Summer*, 导演: 李继贤 Li Jixian
12月20日　《赵先生》 *Mr. Zhao*, 导演: 吕乐Lü Yue; 《共坐白云中》, 导演: Ted Burger (美)
12月27日　《城乡结合部》*Where City and Country Meet*, 导演: 张战庆 Zhang Zhanqing

新锐导演作品1月系列展映
NEW DIRECTORS, JANUARY SERIES

2004年
1月3日　《房子》，导演: 冯晓颖

1月11日　　《今年夏天》 *Fish and Elephant*, 导演: 李玉 Li Yu
1月17日　　《希望之路》 *Railroad of Hope*,　导演: 宁瀛 Ning Ying
1月24日　　《姐姐》 *Elder Sister*, 导演: 李玉 Li Yu, 记录短篇 (documen-
　　　　　　tary short)

新锐导演作品2月系列展映：视频关注

NEW DIRECTORS, FEBRUARY SERIES

2004年
2月7日　　《非常夏日》*A Lingering Face*, 导演: 路学长 Lu Xuechang
2月14日　　《长大成人》 *The Making of Steel*, 导演: 路学长 Lu
　　　　　　Xuechang
2月21日　　《妈妈》 *Mama*, 导演: 张元 Zhang Yuan
2月28日　　《我毕业了》 *I Graduated*, 导演: 王光利 Wang Guangli

新锐导演作品3月系列展映

NEW DIRECTORS, MARCH SERIES

2004年
3月6日　　《车四十四》 *Bus 44*, 导演: 伍仕贤Dayyan Eng; 《安定医院》
　　　　　Anding Hospital, 《敬大爷和他的老主顾》*Grandpa Jing
　　　　　and His Longtime Customers*, 导演: 施润玖 Shi Runjiu;
　　　　　与新锐导演对话: 施润玖
3月13日　　《陌生天堂》*An Estranged Paradise*, 导演: 杨福东 Yang
　　　　　Fudong, 92 min., 英文字幕
3月20日　　《安阳婴儿》 *The Orphan of Anyang*, 导演: 王超 Wang Chao,
　　　　　英文字幕, 100 min.
3月28日　　《香火》 *Incense*, 导演: 宁浩 Ning Hao, 英文字幕

新锐导演作品4月系列展映

NEW DIRECTORS, APRIL SERIES

2004年
4月3日　　《诺玛的十七岁》*When Nuoma Was Seventeen*, 导演: 章家瑞
　　　　　Zang Jiarui, 英文字幕, 主演: 李敏
4月10日　　《一百个》, 导演: 腾华弢, 英文字幕
4月17日　　《车四十四》 *Bus 44*, 导演: 伍仕贤Dayyan Eng, 英文字幕
4月24日　　《缝》, 导演: 李娃克, 英文字幕

新锐导演作品5月系列展映
NEW DIRECTORS, MAY SERIES

2004年
5月1日   《DV CHINA》 *DV China*, 导演: 郑大圣 Zheng Dasheng
5月8日   《拎起大舌头》 *The Secret of My Success*, 导演: 段锦川 Duan
          Jinchuan
5月15日   《闯北京》, 导演: 辛勤
5月22日   《高楼下面》 *Under High-rise Buildings*, 导演: 杜海滨 Du
          Haibin
5月29日   《后革命时代》 *The Post-Revolutionary Age*, 导演: 张扬
          Zhang Yang,   罗拉

新锐导演作品6月系列展映
NEW DIRECTORS, JUNE SERIES

2004年
6月5日   《二弟》 *Drifters*, 导演: 王小帅 Wang Xiaoshuai
6月12日   《希望之路》 *Railroad of Hope*, 导演: 宁瀛 Ning Ying
6月19日   《茶马古道之德拉姆》 *Delamu*, 导演: 田壮壮 Tian Zhuang-
          zhuang
6月26日   《大树乡》 *Big Tree Village*, 导演: 郝志强 Hao Zhiqiang

新锐导演作品7月系列展映
NEW DIRECTORS, JULY SERIES

2004年
7月3日   《任逍遥》 *Unknown Pleasures*, 导演: 贾樟柯 Jia Zhangke
7月10日   《云之南》 *South of the Clouds*, 导演: 朱文 Zhu Wen
7月17日   《长大成人》 *The Making of Steel*, 导演: 路学长 Lu
          Xuechang
7月24日   《香火》 *Incense*, 导演: 宁浩 Ning Hao
7月31日   《旅程》 *Journey*, 导演: 杨超 Yang Chao

Note: Below are films screened after Culture Salon had moved to the Dashanzi
art district in September 2004.

《永远新锐的女导演-宁瀛电影作品展》

A WOMAN DIRECTOR ALWAYS ON THE CUTTING EDGE:
AN EXHIBITION OF NING YING'S WORKS

2004年10月23日
《希望之旅》 *Railroad of Hope* （2001）
《找乐》 *For Fun* （1992）
《民警故事》 *On the Beat* （1995）
《夏日暖洋洋》 *I Love Beijing* （2001）
导演和部分演员到场 director and some actors present

新锐导演电影纪录片系列展映
DOCUMENTARIES FROM NEW DIRECTORS

2004年
12月11日 《横竖横》 *Go for Broke*, 《处女作》 *Maiden Work*, 导演: 王光利 Wang Guangli;
《哭泣的女人》 *Crying Woman*, 导演: 刘冰鉴 Liu Bingjian
12月12日 《好大一对羊》 *Two Great Sheep*, 导演: 刘浩 Liu Hao;
《山清 水秀》, 导演: 甘小二;
《龙套》, 导演: 李然
12月18日 《幸福生活》 *This Happy Life*, 导演: 蒋樾 Jiang Yue;
《拎起大舌头》 *The Secret of My Success*, 导演: 段锦川 Duan Jinchuan;
《平遥》, 导演: 师若
12月19日 《窦豆》 *Dudou*, 《铁路沿线》 *Along the Railroad*, 导演: 杜海滨 Du Haibin;
《安定医院》 *Anding Hospital*, 导演: 施润玖 Shi Runjiu

Films Screened by Formula 3

首届"跨越中国"影像艺术节:中国新女性影像周
THE FIRST VIDEO ART FESTIVAL "CROSSING CHINA": A WEEK ON NEW VISUAL WORKS BY CHINESE WOMEN

崔岫闻 参展影片:《洗手间》
成洁 参展影片:《桥》
石头 参展影片:《女同志游行》
王霓 参展影片:《在路上》
翁秀兰 参展影片:《桃花运》
潇潇 参展影片:《无法追溯的追溯》
曹菲 参展影片:《链》
林美雅 参展影片:《呼吸》
英未未 参展影片:《盒子》 *The Box*, by Ying Weiwei
张微微 参展影片:《手》
张铁梅 参展影片:《鞭打》
枫翎 参展影片:《葳言2002》
何成瑶 参展影片:《行为录象》
庆庆 参展影片:《暧昧》
李红 参展影片:《回到凤凰桥》 *Out of Phoenix Bridge*, by Li Hong
刘冰鉴 参展影片:《哭泣的女人》 *Crying Woman*, by Liu Bingjian
宁瀛 参展影片:《找乐》 *For Fun*, by Ning Ying

中国1949年之前老上海经典电影展播
CLASSIC CHINESE FILMS FROM OLD SHANGHAI PRIOR TO 1949

《劳工之爱情》 *Laborer's Love* 张石川 Zhang Shichuan,1922
《少奶奶的扇子》 *Young Mistress' Fan* 李萍倩 Li Pingqian,1928

《银汉双星》 *Twin Stars of the Silver Screen* 史东山 Shi Dongshan，1931

《脂粉市场》 *The Market of Beauty* 张石川 Zhang Shichuan，1933

《母性之光》 *The Light of Motherhood* 卜万苍 Bu Wancang，1933

《姊妹花》 *Twin Sisters* 郑正秋 Zheng Zhengqiu，1933

《神女》 *Goddess* 吴永刚 Wu Yonggang，1934

《体育皇后》 *Queen of Sports* 孙瑜 Sun Yu，1934

《新女性》 *New Woman* 蔡楚生 Cai Chusheng，1934

《渔光曲》 *Song of the Fishermen* 蔡楚生 Cai Chusheng，1934

《女儿经》 *Bible for Women* 张石川等 Zhang Shichuan et al.，1934

《桃李劫》 *Plunder of Peach and Plum* 应云卫 Ying Yunwei，1934

《风云儿女》 *Children of Troubled Times* 许幸之 Xu Xingzhi，1935

《壮志凌云》 *The Pioneers* 吴永刚 Wu Yonggang，1936

《渔家女》 *Fisherman's Daughter* 卜万苍 Bu Wancang，1936

《摩登女性》 *Modern Woman* 屠光啟 Tu Guangqi，1937

《夜半歌声》 *Singing at Midnight* 马徐维邦 Ma-Xu Weibang，1937

《十字街头》 *Crossroad* 沈西苓 Shen Xiling，1937

《压岁钱》 *New Year's Coin* 张石川 Zhang Shichuan，1937

《武则天》 *Empress Wu Zetian* 方沛霖 Fang Peilin，1939

《一江春水向东流》 *Spring River Flows East* 蔡楚生 Cai Chusheng，郑君里 Zheng Junli，1947

《遥远的爱》 *Faraway Love* 陈鲤庭 Chen Liting，1947

《夜店》 *Night Inn* 黄佐临 Huang Zuolin，1947

《八千里路云和月》 *Eight Thousand Li of Clouds and Moon* 史东山，1947

《天堂春梦》 *Dream in Paradise* 汤晓丹 Tang Xiaodan，1947

《太太万岁》 *Long Live the Mistress* 桑弧 Sang Hu，1947

《不了情》 *Never Ending Love* 桑弧 Sang Hu，1947

《万家灯火》 *Myriad of Lights* 沈浮 Shen Fu，1948

《关不住的春光》 *Springtime Flourishes* 王为一 Wang Weiyi，1948

《乌鸦与麻雀》 *Crows and Sparrows* 郑君里 Zheng Junli，1949

朱传明作品展映及讨论会
ZHU CHUANMING'S WORKS: EXHIBITION AND DISCUSSION

纪录片《北京弹匠》 *Beijing Cotton-Fluffing Artisan*, 58 min.

纪录片《群众演员》 *Extras*, 75 min.

故事片《山上》 *On the Mountain*, 99 min.

赵邈影片展映及座谈会

导演：赵邈，影片：《选择》，该片获2003年国际运动电影电视节金花环奖

苏青、米娜影片展映及座谈会

片名：《白塔》，类型：纪录片，拍摄：2002年，完成：2003年8月，85 min.，导演：苏青，米娜

施润玖影像专场
SHI RUNJIU PICTURES

展出影片:《美丽新世界》*A Beautiful World*，《走到底》*Carry It to the End*
展映作品: 施润玖经典MV、最新DV作品等珍贵影像资料

"不一样的精彩"：关注80后系列论坛之一
ANOTHER KIND OF BRILLIANCE: A FORUM

平泳佳 当CEO遭遇学生电影
《双生》，导演:平泳佳
《诗情》，导演:陈忠，独立制作，104 min.，剧情片

《节日》：2003年第四届迷笛音乐节纪录片展映式
FESTIVAL: A DOCUMENTARY EXHIBITION OF THE FOURTH MIDI MUSIC FESTIVAL, 2003

播放《节日》，导演：孙志强，130 min.，中英文字幕
播放《自由边缘》、《节日》宣传片、《节日》拍摄花絮

划痕：当代中国独立影像作品展播（北京放映片目）
AN EXHIBITION OF INDEPENDENT PICTURES IN CONTEMPORARY CHINA, BEIJING PROGRAM

实验片单元 ：录象与现象（探讨录象艺术家的作品和他们的个人视野的问题）

Experimental unit: videos and phenomena

Group one（第一组）7月16日（周五）18:00–21:00滚动放映，20:00–21:00与外地导演即时网络流.

1 《先死的小丑》彩色/9 min./2004/常伟，郑小平（偶人动画，导演到场）
2 《仿徨》彩色/16 min./2004/翁桢琪（导演到场）
3 《红与蓝》彩色/20 min./2004/徐玲玲（导演与观众即时网络交流）
4 《开火》彩色/6 min./乌尔善（导演到场）
5 《环视》彩色/5 min./乌尔善（导演到场）
6 《脱口而出》黑白/10 min./乌尔善（导演到场）
7 《身体》彩色/10 min./乌尔善（导演到场）
8 《谁是天使》彩色/10 min./陈晓云（导演与观众即时网络交流）
9 《向夜晚延伸的若干个瞬间》黑白/9 min./陈晓云（导演与观众即时网络交流）
10 《红气球》彩色/2 min./2004/刘佳（手绘动画）

Group two（第二组）7月17日（周六）18:00–21:00滚动放映，20:00–21:00与外地导演即时网络交流.

11 《乐园》彩色/10 min./2004/刘佳（导演与观众即时网络交流）
12 《惊蛰》彩色/7 min. /2001/庞璇（导演与观众即时网络交流）
13 《好像那年》彩色/6 min./ 2001/庞璇（导演与观众即时网络交流）
14 《子》彩色/3 min./2004/董钧（导演与观众即时网络交流）
15 《舞者》彩色/10 min./2002/徐巍，徐立（导演与观众即时网络交流）
16 《中国蚂蚁》彩色/5 min./2003/刘旬（2003年北京国际DV论坛获实验单元评审团特别奖，2004年8月雅典视觉艺术奥林匹克大赛）
17 《客厅》彩色/8 min./高世强
18 《卫生间》彩色/10 min./高世强
19 《没有输入》黑白/8 min./常伟，郑小平, 陆磊
20 《Play Go On》彩色/3 min./马秋莎

剧情片单元：7月22日（周四）15:00–20:00放映，20:00–20:20 "后感性"相关材料PowerPoint 示范

Fictional unit: post-sensuality (PowerPoint presentation)

1 《肥皂剧》彩色/90 min./乌尔善 2 《不回头》彩色/30 min./任杰（参加纽约地下电影节，导演到场）
2 《龙江颂》彩色/80 min. /沈晓闽（凤凰卫视中文台中华青年影像大展2002年最佳导演奖，导演到场）
3 《巴洛克》黑白/80 min./2002/董为（参加圣保罗双年展）

纪实与记录片单元：记录与记实（主要关于记录片中的美学的不同层面上的呈现）

Documentary unit: documents and recording

7月23日（周五）15:0–20:00放映

1《乡村摄影师和他的儿子》彩色/53 min./2002/沈晓闽（加州全球艺术院校影像大赛金奖）

2《后房，嘿，天亮了》 *Daybreak in the Back* 黑白/12 min. /2001/杨福东 Yang Fudong

3《城市》彩色/50 min./2002/刘洋（参加以色列双年展作品，导演到场）

4《黑金》彩色/45 min./周渔（导演与观众即时网络交流）

5《参与》黑白/54 min. /赵原冰/2004 (英文字幕，导演与观众即时网络交流)

《五音大鼓》记录片首发式

FIVE-TUNE BIG DRUMS: PREMIERE OF A DOCUMENTARY

导演：魏阿挺 Wei Ating，监制：袁酶，制片人：达君，摄像：孙志强，魏阿挺，剧务：李烨，张莉，史庆刚

记录片《唐唐》首映式

TANG TANG: PREMIERE OF A DOCUMENTARY

导演:张涵子，92 min.

中国以色列影像交流暨作品展映

CHINA-ISRAEL FILM EXCHANGE

专场展映时间及展映作品（导演到场）：

1月15日 15:00（以色列作品）20:00 汪健伟作品《仪式》《蜘蛛》

1月16日 15:00（以色列作品）20:00 李杨作品《盲井》 *Blind Shaft*, by Li Yang

1月17日 15:00（以色列作品）20:00乌尔善作品《肥皂剧》

1月18日 15:00（以色列作品）20:00 孙志强作品《节日》

1月19日 15:00（以色列作品）20:00 邱志杰作品集锦

1月20日 15:00（以色列作品）20:00 吕顺作品《狗日子》

1月21日 15:00（以色列作品）20:00 韩涛作品《宝宝》

Films Screened by Studio Z

与导演对话
CONVERSATIONS WITH FILM DIRECTORS

第一期2002年7月20日王小帅 Wang Xiaoshuai 《十七岁的单车》 *Beijing Bicycle*，国家图书馆，摄像刘杰

第二期2002年7月27日刘浩 Liu Hao 《陈默与美婷》 *Chen Mo and Meiting*，国家图书馆

第三期2002年8月4日贾樟柯 Jia Zhangke 《站台》 *Platform*，国家图书馆，顾峥、王宏伟、赵涛等

第四期2002年8月10日刘冰鉴 Liu Bingjian 《哭泣的女人》 *Crying Woman*，国家图书馆

第五期2002年8月17日杜海滨 Du Haibin 《铁路沿线》 *Along the Railroad*，国家图书馆

第六期2002年8月24日仲华 Zhong Hua 《今年冬天》 *This Winter*，国家图书馆

第七期2002年8月31日高晓松 《那时花开》，国家图书馆

第八期2002年9月7日管虎 Guan Hu 《西施眼》 *The Eyes of Beauty* （首映 premiere），国家图书馆

第九期2002年9月14日孟奇 Meng Qi 《我最中意的雪天》 *My Favorite Snow*，国家图书馆

(The foregoing titles shown inside the National Library)

第十期2002年9月22日马晓颖 Ma Xiaoying 《世界上最疼我的那个人去了》 *Gone Is the One Who Held Me Dearest in the World*，王府井书店，戴锦华教授 presented by Professor Dai Jinhua

十一期2002年10月1日施润玖 Shi Runjiu 《走到底》 *Carry It to the End*，王府井书店

十二期2002年10月5日王超 Wang Chao 《安阳婴儿》 *The Orphan of Anyang*，王府井书店

十三期2002年10月12日伍仕贤 Dayyan Eng《车四十四》 *Bus 44*，王府井书店

(The foregoing titles shown inside a bookstore in Wangfujing)

十四期2002年10月12日贾樟柯 Jia Zhangke 《站台》 *Platform*，北京师范大学，制片人周强，主演赵涛

十五期2002年10月19日贾樟柯/韩杰/卫铁 Jia Zhangke et al.《公共场所》 *In Public*，《过年》，《黄石大道》，王府井书店

十六期2002年10月19日蒋钦民《天上的恋人》(首映)，北京师范大学，刘烨

十七期2002年10月26日王小帅 Wang Xiaoshuai 《扁担姑娘》 *So Close to Paradise*，北京师范大学

十八期2002年10月26日陈大明 Chen Daming 《井盖儿》 *Manhole* (首映 premiere)，王府井书店

十九期2002年11月2日何建军 He Jianjun《邮差》 *Postman*，王府井书店

二十期2002年11月2日刘浩 Liu Hao 《陈默与美婷》 *Chen Mo and Meiting*，北京师范大学

二十一2002年11月9日李虹 Li Hong 《伴你高飞》 *Soaring with You* (黑白)，王府井书店，艾敬，安子

二十二2002年11月9日马晓颖 Ma Xiaoying 《世界上最疼我的那个人去了》*Gone Is the One Who Held Me Dearest in the World*，北京师范大学

二十三2002年11月10日贾樟柯 Jia Zhangke 《站台》 *Platform*，中国人民大学，赵涛，顾峥等

二十四2002年11月16日郑大圣 Zheng Dasheng《王勃之死》 *Death of Wang Bo*，王府井书店

二十五2002年11月17日何建军 He Jianjun 《邮差》 *Postman*，北京师范大学

二十六2002年11月23日王光利 Wang Guangli 《横竖横》 *Go for Broke*，王府井书店

二十七2002年11月24日李虹 Li Hong《黑白》 *Black and White*，北京师范大学

二十八2002年11月25日王小帅 Wang Xiaoshuai 《十七岁的单车》 *Beijing Bicycle*，对外经济贸易大学，李滨，崔林

二十九2002年11月26日贾樟柯 Jia Zhangke 《站台》 *Platform*，对外经济贸易大学

三十2002年11月30日李玉 Li Yu 《今年夏天》 *Fish and Elephant*，北京师范大学

三十一2002年12月1日俞钟 Yu Zhong 《我的美丽乡愁》 *My Beautiful Homesickness*，王府井书店

三十二2002年12月21日李娃克《缝》，王府井书店，杨志超

三十三2002年12月28日胡雪杨 Hu Xueyang《牵牛花》Living Dream，王府井书店

三十四2003年1月4日盛志民《心心》，王府井书店

三十五2003年1月11日蒲盛《净土》(首映)，王府井书店

三十六2003年3月1日路学长 Lu Xuechang 《卡拉是条狗》*Kala My Dog*，王府井书店

三十七2003年3月8日张扬 Zhang Yang 《后革命时代》*The Post-Revolutionary Age* (纪录片 documentary)，王府井书店

三十八2003年3月15日黄军、钟海《太想爱你》《爱情钥匙》(首映)，王府井书店，潘粤明

三十九2003年3月22日龚力《我们的从前》，王府井书店

四十期2003年4月12日章家瑞 Zhang Jiarui《诺玛的十七岁》*When Nuoma Was Seventeen*，国家图书馆

四十一2003年4月19日李继贤 Li Jixian 《王首先的夏天》*High Sky Summer of Wang Shouxian*，国家图书馆

四十二2003年8月9日赵亮《纸飞机》，国家图书馆

四十三2003年8月16日朱传明 Zhu Chuanming 《山上》*On the Mountain* (国内首映 domestic premiere)，国家图书馆

四十四2003年8月23日王小帅 Wang Xiaoshuai《二弟》*Drifters* (国内首映domestic premiere)，国家图书馆

四十五2003年10月24日李杨 Li Yang 《盲井》*Blind Shaft* (国内首映 domestic premiere)，北大图书馆

(The foregoing titles shown in various university campuses in Beijing as well as the National Library and a bookstore in Wangfujing)

2002年12月7日–12月9日首届青年导演作品交流周
THE FIRST YOUNG DIRECTORS' WORKS EXCHANGE WEEK, DECEMBER 7–9, 2002

1 管虎 Guan Hu 《西施眼》*The Eyes of Beauty*

2 刘浩 Liu Hao 《陈默和美婷》*Chen Mo and Meiting*, 75 min. （导演）

3 王小帅 Wang Xiaoshuai 《冬春的日子》*The Days*, 75 min. （导演）

4 王小帅 Wang Xiaoshuai 《极度寒冷》*Frozen* (北京师范大学)

5 贾樟柯 Jia Zhangke 《站台》*Platform* 或《任逍遥》*Unknown Pleasures*,《公共场所》*In Public*, 30 min. （导演）

6 杜海滨 Du Haibin 《高楼下面》*Under High-Rise Buildings* （导演）(北京师范大学)

7 张扬 Zhang Yang 《昨天》*Quitting*, 118 min. （导演不定）

8 刘冰鉴 Liu Bingjian 《哭泣的女人》*Crying Woman* （导演）(北京师范大学)

9 章明 Zhang Ming 《秘语十七小时》 *Weekend Plot*

10 崔子恩 Cui Zi'en 《旧约》 *Old Testaments* (导演) (北京师范大学)

11 伍仕贤 Dayyan Eng 《车四十四》 *Bus 44*, 11 min. (导演) (北京师范大学)

12 何建军 He Jianjun 《悬恋》 *Red Beads* (导演)

13 郑大圣 Zheng Dasheng 《古玩》 *Antique* (电视电影 TV film) (导演) (北京师范大学)

14 吴文光 Wu Wenguang 《流浪北京》 *Bumming in Beijing*, 70 min. (纪录片 documentary)

15 王超 Wang Chao 《安阳婴儿》 *The Orphan of Anyang* (导演) (北京师范大学)

16 唐大年 Tang Danian 《都市天堂》 *City Paradise* (导演)

17 路学长 Lu Xuechang 《长大成人》 *The Making of Steel*

18 仲华 Zhong Hua 《今年冬天》 *This Winter*, 94 min. (纪录片 documentary) (导演) (北京师范大学)

19 孟奇 Meng Qi 《我最中意的雪天》 *My Favorite Snow* (导演) (北京师范大学)

20 辛勤 《闯北京》 (纪录片) (导演) (北京师范大学)

21 潘剑林 《新娘》 48 min. (纪录片) (北京师范大学)

22 程裕苏 Andrew Cheng 《我们害怕》 *Shanghai Panic*, 87 min. (北京师范大学)

23 盛志民 《心心》 90 min. (导演) (北京师范大学)

24 王兵 Wang Bing 《铁西区》 *West of the Tracks*, 180 min. (导演)

25 朱传明 Zhu Chuanming 《群众演员》 *Extras*, 70 min. (导演)

26 杨福东 Yang Fudong 《陌生天堂》 *An Estranged Paradise*, 76 min. (导演)

27 宁瀛 Ning Ying 《希望之路》 *Railroad of Hope*, 56 min. (导演)

28 吕乐 Lü Yue 《赵先生》 *Mr. Zhao* (导演)

2003年3月29日－4月1日 首届中国纪录影片交流周
THE FIRST CHINESE DOCUMENTARY EXCHANGE WEEK, MARCH 29–APRIL 1, 2003

陈苗 Chen Miao 《上海男孩》 *Snake Boy*, 60 min.

崔子恩 Cui Zi'en 《讲故事》 *Story-telling*, 60 min.

段锦川 Duan Jinchuan 《八廓南街16号》 *No. 16 South Barkhor Street*, 73 min.,

《拎起大舌头》 *The Secret of My Success*, 73 min.

杜海滨 Du Haibing 　　　　《高楼下面》 *Under High-Rise Buildings*, 90 min.

冯晓颖 Feng Xiaoyiing 　　　《房子》 30 min.

甘露 Gan Lu 　　　　　　《缘起》 180 min.

黄小娟 Huang Xiaojuan 　　《张博士》 59 min.

胡杰 Hu Jie 　　　　　　《远山》 30 min.，《平原上的山歌》 70 min.

胡庶 Hu Shu 　　　　　　《我不要你管》 *Leave Me Alone*, 70 min.

胡择 Hu Ze 　　　　　　《九位中国艺术家处境》 75 min.

蒋樾 Jiang Yue 　　　　　《彼岸》 *The Other Bank*, 140 min.，
　　　　　　　　　　　《幸福生活》 *This Happy Life*, 93 min.

蒋志 Jiang Zhi 　　　　　《木木在汉城》 6 min.，　《空笼》 25 min.

焦波 Jiao Bo 　　　　　　《哑巴的正月》 90 min.

贾樟柯 Jia Zhangke 　　　　《公共场所》 *In Public*, 30 min.，
　　　　　　　　　　　《狗的状况》 *Condition of a Dog*, 5 min.

李红 Li Hong 　　　　　　《回到凤凰桥》 *Out of Phoenix Bridge*, 113 min.

李娃克 Li Wake 　　　　　《寿衣行为艺术》

李玉 Li Yu 　　　　　　《姐姐》 *Elder Sister*, 20 min.

吕乐 Lü Yue 　　　　　　《怒江，一条丢失的峡谷》 *Nujiang, a Lost Gorge*, 90 min.

宁瀛 Ning Ying 　　　　　《希望之路》 *Railroad of Hope*, 93 min.

潘剑林 Pan Jianlin 　　　　《新娘》 58 min.

潘大为 Pan Dawei 　　　　《姐姐》 13 min.

施润玖 Shi Runjiu 　　　　《安定医院》 *Anding Hospital*, 60 min.

孙曾田 Sun Zengtian 　　　《最后的山神》 *The Last Mountain God*, 30 min.

孙志强 Sun Zhiqiang 　　　《什么最重要》 10 min.

唐丹鸿 Tang Danhong 　　　《夜莺不是唯一的歌喉》 180 min.

王海兵 Wanghaibing 　　　《回家》 50 min.，　《藏北人家》 47 min.

吴文光 Wu Wenguang 　　　《流浪北京》 *Bumming in Beijing*, 70 min.

吴石友 Wu Shiyou 　　　　《红壤》 38 min.

辛勤 Xin Qin 　　　　　　《闯北京》 60 min.

杨志超 Yang Zhichao 　　　《嘉峪关》

英未未 Ying Weiwei 　　　《盒子》 *The Box*, 86 min.

张扬 Zhang Yang 　　　　　《后革命时代》 *The Post-Revolutionary Age*, 90 min.

张勇 Zhang Yong 　　　　　《百年不化》 65 min.

张战庆 Zhang Zhanqing 　　《城乡结合部》 *Where City and Country Meet*

郑大圣 Zheng Dasheng 　　《DV China》 *DV China*, 130 min.

仲华 Zhong Hua 　　　　　《今年冬天》 *This Winter*, 90 min.

朱传明 Zhu Chuanming   《北京弹匠》*The Beijing Cotton-Fluffing Artisan*,
                        60 min.
                        《群众演员》*Extras*, 70 min.
周珏 Zhou Jue   《这里是我朋友家》71 min.

STUDIO Z放映系列活动统计
STUDIO Z DOUBLE FEATURE EVENTS

编号，日期，影片1，影片2，（导演）嘉宾地点

1 2003-11-7《周末情人》*Weekend Lovers*，《紫蝴蝶》*Purple Butter-fly*，娄烨 Lou Ye，北京电影学院标准放映厅

2 2003-11-14《城南旧事》*Memory of Old Beijing*，吴贻弓 Wu Yigong，《世界上最疼我的那个人去了》*Gone Is the One Who Held Me Dearest in the World*，马晓颖 Ma Xiaoying，北京电影学院标准放映厅

3 2003-11-15《黄土地》*Yellow Earth*，陈凯歌 Chen Kaige，《秘语十七小时》*Weekend Plot*，章明 Zhang Ming，北京电影学院标准放映厅

4 2003-11-22《那山，那人，那狗》*Postman in the Mountains*，《蓝色爱情》*A Love of Blueness*，霍建起 Huo Jianqi，北京电影学院标准放映厅

5 2003-11-28《与盗同行》（俄 Russia），《长大成人》*The Making of Steel*，路学长 Lu Xuechang，北京电影学院标准放映厅

6 2003-11-29《黑客帝国III》*The Matrix Revolutions*（美），《青春万岁》*Forever Young*，黄蜀芹，北京电影学院标准放映厅

7 2003-12-12《新龙门客栈》*New Dragon Inn*，《无间道III》*Infernal Affair, III*（香港），北京电影学院标准放映厅

8 2003-12-19《阳光灿烂的日子》*In the Heat of the Sun*，姜文 Jiang Wen，《加勒比海盗》*Pirates of the Caribbean*（美），北京电影学院标准放映厅

(The foregoing titles all projected at the Beijing Film Academy
main theater)

Appendix

The Chinese Underground Film Collection at the University of California, San Diego

Jim Cheng

HISTORICAL BACKGROUND

Any endeavor to create a new collection at an already distinguished academic library requires that essential support be demonstrated by a strong faculty body and academic curricula in the subject area, the library administration's commitment, and, finally, the curator's subject expertise and professional ties to those who will supply the source materials. With an outstanding faculty body and curricula in Chinese film studies at the University of California, San Diego (UCSD), the UCSD Libraries administration's approval, and myself as a librarian with long-standing Chinese film research interests and personal connections with Chinese underground filmmakers,[1] I helped initiate the Chinese Underground Film Collection at the UCSD Libraries in 2002.

An essential part of this collection development, acquisition plan, and technical procedure was to answer the question, "What counts as a Chinese underground film?" Unfortunately, limited publications on the subject as of summer 2003 offered no ready definition,[2] yet a definition had to be fashioned for our collection. So I took it upon myself to offer a definition of Chinese underground film: any film that does not pass or has never been submitted to government censorship institutions but still circulates through unofficial venues, such as private parties, clubs, bars, university campuses, and international film festivals. I presented this definition in a panel discussion with other participating scholars at the Chinese Underground Film Festival at UCSD in 2003.[3]

As a film movement, Chinese underground films first appeared in the early 1990s when the Chinese government opened the door for private filmmakers. This policy change—along with economic reforms—provided a necessary economic foundation and a "gray-zone" political environment for a fledgling underground film movement. This was the first time since 1952 that a director could seek nongovernmental funding to make a film inside China. However, this also meant that if a film did not pass censorship, it could not be officially distributed and exhibited to the public, although the director could still keep the film and show it in unofficial venues. Before the 1990s, if any government-funded film (normally produced by a state-owned film studio) did not pass censorship or was banned, the studios would shelve the film and make it "disappear" from public view. However, with a few exceptions, Chinese underground films are now typically funded by private, sometimes foreign, sources. The first Chinese film to be commonly acknowledged as "underground" or "independent" is Zhang Yuan's *Beijing Bastards* (1993).[4] As we enter the twenty-first century, for various reasons, many film directors and critics in China have used the less politically sensitive term "independent film" instead of "underground film" (see Chen Mo and Zhiwei Xiao's chapter).

Acquiring a representative body of Chinese underground films is by no means an easy task. By definition, these films do not pass Chinese censorship channels, so there are no reliable distributors and no box office incomes for them in China. However, a few directors have found foreign distributors and have exhibited their films overseas. Two such examples are Wang Xiaoshuai and Jia Zhangke. As a result of restrictions mentioned above, we have to collect these films directly from the directors themselves through personal connections and contacts and have to pay a relatively high price. But this price is justified considering how difficult it is for the directors to get funding and survive without regular box office incomes, let alone deal with potential buyers without a distribution agent. Of course, meeting high standards for teaching and research is our primary objective in this collection, but as a means of supporting alternative and progressive media in China, our acquisition endeavor also seeks to promote a democratic society, both here and abroad.

CURRENT STATUS OF THE COLLECTION

The Size of the Collection

Based on our definition of Chinese underground film, we collected 152 titles by June 2004. The collection includes films that did not pass the censorship process initially but may have passed at a later date. Among such films are He Jianjun's *Postman* (1995) and A Nian's *Love in the City* (1997). Films that have never been submitted to censorship are also represented in the collection. These include films by Cui Zi'en and films made by students of the Beijing Film Academy. As a rule, we try to acquire the original versions directly from the directors themselves.

The front of a Beijing film club postcard advertising He Jianjun's Postman (1995)

Types of Films Represented

There were seventy-five fictional films, seventy documentary films, six experimental films, and one animated film in the initial collection.

Formats Represented

Of all films in the original collection, twenty-nine are in VCD or DVD and 134 in VHS/PAL, while some titles are available in both VCD/DVD and VHS formats.

Languages Represented

More than two-thirds of the films carry English subtitles, and some of the films feature English narration.

Content and Characteristics

In terms of content, most films depict aspects of Chinese life that have been ignored by the official or mainstream media, aspects such as religious practices, gay sexuality, environmental problems, labor issues (unemployment, migrant workers, retirees, etc.), and prostitution. British film critic Tony Rayns lists five special features of Chinese underground film: documentary methods, street realism, improvised filmmaking, fractured narration, and the ontology of images (see Yingjin Zhang's chapter).[5] However, there is a paramount, albeit unwritten or self-imposed, rule observed by nearly all Chinese underground directors. As Paul Pickowicz pointed out in an interview with the National Public Radio film critic Beth Accomando, "You cannot criticize the Chinese Communist Party. You cannot criticize the government and state."[6] In other words, films that directly criticize the party-state or substantially deal with politically sensitive subjects are still very much off limits to most directors (see Paul Pickowicz's chapter).

Access Policy

Scholars and students are welcome to use the Chinese Underground Film Collection inside the UCSD Libraries. We provide viewing facilities, but we prohibit taking the titles out of the library building. Due to copyright issues and the difficulties in film acquisition and replacement, there is no interlibrary loan service available for the Chinese Underground Film Collection.

FUTURE PLANS FOR THE COLLECTION

Entering the twenty-first century under the banner of "independent filmmaking," an increasing number of professional and amateur filmmakers in China are making their own films with the aid of recent developments in new DV technology, which dramatically reduces filmmaking budgets and technical requirements, and makes it less necessary to seek financial support from private and foreign sources (see Chris Berry's chapter). The UCSD Libraries are committed to continuing the acquisition of Chinese underground and independent films and have devised plans for developing an infrastructure necessary for providing electronic access to these materials for the UCSD campus and beyond, when copyright and technical issues are resolved. The number of titles in the collection grew to more than three hundred by July 2005, and the latest catalogue information can be accessed at http://gort.ucsd.edu/EAFC/ChinUnderIndeFilm.html. We estimate that by the end of 2006 the collection will consist of more than five hundred titles.

NOTES

1. See Jim Cheng, *An Annotated Bibliography for Chinese Film Studies* (Hong Kong: Hong Kong University Press, 2004).

2. Due to censorship and access restrictions, no book-length studies of Chinese underground film were published in China or abroad in the last century. By the time of the UCSD film festival in 2003, I found the following books, which prefer the term "underground" to "independent": Cheng Qingsong and Huang Ou, *Wode sheyingji bu sahuang: xianfeng dianying ren dang'an—shengyu 1961–1970* [My Camera Doesn't Lie: Documents on Avant-garde Filmmakers Born between 1961 and 1970] (Beijing: Zhongguo youyi chuban gongsi, 2002); Cui Zi'en, *Diyi guanzhong* [The First Audience] (Beijing: Xiandai chubanshe, 2003); Lin Xudong et al., eds., *Jia Zhangke dianying: guxiang sanbuqu zhi "Xiao Wu"* [Jia Zhangke's Films: Hometown Trilogy, *Xiao Wu*] (Beijing: Mangwen chubanshe, 2003, 3 vols.). In 2003, two European directors, Solveig Klassen and Katharina Schneider-Roos, produced an important documentary film on Chinese underground film, *My Camera Doesn't Lie*, which contains interviews with twelve major Chinese independent directors. However, no clear definition of Chinese underground or independent film appears in these works.

3. The UCSD Libraries and a number of cosponsors hosted the underground film festival on October 8–10, 2003. The festival featured thirteen films and four panel discussions led by Cui Zi'en, a film director from the Beijing Film Academy, and by scholars from UCSD; UCLA; California State University, San Marcos; and the University of Montreal. Detailed information about the event can be found at the festival's website: http://cuff.ucsd.edu.

4. See Cheng Qingsong and Huang Ou, *Wode sheyingji*, 101.

5. Cheng Qingsong and Huang Ou, *Wode sheyingji*, 6–7.

6. For this interview, see BBC/NPR, "The World: Chinese Film Report" (Nov. 17, 2003), www.theworld.org/latesteditions/20031117.shtml.

FILMOGRAPHY

What follows is the filmography of the Chinese underground films collected by the UCSD Libraries as of June 2004. It includes crucial information regarding directors, titles, lengths, formats, dates, types, languages, and brief plot summaries. However, due to space limits, nonessential information, such as producers, screenwriters, cast, and distributors, is omitted here. A more detailed bibliographic record of these films is available at "Roger," the UCSD Libraries' online catalogue: http://roger.ucsd.edu.

Film Titles

All film titles and the orders of their appearance in each title field were strictly copied down from the original films, and I do not provide my own English translations of them. For this reason, some English titles may be grammatically awkward, and many titles may differ from those widely circulated in the media and the academy in the West. For standardized English titles (as well as different versions with varied running times), the reader is advised to consult the filmography that immediately follows this appendix.

Director	Title	Time	Format	Date	Type	Language	Summary
A, Nian/ 阿年	Cheng shi ai qing/ 城市爱情 = Love in the City	90 min.	VHS/ PAL	1997	FIC	Chinese dialogue with English subtitles	Individual stories of a group of people born in the 1960s and how they live their lives in today's China.
Bai, Fujian/ 白福坚	Deng/ 等	45 min.	VCD	2003	FIC	Chinese dialogue with Chinese subtitles	A village boy waits on the beach for a fisherman (who saved his grandfather's life at sea), holding the fisherman's favorite cigarettes his grandfather had saved.
Bai, Fujian/ 白福坚	Gan zhe/ 甘蔗	25 min.	VCD	2003	FIC	Chinese dialogue with Chinese subtitles	A college student comes from Beijing to visit her parents in a small village and teaches English to local children. One local kid, who lives with his grandfather, wants to join the class.
Bai, Fujian/ 白福坚	Hou yuan de hai tan/ 后院的海滩 = Beach in the Back Yard	40 min.	VHS/ PAL	2002	FIC	Chinese dialogue with Chinese subtitles	A young university graduate is laid off from his job in the city and returns to his hometown, a small seaside village, where he faces many challenges.

Table Continued

Director	Title	Time	Format	Date	Type	Language	Summary
Chen, Miao (Michelle Chen)/ 陈苗	Ye Shanghai/ 夜上海 = Shanghai Dreams	60 min.	VHS/ PAL	2001	DOC	English narration, Chinese and English dialogue with English subtitles	Documentary film about a private club owner, an American actor, a beauty salon owner, and a taxi driver trying to pursue their individual dreams in Shanghai.
Chen, Miao (Michelle Chen)/ 陈苗	Shanghai nan hai/ 上海男孩 = The Snake Boy	60 min.	VHS/ PAL	2002	DOC	Chinese and English dialogue with English subtitles	A documentary about Coco, a popular gay Chinese jazz singer in Shanghai.
Chen, Yingshan (Rebecca Chen)/ 陈映珊 and others	Yan jing, Xun sheng, Taluo pai zhi mi, Mi li dang an/ 眼睛，循声，塔罗牌之谜，迷离档案	15 min.	VHS/ PAL	2002	FIC	Chinese narration and Chinese dialogue	Four short episodes reflect the director's spiritual scenarios.
Cheng, Yusu (Andrew Y. S. Cheng)/ 程裕苏	Mu di di, Shanghai/ 目的地，上海 = Welcome to Destination Shanghai	90 min.	VHS/ PAL	2003	FIC	Chinese dialogue with English subtitles	A young man's life as a call boy in Shanghai.

Author / Director	Title	Duration	Format	Year	Type	Language	Description
Cheng, Yusu (Andrew Y. S. Cheng)/ 程裕苏	Wo men hai pa/ 我们害怕 = Shanghai Panic	90 min.	VHS/ PAL	2002	FIC	Chinese dialogue with English subtitles	Night life, sex, AIDS, drugs, and love in today's Shanghai.
Cui, Zi'en/ 崔子恩	Ai ya ya, qu bu ru/ 哎呀呀, 去哺乳 = Feeding Boys, Ayaya	80 min.	VHS/ PAL	2003	FIC	Copy 1: Chinese dialogue; copy 2: Chinese dialogue with English subtitles	Dabing and his girlfriend, Wenwen, want to save his brother and other male prostitutes working on city streets.
Cui, Zi'en/ 崔子恩	Chou jue deng chang/ 丑角登场 = Enter the Clowns	100 min.	VHS/ PAL	2001	FIC	Chinese dialogue with English subtitles	Xiao Bo feeds sermons like milk to his dying father, while Nana (a transsexual) can't find a partner.
Cui, Zi'en/ 崔子恩	Jiang gu shi/ 讲故事 = Story Time	45 min.	Copy 1: VHS/ PAL; copy 2: VCD	2003	FIC	Copy 1: Chinese dialogue; copy 2: Chinese dialogue with English subtitles	A group of students telling their own stories.
Cui, Zi'en/ 崔子恩	Lian bu bian se xin bu tiao/ 脸不变色心不跳 = Keep Cool and Don't Blush	70 min.	VHS/ PAL	2002	FIC	Copy 1: Chinese dialogue; copy 2: Chinese dialogue with English subtitles	A couple attempts to kill their illegitimate child, who is saved by a fairy and returns for revenge.

Table Continued

Director	Title	Time	Format	Date	Type	Language	Summary
Cui, Zi'en/ 崔子恩	Wu yu/ 雾语 = The Narrow Path	75 min.	VHS/ PAL	2003	FIC	Copy 1: Chinese dialogue; copy 2: Chinese dialogue with English subtitles	Stories of an alien who comes to Earth from Mars.
Cui, Zi'en/ 崔子恩	Xing xing xiang xi xi/ 星星相吸惜 = Star Appeal	105 min.	VHS/ PAL	2003	FIC	Copy 1: Chinese dialogue; copy 2: Chinese dialogue with English subtitles	A love triangle between ET from Mars, Xiao Bo, and his girlfriend Wenwen.
Cui, Zi'en/ 崔子恩	Jiu yue/ 旧约 = Old Testament	Copy 1: 100 min.; copy 2: 75 min.	VHS/ PAL and VHS/ NTSC	2001	FIC	Chinese dialogue with English subtitles	This film has three parts: Poem 1991, Proverb 2001, and Chant 2011. It describes the lives of homosexuals in China in the past, present, and future.
Cui, Zi'en/ 崔子恩	Si wang de nei jing/ 死亡的内景 = An Interior View of Death	65 min.	VHS/ PAL	2003	FIC	Copy 1: Chinese dialogue; copy 2: Chinese dialogue with English subtitles	Using photography and imaginary description, this film tries to present realistic views of death.
Cui, Zi'en/ 崔子恩	WC hu hu ha hei/ WC 呼呼哈嘿 = WC Houhouha-hei	80 min.	VHS/ PAL	2003	FIC	Chinese dialogue with English subtitles	A comedy that systematically describes the function and management of each kind of public restroom.

Director	Title	Duration	Format	Year	Type	Language	Description
Cui, Zi'en/ 崔子恩	Ye jing/ 夜景 = Night Scene	80 min.	VHS/ PAL	2003	FIC	Copy 1: Chinese dialogue; copy 2: Chinese dialogue with English subtitles	A story about a male prostitute who finds out that his father is gay and that he is gay himself.
Du, Bo/ 杜波	Beijing gu shi/ 北京故事	30 min.	VCD	2003	DOC	Chinese dialogue	People's life in Beijing during the April 2003 SARS epidemic.
Du, Bo/ 杜波	Kan shang qu hen mei/ 看上去很美	52 min.	VCD	2000	FIC	Chinese dialogue	A street singer meets a young prostitute in the city.
Du, Haibin/ 杜海滨	Beijing ji shi/ 北京纪事 = Life in Beijing	25 min.	VHS/ PAL	2003	FIC	Chinese dialogue with Chinese subtitles	The life of a street prostitute in Beijing.
Du, Haibin/ 杜海滨	Gao lou xia mian/ 高楼下面	60 min.	VHS/ PAL	2002	DOC	Chinese dialogue	The stories of two workers who live in the underground basement of a high-rise building and who work for a real estate management company.
Du, Haibin/ 杜海滨	Tie lu yan xian/ 铁路沿线 = Along the Railway	60 min.	VCD	2000	DOC	Chinese dialogue with English subtitles	The life of a group of homeless youths living along the railway.

Table Continued

Director	Title	Time	Format	Date	Type	Language	Summary
Duan, Jinchuan/ 段锦川	Bakuo Nanjie shi liu hao/ 八廓南街十六号	80 min.	VHS/ PAL	1996	DOC	Chinese dialogue	Things happen at No. 16 South Barkhor Street in Lhasa, Tibet, which houses the local neighborhood committee, the smallest unit in the Chinese government.
Duan, Jinchuan/ 段锦川	Lin qi da she tou/ 拎起大舌头 = The Secret of My Success	75 min.	VHS/ PAL	2002	DOC	Chinese dialogue with English subtitles	A documentary about a villager, Lu Guohua, who is in charge of local birth control enforcement, and then becomes the village head.
Fang, Xiangming/ 方向明	Mo jing/ 魔镜	30 min.	VCD	2003	FIC	Chinese dialogue	A young man with a magic mirror that reflects different images of himself.
Fang, Zheng/ 方正	Jie jue/ 子子	32 min.	VHS/ PAL	2001	FIC	Chinese dialogue	A man finds a young lady's lost handbag on the subway. There are many private items in the bag, including a videotape.
Feng, Shunxu/ 冯舜旭	Guan yu Feng yu Shan de gu shi/ 关于峰与珊的故事	15 min.	VHS/ PAL	2002	FIC	Chinese dialogue with Chinese subtitles	A short love story between a student, Feng, and his girlfriend, Shan.

Director	Title	Duration	Format	Year	Type	Language	Description
Feng, Xiaoying/ 冯小影	Fang zi/ 房子 = The House	30 min.	VHS/ PAL	2001	DOC	Chinese dialogue with English subtitles	Lao Zhang's present house must be torn down and his life has to start anew.
Gan, Xiao'er/ 甘小二	Shan qing shui xiu/ 山清水秀 = The Only Sons	90 min.	VHS/ PAL	2003	FIC	Chinese dialogue with Chinese and English subtitles	A humble man and his life selling his blood, children, and wife, until he, himself, dies.
Geng, Jun/ 耿军	Shan zha/ 山楂 = The Hawthorn	36 min.	VHS/ PAL	2002	FIC	Chinese dialogue with Chinese and English subtitles	A migrant worker struggling to survive in the city.
Gong, Li/ 龚力	Bu ji de qing chun/ 不羁的青春	90 min.	VHS/ PAL	1996	FIC	Chinese dialogue	The story of first love between two high school students.
Guan, Hu/ 管虎	Xi Shi yan/ 西施眼 = Eyes of Beauty	90 min.	VHS/ PAL	2001	FIC	Chinese dialogue with English subtitles	Stories of three beautiful women in the hometown of the famous ancient beauty, Xi Shi.
Han, Kaichen (Condor Han)/ 韩凯臣	Fu hua shi jie/ 浮华世界 = The Flush World	145 min.	VHS/ PAL	2003	FIC	Chinese dialogue with Chinese and English subtitles	A deformed man's life in the real world with a young prostitute, and in his imaginary world with three famous historical women in Beijing.
Han, Yeqiang/ 韩烨强	Bu zai fu wu qu/ 不在服务区 = Out of Service	58 min.	VHS/ PAL	2002	FIC	Chinese dialogue with English subtitles	A young migrant worker struggles to live an honest life in the city.

Table Continued

Director	Title	Time	Format	Date	Type	Language	Summary
Hao, Zhiqiang/ 郝志强	Dashu Xiang/ 大树乡 = Big Tree Village	50 min.	VHS/ PAL	1993	DOC	Chinese dialogue with English subtitles	A documentary about environmental pollution in Big Tree Village, which used to have many trees.
Hao, Zhiqiang/ 郝志强 (Chu, Han/ 楚汉 is used as the director's name in the film)	Feng/ 风 = Wind	25 min.	VHS/ PAL	1988	ANI	No dialogue or narration	A symbolic animated film about the "wind" in Chinese culture and history.
He, Jianjun/ 何建军	Man yan/ 蔓延 = Pirated Copy	84 min.	VHS/ PAL	2003	FIC	Chinese dialogue with Chinese and English subtitles	The stories of a vendor and his customers dealing in pirated DVDs.
He, Jianjun/ 何建军	Xuan lian/ 悬恋 = Red Beads	90 min.	VHS/ PAL	1993	FIC	Chinese dialogue with English subtitles	Stories about a care-giver and his mentally ill patient.
He, Jianjun/ 何建军	You chai/ 邮差 = Postman	98 min.	VHS/ PAL	1995	FIC	Chinese dialogue with English subtitles	Xiao Dou, a postman, opens and reads the letters that he is supposed to deliver and struggles with his strange relationships with his sister and a female colleague.

Author	Title	Duration	Format	Year	Type	Language	Description
Hu, Jie/ 胡杰	2002 Shai tai yang/ 2002 晒太阳	45 min.	VHS/ PAL	2002	DOC	Chinese dialogue with Chinese subtitles	On an island near Nanjing, in the spring of 2002, a group of artists organize and participate in an unofficial avant-garde art program called "Under the Sun."
Hu, Jie/ 胡杰	Mei po/ 媒婆	45 min.	VHS/ PAL	Shot in 1997, edited in 2002	DOC	Chinese dialogue with Chinese subtitles	The stories of a matchmaker and her business practices in the countryside of Shandong province, China.
Hu, Jie/ 胡杰	Xun zhao Lin Zhao de ling hun/ 寻找林昭的灵魂	100 min.	VHS/ PAL	2004	DOC	Chinese dialogue	A documentary film about Lin Zhao, a student at Beijing University. As a rightist in 1957, she was jailed and executed for her democratic beliefs.
Hu, Jie/ 胡杰	Yuan shan/ 远山	60 min.	VHS/ PAL	1995	DOC	Chinese dialogue	A documentary film about a small mining town and the life of miners there.
Hu, Shu/ 胡庶	Wo bu yao ni guan/ 我不要你管 = Leave Me Alone	70 min.	VHS/ PAL	2001	DOC	Chinese narration, Chinese dialogue with English subtitles	The true story of three girls who migrate to the big city to seek their fortunes. They work at night clubs, a beauty salon, and a massage parlor, rendering their "services" on the side.

Table Continued

Director	Title	Time	Format	Date	Type	Language	Summary
Hu, Xiaoding/ 胡小钉	Lai le/ 来了 = I Am Here	90 min.	VHS/PAL	2002	FIC	Chinese dialogue with English subtitles	A male dancer's relationship with his two female friends.
Hu, Ze/ 胡泽	Beijing jiao qu/ 北京郊区 = Beijing Suburb	86 min.	VHS/PAL	2001/2002	DOC/FIC	Chinese dialogue with English subtitles	A documentary-fictional film in which the protagonists, residents of an artist community in suburban Beijing, play themselves.
Hu, Ze/ 胡泽	Chu jing/ 处境 = Circumstances	78 min.	VHS/PAL	1999	DOC	Chinese dialogue with English subtitles	Interviews with two art and literary critics.
Huang, Jianzhong/ 黄建中	Da hong mi dian/ 大鸿米店	100 min.	DVD	2003	FIC	Chinese dialogue	The story surrounding a rice-store manager's apprentice and his unusual life.
Huang, Xiaojuan/ 黄小娟	Zhang bo shi/ 张博士 = Dr. Zhang	59 min.	VHS/PAL	2002	DOC	Chinese dialogue with English subtitles	A documentary about a person who misses his educational opportunity during the Cultural Revolution but later spends 17 years auditing classes at a university.
Jia, Zhangke/ 贾樟柯	Gou de zhuang kuang/ 狗的状况 = La Condition Canine	5 min.	VHS/PAL	2001	DOC	Chinese dialogue	A documentary film about a dog market in China.

Jia, Zhangke/ 贾樟柯	Ren xiao yao/ 任逍遥 = Unknown Pleasures	110 min.	VHS/ PAL	2002	FIC	Chinese dialogue with English subtitles	Two nineteen-year-old youths, children of laid-off government mine workers, are now living in the city and pursuing their pleasures.
Jia, Zhangke/ 贾樟柯	Xiao Wu/ 小武 = Artisan Pickpocket	104 min.	VHS/ PAL	1997	FIC	Chinese dialogue with English subtitles	The story of Xiao Wu, a pickpocket, in a small inland Chinese city.
Jia, Zhangke/ 贾樟柯	Zhan tai/ 站台 = Platform	148 min.	VHS/ PAL and DVD	2000	FIC	Copy 1: VHS: Chinese dialogue with Chinese and English subtitles; copy 2: DVD: Chinese dialogue with Chinese and Japanese subtitles	Follows the lives of four friends over a turbulent ten-year period from 1979 to 1989 in a small city in China.
Jia, Zhangke/ 贾樟柯	Gong gong kong jian/ 公共空间 = Public Space	50 min.	VHS/ PAL	2002	DOC	Chinese dialogue with English subtitles	A documentary on public spaces, such as bus stations, restaurants, and game rooms, in Datong, China.
Jiang, Wen/ 姜文	Gui zi lai le/ 鬼子来了 = Devils Are Here	90 min.	DVD	2002	FIC	Chinese and Japanese dialogue with Japanese subtitles	The story of the strange relationship between a Chinese peasant and Japanese soldiers in a small Chinese village during WWII.

Table Continued

Director	Title	Time	Format	Date	Type	Language	Summary
Jiang, Yue/ 蒋樾	Bi an/ 彼岸 = Faramita	90 min.	VHS/ PAL	1995	DOC	Chinese dialogue with English subtitles	Real stories about a group of young students who fail their college entrance exams and come to Beijing pursuing their dreams of getting into the Beijing Film Academy by trying to stage a drama.
Jiang, Yue/ 蒋樾	Xing fu sheng huo/ 幸福生活 = Happy Life	45min.	VHS/ PAL	2000	DOC	Chinese dialogue with English subtitles	What does a "happy life" mean to two normal workers in the Zhengzhou Railway Station?
Jiang, Zhi/ 蒋志	Fei ba, fei ba/ 飞吧, 飞吧	6 min.	VHS/ PAL	1997	EXP	Chinese dialogue	When a person is isolated, how can he solve the contradiction between reality and fantasy?
Jiang, Zhi/ 蒋志	Shi zhi/ 食指	45 min.	VHS/ PAL	1999	DOC	Chinese dialogue	interviews with the poet, Shi Zhi.
Jiang, Zhi/ 蒋志	You xi zhi di/ 游戏之地	6 min.	VHS/ PAL	1998	DOC	Chinese dialogue	Children at play in the playground.
Jin, Yan/ 金燕 (Wei, La/ 维拉 is used as the director's name in the film)	Bi zhe yan jing shuo hua/ 闭着眼睛说话	60 min.	VHS/ PAL	2002	DOC	Chinese dialogue with Chinese subtitles	The life of a blind musician, Lan Yue.

Kang, Feng/ 康峰	Shei jian guo ye sheng dong wu de jie ri/ 谁见过野生动 物的节日 = Who's Ever Seen the Wild Animal Day	83 min.	VHS/ PAL	1998	FIC	Chinese dialogue with English subtitles	Seventeen-year-old Jiang Zi is blatantly teased by a man in a park restroom. Afterward, he is labeled a homosexual due to this experience. Driven by his fears and a desire to change his reputation, he seeks retribution and accidentally kills the man.
Klassen, Solveig, and Schneider-Roos, Katharina	Wo de she ying ji bu sa huang/ 我的摄影机不撒谎 = My Camera Doesn't Lie	92 min.	VHS/ PAL and VCD/ NTSC	2003	DOC	Chinese dialogue with English subtitles	A film about Chinese underground filmmakers who were the first to express their realistic views on China from 1989 to 2003. Includes interviews with twelve film directors and clips from various films.
Li, Hong/ 李虹	Hei bai she ying gong zuo shi sha ren shi jian/ 黑白摄影工作室 杀人事件 = Murder Case in the Black Room	84 min.	VHS/ PAL	2001	FIC	Chinese dialogue	A murder occurs in a black-and-white portrait studio, but who is the murderer?

Table Continued

Director	Title	Time	Format	Date	Type	Language	Summary
Li, Hong/ 李红	Hui dao Feng Huang Qiao/ 回到凤凰桥	120 min.	VHS/ PAL	1997	DOC	Chinese dialogue	Living with four nannies from Anhui province who are now working in Beijing: their stories and lives.
Li, Jixian/ 李继贤	Wang Shouxian de xia tian/ 王首先的夏天 = A High Sky Summer	90 min.	VHS/ PAL	2002	FIC	Chinese dialogue	A twelve-year-old boy living in the countryside has been selected to pay a role in a film.
Li, Yu/ 李玉	Jin nian xia tian/ 今年夏天 = Fish and Elephant	106 min.	VHS/ PAL	2000	FIC	Chinese dialogue with English subtitles	Elephant trainer Xiao Qun falls in love with a woman. Her mother can't understand this relationship and introduces some men to her.
Liu, Bingjian/ 刘冰鉴	Ku qi de nü ren/ 哭泣的女人 = Cry Woman	100 min.	VHS/ PAL	2002	FIC	Chinese dialogue with English subtitles	Wang Guixiang becomes a famous professional mourner for local funerals and manages to save enough money to bribe the local prison director to have her husband released earlier.

Director	Title	Duration	Format	Year	Type	Language	Description
Liu, Bingjian/ 刘冰鉴	Nan nan nü nü/ 男男女女 = Men and Women	100 min.	VHS/ PAL	1999	FIC	Chinese dialogue with English subtitles	Xiao Bo comes to Beijing as a migrant worker and stays in his female boss's home. The husband of his boss thinks he is a gay and tries to rape him, causing Xiao Bo to quit his job and move into a gay friend's home.
Liu, Ming/ 刘铭	Zha zi/ 渣子 = Rubbish	16 min.	VHS/ PAL	2003	FIC	Chinese dialogue with Chinese and English subtitles	Garbage is the theme of an artist's teaching, poetry, and artwork.
Liu, Ran/ 刘然	Bang mang/ 帮忙	30 min.	VHS/ PAL	2003	DOC	Chinese dialogue with Chinese subtitles	A documentary about a wedding ceremony.
Lou, Ye/ 娄烨	Suzhou He/ 苏洲河 = Suzhou River	90 min.	VHS/ PAL	1997, completed in 2000	FIC	Chinese dialogue with English subtitles	The story about a delivery-man in Shanghai and a mysterious girl he loves.
Lu, Xuechang/ 路学长	Zhang da cheng ren/ 长大成人 = The Making of Steel	90 min.	VHS/ PAL	1997	FIC	Chinese dialogue with Chinese and English subtitles	An initiation story of a young man in a tough Beijing environment between 1970 and 2000.
Lü, Yue/ 吕乐	Zhao xian sheng/ 赵先生 = Mr. Zhao	90 min.	VHS/ PAL	1998	FIC	Chinese dialogue with English subtitles	The stories of the relationships between a university professor and his wife, lover, and dream lover.

Table Continued

Director	Title	Time	Format	Date	Type	Language	Summary
Lü, Yue/ 吕乐	Nu Jiang, yi tiao diu shi de xia gu/ 怒江，一条丢失的峡谷 = Nujiang, LA Vallee Perdue	80 min.	VHS/ PAL	1987	DOC	Chinese dialogue with French subtitles	The culture and religious practice of the minorities living in the Nujiang area.
Meng, Qi/ 孟奇	Wo zui zhong yi de xue tian/ 我最中意的雪天	90 min.	VHS/ PAL	2002	FIC	Chinese dialogue	An ordinary city person's life in today's China.
Ning, Hao/ 宁浩	Xiang huo/ 香火 = Incense	70 min.	VHS/ PAL	2003	FIC	Chinese dialogue with Chinese and English subtitles	A story about a young monk in a small Chinese village who tries to rekindle interest in Buddhism and keep the incense burning in his small temple.
Ning, Hao/ 宁浩	Xing qi si, xing qi san/ 星期四，星期三 = Thursday, Wednesday	66 min.	VHS/ PAL	2001	FIC	Chinese dialogue with English subtitles	There are three parts: street youths, a girl who wants to go abroad, and poor musicians.
Ning, Ying/ 宁瀛	Xi wang zhi lu/ 希望之路	60 min.	VHS/ PAL	2002	DOC	Chinese dialogue	Interviews with migrant cotton pickers on the train from Sichuan to Xinjiang during the cotton harvest season.

Director	Title	Duration	Format	Year	Type	Language	Synopsis
Pan, Jianlin/ 潘剑林	Zao an, Beijing/ 早安，北京 = Good Morning, Beijing	84 min.	VHS/ PAL	2003	FIC	Chinese dialogue with English subtitles	In Beijing, a young woman is kidnapped, and her boyfriend spends a whole night trying to locate her.
Pan, Zhaolin/ 潘钊林	Xin niang/ 新娘	60 min.	VHS/ PAL	2001	DOC	Chinese dialogue	A newly wed migrant couple is separated after being detained by police in the city.
Peng, Tao/ 彭韬	Dong tian li de gu shi/ 冬天里的故事 = Winter Story	30 min.	VHS/ PAL	2003	FIC	Chinese dialogue	Two laid-off workers buy a BB gun, shoot women from the roof for fun, and are caught.
Pu, Sheng/ 蒲盛	Jing tu/ 净土 = Pure Land	85 min.	VHS/ PAL	2003	FIC	Chinese dialogue with English subtitles	An underworld boss decides to give up his criminal career and work as a normal laborer in order to seek his spiritually "pure land."
Sheng, Zhimin/ 盛志民	Xin xin/ 心心 = Two Hearts	95 min.	VHS/ PAL	2002	FIC	Chinese dialogue with English subtitles	The stories of two young girls in Beijing: Xinxin, who will soon go to Canada to study, and Dingding, who is a phone-sex worker.

Table Continued

Director	Title	Time	Format	Date	Type	Language	Summary
Shi, Runjiu/ 施润玖	An ding yi yuan/ 安定医院 = Anding Hospital	60 min.	VHS/PAL	2002	DOC	Chinese dialogue	Anding hospital in Beijing is the biggest mental hospital in Asia.
Sun, Zengtian/ 孙增田	Zui hou de shan shen/ 最后的山神	45 min.	VHS/PAL	1992	DOC	Chinese narration and Chinese subtitles	The stories about the last shaman of the Erlunchun tribe in the northeast mountain and forest areas of China.
Sun, Zengtian/ 孙增田	Shen lu a, shen lu/ 神鹿啊，神鹿	55 min.	VHS/PAL	1997	DOC	Chinese narration and English subtitles	How a female artist finds the meaning of life in her native land and with her native people, the Erlunchun tribal people.
Tang, Xiaobai/ 唐晓白	Dong ci bian wei/ 动词变位 = Conjugation	97 min.	VHS/PAL	2001	FIC	Chinese dialogue with English subtitles	The story of a young college graduate who lives with his girlfriend in Beijing right after the famous student movement in 1989.
Wang, Bing/ 王兵	Tiexi Qu/ 铁西区	330 min.	VCD	2001	DOC	Chinese dialogue with English subtitles	Tiexi district is a heavy industrial area in Shenyang, NE China. Many government-owned factories are ready to file bankruptcy, and people there are trying to find their own ways of working and living during this transition period.

Director	Title	Duration	Format	Year	Type	Language	Description
Wang, Chao/ 王超	Anyang ying er/ 安阳婴儿 = Anyang Orphan	80 min.	VHS/ PAL	2001	FIC	Chinese dialogue with English subtitles	The story of a laid-off worker who picks up an abandoned infant, later meets the mother, a prostitute, and the biological father, a mob boss.
Wang, Guangli/ 王光利	Chu nü zuo/ 处女作	90 min.	VHS/ PAL	1997	FIC	Chinese dialogue	The story of the relationship between a poor artist and his two lesbian friends.
Wang, Guangli/ 王光利	Wo bi ye le/ 我毕业了	60 min.	VHS/ PAL	1992	DOC	Chinese dialogue with Chinese subtitles	Interviews with seniors from several universities in Beijing before their graduations.
Wang, Kaiwen/ 王凯文	Shao kao/ 烧烤 = What's Wrong	60 min.	VCD	2003	FIC	Chinese dialogue with Chinese subtitles	A story of a young man who wants to start as a street vendor selling barbeque.
Wang, Xiaoshuai/ 王小帅	Bian dan gu niang/ 扁担姑娘 Close to Paradise	90 min.	VHS/ NTSC	1998	FIC	Chinese dialogue with English subtitles	Two young migrant workers come together in the city to better their lives, and they get involved with a girl singing at a bar.

Table Continued

Director	Title	Time	Format	Date	Type	Language	Summary
Wang, Xiaoshuai/ 王小帅	Dong Chun de ri zi/ 冬春的日子 = The Days	90 min.	VHS/ NTSC	1993	FIC	Chinese dialogue with English subtitles	Dong and Chun are a couple who were high school sweethearts, but they realize that their separation is inevitable.
Wang, Xiaoshuai/ 王小帅	Shi qi sui de dan che/ 十七岁的单车 = Beijing Bicycle	110 min.	VHS/ NTSC	2000	FIC	Chinese dialogue with English subtitles	A seventeen-year-old worker from the countryside loses the new bicycle assigned to him by his company in Beijing.
Wang, Xiaoshuai/ 王小帅 (Wu, Ming/ 无名 is used as the director's name in the film)	Ji du han leng/ 极度寒冷 = Frozen	95 min.	DVD	1999	FIC	Chinese dialogue with English subtitles	An artist plans to end his life through a performance art program.
Wang, Zi/ 王子	Wo men zhang da le/ 我们长大了	10 min.	VCD	2001?	FIC	Chinese dialogue with Chinese subtitles	A story between one girl and two brothers.
Wei, Xiaojun/ 魏晓军	Er yue hua yu/ 二月话语	25 min.	VCD	2003	DOC	Chinese dialogue with Chinese subtitles	Two young artists talking about making films.
Wei, Xing/ 魏星	Wang ji ta shi ta/ 忘记他是她	14 min.	VHS/ PAL	2003	DOC	Chinese dialogue with Chinese subtitles	Interviews with a group of gay men in China.
Wei, Xing/ 魏星	Yesu bao you nin/ 耶稣保佑您 = Jesus Bless You	45 min.	VHS/ PAL	2002	DOC	Chinese dialogue with Chinese subtitles	A documentary film about Christian practice in a rural village in Shandong province.

Creator	Title	Duration	Format	Year	Type	Language	Description
Wen, Pulin/ 温普林	Bajiao Jie/ 八角街	60 min.	VCD	2000	DOC	Chinese and Tibetan dialogue	The lives of Buddhists, prayers, monks, landlords, street performers, craftsmen, and merchants on Bajiao Street, a religious, cultural, commercial, and tourist center in Lhasa, Tibet.
Wen, Pulin/ 温普林	Chong jian Gong de lin/ 重建功德林	60 min.	VCD	2001	DOC	Tibetan dialogue	The practice and recovery of a Tibetan Buddhist monastery school.
Wen, Pulin/ 温普林	Damu tian zang tai/ 达木天葬台 = Celestial Burial	150 min.	VCD (2)	2001	DOC	English narration, Tibetan and Chinese dialogue with English subtitles	Documentation of the Tibetan celestial burial in Damu Monastery.
Wen, Pulin/ 温普林	Gama Baqin/ 噶玛巴钦 = Karmapa Bless You	200 Min	VCD (3)	1995	DOC	English narration, Tibetan and Chinese dialogue with English subtitles	Documentation of the teaching and religious practices at the Tibetan Karmapa's Buddhist monastery school.
Wen, Pulin/ 温普林	Meng hui Axu/ 梦回阿须	80 min.	VCD	1999?	DOC	Chinese narration, Chinese and Tibetan dialogue with Chinese subtitles	The stories of two Chinese brothers who befriend a living Buddha and their joint effort to establish a Buddhist temple in the Axu grasslands of Tibet.

Table Continued

Director	Title	Time	Format	Date	Type	Language	Summary
Wen, Pulin/ 温普林	Minqiong an a ni/ 敏琼庵阿尼	80 min.	VCD	1999?	DOC	Chinese narration, Tibetan dialogue with Chinese subtitles	The lives of a group of Tibetan Buddhist nuns in the Minqiong monastery, Lhasa, Tibet.
Wen, Pulin/ 温普林	Qingpu/ 菁朴 = The Sacred Site for Asceticism: Mt. Chims-phu	80 min.	VCD	1993?	DOC	Chinese narration, Tibetan and Chinese dialogue with English subtitles	A pilgrimage journey to the sacred site of asceticism, Mt. Chims-phu, and the life of a group of Tibetan Buddhist monks and nuns who live and practice their religion there.
Wen, Pulin/ 温普林	Tian zhu zai Xizang/ 天主在西南 = Catholicism in Tibet	60 min.	VCD	1999?	DOC	Tibetan and Chinese dialogue	The history and current situation of the only Catholic church in Tibet.
Wen, Pulin/ 温普林	Zai Zang shi nian/ 在藏十年 = Tibet 10 Years	160 min.	VCD (2)	1999	DOC	English narration, Tibetan and Chinese dialogue with English subtitles	A documentary film about Wen Pulin, a graduate of the Central Arts and Crafts Academy in Beijing, and his ten years (1989–1999) in Tibet.
Wen, Pulin/ 温普林	Zhongguo xing dong/ 中国行动	80 min.	VCD	1999	DOC	Chinese narration with Chinese subtitles	A documentary film about Chinese avant-garde art movements in the 1980s and 1990s.

Wen, Pulin/ 温普林	Zhu shen xia fan/ 诸神下凡	60 min.	VCD	1998?	DOC	Tibetan and Chinese dialogue	The lives of a group of Tibetan religious dance performers.
Weng, Shouming/ 翁首鸣	Mo li hua Haiwan/ 茉莉花海湾 = Jasmine Bay	18 min.	VHS/ PAL	2003	FIC	Chinese dialogue with English and Chinese subtitles	Past and current stories of a young college student growing up in a small village beside Jasmine Bay.
Wu, Di/ 邬迪	Huang jin yu/ 黄金鱼 = Goldfish	70 min.	VHS/ PAL	1995	FIC	Chinese dialogue with English subtitles	A young goldfish vendor tries to live his own life instead of following his girlfriend and his wife who move to the United States.
Wu, Ershan/ 乌尔善	Shu zi, ren qun, lao ren, peng zhuang/ 数字、人群、老人、碰撞	20 min.	VHS/ PAL	2002	EXP	No dialogue or narration	Four short pieces of moving numbers and images of a mouse, a man, an old man, and others. Alternative music soundtrack.
Wu, Ershan/ 乌尔善	Huan gu/ 环顾 = Looking Around	5 min.	VHS/ PAL	1997	EXP	Chinese dialogue with English subtitles	A montage of altered images and background sounds at a restaurant wedding banquet.
Wu, Shixian/ 武仕贤	Che si shi si/ 车四十四 = Bus 44	11 min.	VHS/ PAL	2001	FIC	Chinese dialogue with English subtitles	Robbery and rape happen on Bus 44. What is the reaction of the passengers and driver?

Table Continued

Director	Title	Time	Format	Date	Type	Language	Summary
Wu, Wenguang/ 吴文光	1966, Wo de hong wei bing shi dai/ 1966, 我的红卫兵时代 = 1966, My Time in the Red Guards	165 min.	VHS/ PAL	1993	DOC	Chinese dialogue with English subtitles	A documentary based on several former Red Guards' experiences during the Cultural Revolution.
Wu, Wenguang/ 吴文光	Si hai wei jia/ 四海为家 = At Home in the World	170 min.	VHS/ PAL	1995	DOC	Chinese dialogue with English subtitles	A five-year follow-up to the documentary film *Bumming in Beijing*, it describes the experiences of five young artists in Beijing, France, Italy, the United States, and Austria during the 1990s.
Wu, Wenguang/ 吴文光	Liu lang Beijing/ 流浪北京 = Bumming in Beijing, the Last Dreamers	90 min.	VHS/ PAL	1990	DOC	Chinese dialogue with English subtitles	Leaving their officially assigned jobs behind during the 1980s, five young artists come to Beijing after graduating from college in search of their dreams.

Author	Title	Duration	Format	Year	Type	Language	Description
Wu, Wenguang/ 吴文光	He min gong tiao wu/ 和民工跳舞 = Dance with Farm Workers	60 min.	VHS/ PAL	2001	DOC	Chinese dialogue with English subtitles	Wu Wenguang choreographs dances utilizing thirty farm workers who simulate the movements of their daily work.
Wu, Wenguang/ 吴文光	Jiang hu/ 江湖 = Life on the Road	120 min.	VHS/ PAL	1999	DOC	Chinese dialogue with English subtitles	A documentary of the Yuanda Song and Dance Tent Show, a wandering troupe from the countryside of Henan province that is on the road all four seasons of the year.
Wu, Wenguang/ 吴文光	Ri ji—yi jiu jiu ba nian shi yi yue er shi yi ri, xue/ 日记——九九八年十一月二十一日, 雪 = Diary—Snow, Nov. 21, 1998	14 min.	VHS/ PAL	1999	DOC	Partially silent with some Chinese dialogue and one brief English interview; English and Chinese captions	An impressionistic documentary recounting a visit to Beijing's Ancestral Temple for an art exhibition, which ends up being cancelled for "official" reasons.
Xin, Qin/ 辛勤	Chuang jiang hu de ji jian shi/ 闯江湖的几件事 = Things I Came Across in My Experience	60 min.	VHS/ PAL	2003	DOC	Chinese dialogue with Chinese and English subtitles	The stories of a puppet show family that leaves its hometown to perform in Beijing during the Spring Festival of 2002.

Table Continued

Director	Title	Time	Format	Date	Type	Language	Summary
Yan, Lei/ 颜磊	1500 li mi/ 1500 厘米 = 1500 cm.	35 min.	VCD	1994	EXP	No dialogue or narration	A man washes a plastic tape measuring 1,500 cm, swallows it, pulls it out of his mouth, and inserts it into a glass bottle.
Yang, Fudong/ 杨福东	Mo sheng tian tang/ 陌生天堂 = An Estranged Paradise	70 min.	VHS/ PAL	2002	FIC	Chinese dialogue with English subtitles	Depicts urban intellectual life during the 1970s.
Yang, Tianyi/ 杨天乙	Lao tou/ 老头 = Old Men	94 min.	VHS/ PAL	1999	DOC	Chinese dialogue	A documentary about a group of retired old men gathering daily on a street corner.
Yang, Zhichao/ 杨志超	Jiayuguan/ 嘉峪关	30 min.	VHS/ PAL	2000	DOC	Chinese dialogue	A documentary about a patient's experience of being checked into a mental hospital.
Ying, Weiwei/ 英未未	He zi/ 盒子 = The Box	90 min.	VHS/ PAL	2001	DOC	Chinese dialogue with English subtitles	This documentary film describes two lesbians' simple and fragile daily lives.
Yu, Xiaoyang/ 于小洋	Mi an/ 迷岸	50 min.	VHS/ PAL	1996	FIC	Chinese dialogue	An artist's life in modern China mixed with his poetic memories of childhood, fairy tales, and his imaginary world.

Director	Title	Duration	Format	Year	Type	Language	Synopsis
Zhang, Huilin/ 张晖林	Tiao you/ 条友 = Hi, Guys	35 min.	VHS/ PAL	2002	DOC	Chinese dialogue with English subtitles	The life of a film and music CD/ DVD pirate in Guangzhou.
Zhang, Ming/ 章明	Mi yu shi qi xiao shi/ 密语十七小时	80 min.	VHS/ PAL	2002	FIC	Chinese dialogue with English subtitles	A group of friends come from Beijing to the Yangtze River for an eventful summer weekend.
Zhang, Ming/ 章明	Wu Shan yun yu/ 巫山云雨 = In Expectation	95 min.	VHS/ PAL	1996	FIC	Chinese dialogue with English subtitles	A single man living in a lonely lighthouse falls in love with a widow who lives across the Yangtze River.
Zhang, Tielin/ 张铁林	Yi zi/ 椅子 = The Chair	80 min.	VHS/ PAL	1996	FIC	Chinese dialogue with Chinese and English subtitles	The story of a newly retired editor and the antique chair he purchased.
Zhang, Yuan/ 张元	Beijing za zhong/ 北京杂种 = Beijing Bastards	85 min.	VHS/ PAL	1993	FIC	Chinese dialogue with English subtitles	A rock musician breaks up with his girlfriend because they disagree on what to do about her pregnancy.
Zhang, Yuan/ 张元	Dong gong xi gong/ 东宫西宫 = East Palace, West Palace	90 min.	VHS/ NTSC	1996	FIC	Chinese dialogue with English subtitles	A young gay Chinese writer, A-Lan, faces a whole night of detention and interrogation by a young policeman he is attracted to.

Table Continued

Director	Title	Time	Format	Date	Type	Language	Summary
Zhang, Yuan/ 张元	Er zi/ 儿子 = Sons	95 min.	VHS/ PAL	1996	FIC	Chinese dialogue with English subtitles	Two sons try to live with their alcoholic father in today's Beijing.
Zhang, Yuan/ 张元	Feng kuang ying yu/ 疯狂英语 = Crazy English	90 min.	VHS/ PAL	1998	DOC	Chinese dialogue with English subtitles	A documentary on the nationwide "Crazy English" lecture tours given by Li Yang.
Zhang, Yuan/ 张元	Jin Xing xiao jie/ 金星小姐	30 min.	VHS/ PAL	2000	DOC	Chinese dialogue	A documentary about a transsexual, Miss Jin Xing, who works as a professional dancer and choreographer in Beijing.
Zhang, Zhanqing/ 张战庆	Cheng xiang jie he bu/ 城乡结合部 = Where City and Country Meet	60 min.	VHS/ PAL and VCD	2001	DOC	Chinese dialogue with English subtitles	This documentary film describes the life of Guan Chunqi, a struggling migrant, and his family, living in the outskirts of Beijing.
Zhao-Yan, Guozhang/ 赵燕国彰	Qia tong xue shao nian/ 恰同学少年 = A Dream of Youth	90 min.	VHS/ PAL	2000	FIC	Chinese dialogue with English subtitles	The stories of a group of students in the Beijing Film Academy.
Zheng, Dasheng/ 郑大圣	Xing zhe I, II, III/ 行者 1, 2, 3 = Wanderer 1, 2, 3	12 min.	VHS/ PAL	1993	EXP	No dialogue or narration	Montage of the images of traffic, pedestrians, signs, and buildings.

Director	Title	Duration	Format	Year	Type	Language	Description
Zheng, Dasheng/ 郑大圣	DV China	90 min.	VCD	2002	DOC	Chinese dialogue with English subtitles	A documentary about a local cultural official who, by using DV technology, tries to make martial arts films with local people.
Zhong, Hua/ 仲华	Jin nian dong tian/ 今年冬天 = This Winter	90 min.	VHS/ PAL	2001	DOC	Chinese dialogue with English subtitles	Four soldiers in a military police unit finish their service and are ready to leave.
Zhong, Hua/ 仲华	Mao Shan hao zi/ 茅山号子	60 min.	VHS/ PAL	2002	DOC	Chinese dialogue with Chinese subtitles	A documentary about folk music in the Maoshan area.
Zhou, Hongxiang/ 周弘湘	Hong qi piao/ 红旗飘 = The Red Flag	70 min.	VCD	2002	EXP	Chinese dialogue with English subtitles	They are the children of Marx and Coca-Cola, who inherit Mao and Microsoft, and they answer questions about the meanings of luck, love, money, future, power, wealth, and God.
Zhou, Jue/ 周玨	Zhe li shi wo peng you jia/ 这里是我朋友家 = Here Is My Friend's House	71 min.	VHS/ PAL	2003	DOC	Chinese dialogue with English subtitles	The director spends one afternoon in the house of his friend, Peng Yue, an artist in Beijing.
Zhu, Chuanming/ 朱传明	Qun zhong yan yuan/ 群众演员	70 min.	VHS/ PAL	2001	DOC	Chinese dialogue with Chinese subtitles	The lives of a group of people who try to find jobs as film extras in Beijing.

Abbreviations
ANI = Animated   DOC = Documentary   EXP = Experimental   FIC = Fictional

Filmography

Note: The following Chinese film titles, including DV and video works, are cited in the book (except for the appendixes in chapter 8 and the filmography in the appendix) and are arranged chronologically under the alphabetic listings of directors' names. All films are fictional unless otherwise identified. Technical specifications are given where available, and approximate running times may vary according to particular versions.

A Nian 阿年 (Xu Hongyu 许宏宇, b. 1965). *Chengshi aiqing* 城市爱情 (Love in the City). 87 min. 35mm. Hangzhou: Zhejiang Studio, 1997.

Chen Kaige 陈凯歌. *Huang tudi* 黄土地 (Yellow Earth). 87 min. 35mm. Nanning: Guangxi Studio, 1984.

Chen Miao (Michelle Chen 陈苗). *Shanghai nanhai* 上海男孩 (The Snake Boy). Documentary. 63 min. 2001.

Cui Zi'en 崔子恩 (b. 1958). *Choujue dengchang* 丑角登场 (Enter the Clowns). 103 min. DV. Beijing: Cuizi Studio, 2001.

——. *Jiuyue* 旧约 (Old Testament). 75 min./100 min./138 min. DV. Beijing: Cuizi Studio, 2001.

Du Haibin 杜海滨 (b. 1972). *Tielu yanxian* 铁路沿线 (Along the Railroad). Documentary. 60 min./98 min./137 min. Hi8. 2000.

Duan Jinchuan 段锦川 (b. 1962) with Zhang Yuan. *Guangchang* 广场 (The Square). Documentary. 100 min. 35mm. 1994.

——. *Bakuo nan jie 16 hao* 八廓南街16号 (No. 16 South Barkhor Street). Documentary. 30 min./80 min./100 min. Video. Lhasa: Tibetan Cultural Communication, 1997.

——. *Linqi da shetou* 拎起大舌头 (The Secret of My Success). Documentary. 75 min. Beijing: China Memo Films, 2002.

Guan Hu 管虎 (b. 1967). *Toufa luanle* 头发乱了 (Dirt). 97 min. 35mm. Hohhot: Inner Mongolia Studio/Beijing: Golden Bridge (金桥) International Trading Co., 1994.

He Jianjun 何建军 (He Yi 何一, b. 1960). *Xuanlian* 悬恋 (Red Beads). 92 min. Hong Kong: Shu Kei 舒琪 Creative Workshop 创造社, 1993.

——. *Youcai* 邮差 (Postman). 98 min. 1995.

——. *Manyan* 蔓延 (Pirated Copy). 84 min. Beijing: Fanhall 现象, 2004.

Hu Shu 胡庶 (b. 1967). *Wo bu yao ni guan* 我不要你管 (Leave Me Alone). Documentary. 70 min. DV. 2001.

Hu Xueyang 胡雪杨 (b. 1963). *Yanmo de qingchun* 淹没的青春 (The Drowned Youth). 35mm. Shanghai: Shanghai Studio, 1994.

Huang Shuqin 黄蜀芹. *Qingchun wansui* 青春万岁 (Forever Young). 35mm. Shanghai: Shanghai Studio, 1983.

Huo Jianqi 霍建起. *Nashan, Naren, Nagou* 那山, 那人, 那狗 (Postman in the Mountains). 35mm. Changsha: Xiaoxiang Studio and Hunan Provincial Post Office/Beijing: Beijing Studio, 1998.

——. *Nuan* 暖 (Nuan). 90 min. 35mm. Beijing: Jinha fangzhou 金海方舟/Japan: JCP, 2003.

Jia Zhangke 贾樟柯 (b. 1970). *Xiao Wu* 小武 (Xiao Wu, aka Artisan Pickpocket). 107 min. 16mm. Hong Kong: Hutong 胡同, 1997.

——. *Zhantai* 站台 (Platform). 154 min./193 min. 35mm. Hong Kong: Hutong/Japan: T-Mark, 2000.

——. *Gonggong changsuo* 公共场所, aka *Gonggong kongjian* 公共空间 (In Public). Documentary. 31 min./50 min. DV. South Korea: SIDUS, 2001.

——. *Ren xiaoyao* 任逍遥 (Unknown Pleasures). 117 min. DV/35mm. Hong Kong: Hutong/Japan: Office Kitano 北野武/France: Lumen/South Korea: E-Pictures, 2002.

——. *Shijie* 世界 (The World). 143 min. 35mm. Shanghai: Shanghai Studio/Japan: Office Kitano/France: Lumen, 2004.

Jiang Wen 姜文 (b. 1963). *Yangguang canlan de rizi* 阳光灿烂的日子 (In the Heat of the Sun). 35mm. Beijing: China Co-Production/Hong Kong: Ganglong 港龙/Taipei: Xiehe 协和, 1994.

——. *Guizi laile* 鬼子来了 (Devils on the Doorstep). 139 min./162 min. 35mm. b/w. Beijing: Huayi Brothers and Taihe 华谊兄弟太合, 2000.

Jiang Yue 蒋樾 (b. 1962). *Bi an* 彼岸 (The Other Bank). Documentary. 90 min./140 min. 1995.

——. *Xingfu shenghuo* 幸福生活 (This Happy Life). Documentary. 45 min. Beijing: China Memo Films, 2002.

Ju Anqi 雎安奇 (b. 1975). *Beijing de feng henda* 北京的风很大 (There's a Strong Wind in Beijing). Documentary. 49 min. Beijing: Haogou (壕沟) Film Group, 2000.

Klassen, Solveig, and Katharina Schneidere-Roos. *Wode sheyingji bu sahuang* 我的摄影机不撒谎 (My Camera Doesn't Lie). Documentary. 92 min. DV. 2003.

Li Dan 李丹. *Laorenmen* 老人们 (Old People). Documentary. 2000.

Li Hong 李红 (b. 1967). *Huidao Fenghuang qiao* 回到凤凰桥 (Out of Phoenix Bridge). Documentary. 120 min. 1997.

——. *He ziji tiaowu* 和自己跳舞 (Dancing with Myself). Documentary. 2002.

Li Yang 李杨. *Mangjing* 盲井 (Blind Shaft). 92 min. 35mm. Beijing: Li Yang/Tang Splendor Films 盛唐, 2002.

Li Yu 李玉 (b. 1973). *Jinnian xiatian* 今年夏天 (Fish and Elephant). 106 min. 2000.

Lin Nong 林农 (b. 1918). Dang de nü'er 党的女儿 (Daughter of the Party). 110 min. 35mm. Changchun: Changchun Studio, 1958.

Liu Weiqiang (刘伟强 Andrew Lau) and Mai Zhaohui (麦兆辉 Alan Mak). *Wujian dao III* 无间道 III (Infernal Affairs III). 117 min. 35mm. Hong Kong: Media Asia 寰亚, 2003.

Lou Ye 娄烨 (b. 1965). *Zhoumo qingren* 周末情人 (Weekend Lovers). 96 min. 35mm. Fuzhou: Fujian Studio/Hai'nan: Star and Sea (星海) Real Estate Co., 1994.

——. *Suzhou he* 苏州河 (Suzhou River). 90 min. 16mm/35mm. Beijing: China Co-Production/Germany: Essential Filmprodukton, 1997, 2000.

Lu Xuechang 路学长 (b. 1964). *Zhangda chengren* 长大成人 (The Making of Steel). 90 min. 35mm. Beijing: Beijing Studio/Great Wall (长城) International Advertising Co., 1995, 1997 (released).

Lü Yue 吕乐 (b. 1957). *Zhao xiansheng* 赵先生 (Mr. Zhao). 90 min. 1998.

Ning Dai 宁岱. *Tingji* 停机 (Shutting Down). Documentary. Video. 1993.

Ning Ying 宁瀛. *Zhaole* 找乐 (For Fun). 93 min. 35mm. Beijing: Beijing Studio/Hong Kong: Vanke 万科, 1992.

Shi Jian 时间 (b. 1963) et al. *Tiananmen* 天安门 (Tiananmen). Documentary in 8 parts. 1991.

———. *Wo biye le* 我毕业了 (I've Graduated). Documentary. 1992.

Tang Xiaobai 唐晓白 (Emmy Tang). *Dongci bianwei* 动词变位 (Conjugation). 97 min. 16mm. 2001.

Tian Zhuangzhuang 田壮壮 (b. 1952). *Daoma zei* 盗马贼 (Horse Thief). 83 min. 35mm. Xi'an: Xi'an Studio, 1986.

———. *Lan fengzheng* 蓝风筝 (The Blue Kite). 140 min. 35mm. Beijing: Beijing Studio/Hong Kong: Longwick 长威, 1993.

———. *Xiaocheng zhi chun* 小城之春 (Springtime in a Small Town). 116 min. 35mm. Beijing: Beijing Studio, 2000.

———. *Delamu* 德拉姆 (Delamu). Documentary. 110 min. Japan: NHK, 2003.

Wang Bing 王兵 (b. 1967). *Tiexi qu* 铁西区 (West of the Tracks). Documentary in 3 parts. 330 min./450 min. DV. 2001.

Wang Chao 王超 (b. 1964). *Anyang yinger* 安阳婴儿 (The Orphan of Anyang). 81 min. 35mm. Netherlands: Cineco Film, 2001.

Wang Fen 王芬 (b. 1978). *Bu kuaile de bu zhi yige* 不快乐的不止一个 (Unhappiness Doesn't Stop at One). Documentary. DV. 2000.

Wang Guangli 王光利 (b. 1966). *Heng shu heng* 横竖横 (Go for Broke). 35mm. Shanghai: Shanghai Studio, 2000.

Wang Jiawei 王家卫 (Wong Kar-Wai, b. 1958). *Chongqing senlin* 重庆森林 (Chunking Express). 102 min. 35mm. Hong Kong: Jet Tone 泽东, 1994.

———. *Dongxie xidu* 东邪西毒 (Ashes of Time). 98 min. 35mm. Hong Kong: Jet Tone/Beijing: Beijing Studio, 1994.

Wang Quan'an 王全安 (b. 1965). *Yueshi* 月蚀 (Lunar Eclipse). 35 mm. Beijing: Beijing Studio/ Yuanguang (远光) Film and TV, 1999.

Wang Xiaoshuai 王小帅 (b. 1966). *Dong Chun de rizi* 冬春的日子 (The Days). 90 min. 35mm. b/w. Beijing: Yinxiang 印象/Hong Kong: Shu Kei Creative Workshop, 1993.

———. (Wu Ming 无名). *Jidu hanleng* 极度寒冷 (Frozen). 95 min. 16mm. Hong Kong: Shu Kei Creative Workshop/Hubert Bals Foundation, 1997.

———. *Biandan guniang* 扁担姑娘 (So Close to Paradise). 91 min. 35mm. Beijing: Jindie (金碟) Film and TV/Beijing Studio, 1998.

———. *Shiqi sui de dan danche* 十七岁的单车 (Beijing Bicycle). 110 min. 35mm. Beijing: Beijing Studio/Taipei: Arch Light 吉光/France: Pyramide Productions, 2000.

Wei Ating 魏阿挺. *Wuyin dagu* 五音大鼓 (Five-Tune Big Drums). Documentary. 2004.

Wu Wenguang 吴文光 (b. 1956). *Liulang Beijing: zuihou de mengxiangzhe* 流浪北京: 最后的梦想者 (Bumming in Beijing: The Last Dreamers). Documentary. 70 min./90 min. 1990.

———. *1966, Wo de hong weibing shidai* 1966, 我的红卫兵时代 (1966, My Time in the Red Guards). Documentary. 165 min. Beijing: Wu Documentary Studio, 1993.

———. *Sihai weijia* 四海为家 (At Home in the World). Documentary. 170 min. Beijing: Dragon Films, 1995.

———. *Jiang Hu* 江湖 (Jiang Hu: Life on the Road). Documentary. 58 min./120 min. DV. Beijing: Wu Documentary Studio, 1999.

———. *He mingong yiqi tiaowu* 和民工一起跳舞 (Dance with Migrant Workers). Documentary. 60 min. DV. Beijing: Wu Documentary Studio, 2001.

———. *Dianying shi shenme* 电影是什么 (What is Film?). Documentary. DV. Beijing: Wu Documentary Studio, 2002.

———. *Cao tama de dianying* 操他妈的电影 (Fuck the Movies). Documentary. DV. Beijing: Wu Documentary Studio, 2004.

Yang Chao 杨超. *Daibi* 待避 (Runaway). Student feature. 30 min. 2001.

Yang Dechang 杨德昌 (Edward Yang, b. 1947). *Gulingjie shaonian sharen shijian* 牯岭街少年 杀人事件 (A Brighter Summer Day). 180 min. 35mm. Taipei: Central Motion Picture Corporation, 1991.

Yang Tianyi (Yang Lina) 杨天乙 (杨荔纳, b. 1972). *Laotou* 老头 (Old Men). Documentary. 94 min. DV. 1999.

Ying Weiwei 英未未 (Echo Y. Windy, b. 1970). *Hezi* 盒子 (The Box). Documentary. 88 min. DV. 2001.

Zhang Ming 章明 (b. 1961). *Wushan yunyu* 巫山云雨 (Rainclouds over Wushan, aka In Expectation). 95 min. 35mm. Beijing: Beijing Studio/Eastern Land (东方大地) Cultural Development, 1996.

Zhang Yang 张杨 (b. 1967). *Xizao* 洗澡 (Shower). 94 min. 35mm. Xi'an: Xi'an Studio/Imar 艺码, 1999.

———. *Zuotian* 昨天 (Quitting). 35mm. Xi'an: Xi'an Studio/Imar, 2001.

Zhang Yimou 张艺谋 (b. 1950). *Wo de fuqin muqin* 我的父亲母亲 (The Road Home). 90 min. 35mm. Nanning: Guangxi Studio/Columbia Asia, 1999.

———. *Yingxiong* 英雄 (Hero). 99 min. 35mm. Beijing: New Picture 新画面/Hong Kong: Elite Group 精英, 2002.

———. *Shimian maifu* 十面埋伏 (House of the Flying Daggers). 117 min. 35mm. Beijing: New Picture/Hong Kong: Elite Group, 2004.

Zhang Yuan 张元 (b. 1963). *Mama* 妈妈 (Mama). 83 min. 35mm. Xi'an: Xi'an Studio, 1991.

———. *Beijing zazhong* 北京杂种 (Beijing Bastards). 95 min. 35mm. 1993.

———. with Duan Jinchuan. *Guangchang* 广场 (The Square). Documentary. 100 min. 35mm. 1994.

———. *Erzi* 儿子 (Sons). 95 min. 35mm. Beijing: Biaoqing wenhua 表情文化, 1996.

———. *Donggong xigong* 东宫西宫 (East Palace, West Palace). 94 min. 35mm. France: Quelqu'un d'autre Productions, 1996.

———. *Guonian huijia* 过年回家 (Seventeen Years). 90 min. 35mm. Xi'an: Xi'an Studio/Beijing: Duozhong xixun 多种喜讯, 1998.

———. *Dingzi hu* 钉子户 (Resisting Eminent Domain). Documentary. 81 min. Beta-Cam. 1998.

———. *Fengkuang yingyu* 疯狂英语 (Crazy English). Documentary. 90 min. 35mm. Xi'an: Xi'an Studio/Beijing: Shiji xixun 世纪喜讯, 1999.

———. *Jin Xing xiaojie* 金星小姐 (Miss Jin Xing). Documentary. 31 min. 35mm. Beijing: Shiji xixun, 2000.

———. *Wo ai ni* 我爱你 (I Love You). 97 min. 35mm. Beijing: Beida Huayi 北大华亿/Duozhong xixun, 2002.

———. *Jiang jie* (Sister Jiang, a Revolutionary Martyr). Filmed stage play. Beijing: Duozhong xixun, 2002.

———. *Lücha* 绿茶 (Green Tea). 83 min. 35mm. Beijing: Beida Huayi, 2003.

Zheng Dasheng 郑大圣. *DV Zhongguo* DV中国, aka *Yige nongmin de daoyan shengya* 一个农民的导演生涯 (DV China). Documentary. 90 min. 2003.

Zhu Chuanming 朱传明 (b. 1971). *Beijing tanjing* 北京弹匠 (Beijing Cotton-Fluffing Artisan). Documentary. 60 min. Hi8. 1999.

———. *Qunzhong yanyuan* 群众演员 (Extras). Documentary. 70 min. DV. 2001.

Zhu Wen 朱文 (b. 1967). *Haixian* 海鲜 (Seafood). 83 min. DV/35mm. 2001

Bibliography

Note: This bibliography includes books and articles referenced in the chapters and the appendix. Chinese characters for these frequently cited periodicals and newspapers in print are given only once below.

Beijing dianying xueyuan xuebao 北京电影学院学报 (Journal of the Beijing Film Academy), bimonthly, Beijing

Dangdai dianying 当代电影 (Contemporary Film), bimonthly, Beijing

Dianying yishu 电影艺术 (Film Art), bimonthly, Beijing

Dushu 读书 (Reading), monthly, Beijing

Ershiyi shiji 二十一世纪 (Twenty-first Century), bimonthly, Hong Kong

Nanfang dushi bao 南方都市报 (South Metropolis Daily), Guangzhou

Nanfang zhoumo 南方周末 (Southern Weekend), Guangzhou

Barmé, Geremie R. *In the Red: On Contemporary Chinese Culture*. New York: Columbia University Press, 1999.

Bauman, Zygmunt. *Globalization: The Human Consequences*. New York: Columbia University Press, 1998.

Bazin, André. *Qu'est-ce le cinéma?* Paris: Les Éditions du cerf, 2002.

Berry, Chris. "Miandui xianshi: Zhongguo de jilupian, Zhongguo de hou shehui zhuyi" 面对现实: 中国的纪录片, 中国的后社会主义 (Facing Reality: Chinese Documentaries, Chinese Postsocialism). Trans. Liu Zijia 刘子佳 and Wen Jin'gen 温晋根. *Southern Entertainment* 南方网娱乐 (2003). www.southcn.com/ent/zhuanti/gzart1/doc/200301140008.htm (accessed July 23, 2005).

———. *Postsocialist Cinema in Post-Mao China: The Cultural Revolution after the Cultural Revolution*. London: Routledge, 2004.

——— "The Sacred, the Profane, and the Domestic in Cui Zi'en's Cinema." *Positions* 12, no. 1 (2004): 195–201.

———. "Getting Real: Chinese Documentaries, Chinese Postsocialism." In Zhen Zhang, *The Urban Generation*.

"Bieren yanzhong de Zhou Yuanqiang" 别人眼中的周元强 (Zhou Yuanqiang in Other People's Views). *Our DV*, March 8, 2004. www.tosin163.com/xinwen/html/dv_r%5C2004-3-8/200438213634.shtml.

Bourdieu, Pierre. *The Field of Cultural Production: Essays on Art and Literature*. Edited and introduced by Randal Johnson. New York: Columbia University Press, 1993.

——. "Bungakuba no seisei to kozo" 文学場の生成と構造 (Genesis and Structure of the Literary Field). *Bungaku* 文学 5, no. 1 (1994): 54–65.

——. *The Rules of Art: Genesis and Structure of the Literary Field.* Stanford, Calif.: Stanford University Press, 1996.

Bourdieu, Pierre, and Loic J. D. Wacquant. *An Invitation to Reflexive Sociology.* Chicago, Ill.: University of Chicago Press, 1992.

Chen, Xiaomei. *Occidentalism: A Theory of Counter-Discourse in Post-Mao China.* New York: Oxford University Press, 1995.

Chen Xihe 陈犀禾 and Shi Chuan 石川, eds. *Duoyuan yujing zhong de xinshengdai dianying: Zhongguo xinshengdai dianying lunwen ji* 多元语境中的新生代电影: 中国新生代电影研究论文集 (Newborn Generation Films in Multiple Contexts: Essays on Chinese Newborn Generation Film). Shanghai: Xuelin chubanshe, 2003.

Chen Xuguang 陈旭光. *Zhongguo dangdai yingshi wenhua yanjiu* 中国当代影视文化研究 (A Study of Film and Television Culture in Contemporary China). Beijing: Beijing daxue chubanshe, 2004.

Cheng, Jim. *An Annotated Bibliography for Chinese Film Studies.* Hong Kong: Hong Kong University Press, 2004.

Cheng Qingsong 程青松. *Kandejian de yingxiang* 看得见的影像 (Films Permitted for Watching). Shanghai: Sanlian shudian, 2004.

Cheng Qingsong 程青松 and Huang Ou 黄鸥. *Wode sheyingji bu sahuang: xianfeng dianying ren dang'an—shengyu 1961–1970* 我的摄影机不撒谎: 先锋电影人档案—生于1961–1970 (My Camera Doesn't Lie: Documents on Avant-garde Filmmakers Born between 1961 and 1970). Beijing: Zhongguo youyi chuban gongsi, 2002.

China Daily. "'Underground' Movie Directors Emerge." *China Daily,* April 26, 2004.

Chow, Rey. *Primitive Passions: Visuality, Sexuality, Ethnography, and Contemporary Chinese Cinema.* New York: Columbia University Press, 1995.

Chun Shu 春树. *Beijing wawa: shiqisui shaonü de canku qingchun zibai* 北京娃娃: 十七岁少女的残酷青春自白 (Beijing Doll: Confession of Cruel Youth by a Seventeen-Year-Old Girl). Hohhot: Yuanfang chubanshe, 2002.

Chun, Sue. *Beijing Doll: A Novel.* Translated by Howard Goldblatt. New York: Riverhead Books, 2004.

Chute, David. "Beyond the Law." *Film Comment* 30, no. 1 (1994): 60–62.

Ci, Jiwei. *Dialectic of the Chinese Revolution: From Utopianism to Hedonism.* Stanford, Calif.: Stanford University Press, 1994.

Clark, Paul. *Chinese Cinema: Culture and Politics since 1949.* Cambridge, England: Cambridge University Press, 1987.

Cornelius, Sheila, with Ian Haydn Smith. *New Chinese Cinema: Challenging Representations.* London: Wallflower, 2002.

Crane, Diana. "Reward Systems in Art, Science, and Religion." In *The Production of Culture,* edited by Richard A. Peterson, 57–72. Beverly Hills, Calif.: Sage, 1976.

Cui, Shuqin. "Working from the Margins: Urban Cinema and Independent Directors in Contemporary China." *Post Script* 20, nos. 2–3 (2001): 77–93.

Cui Weiping 崔卫平. "Zhongguo dalu duli zhizuo jilupian de shengzhang kongjian" 中国大陆独立制作纪录片的生长空间 (Space for the Growth of the Independent Documentary in Mainland China). *Ershiyi shiji* 77 (June 2003): 84–94.

Cui Zi'en 崔子恩. "Dianying minjian sheng" 电影民间声 (Unofficial Voices from Film). *Yinyue yu biaoyan* 音乐与表演, 2001, no. 3:32–38.

——. "Yese liaoren: Zhongguo duli dianying de xiao quanjing he da texie" 夜色撩人: 中国独立电影的小全景和大特写 (Tantalizing Night: Independent Film in China in a Small Panorama and a Big Close-Up). *Furong* 芙蓉, 2002, no. 2:70–80.

———. *Diyi guanzhong* 第一观众 (The First Audience). Beijing: Xiandai chubanshe, 2003.

Dai Jinhua 戴锦华. *Wuzhong fengjing*雾中风景 (A Scene in the Fog). Beijing: Beijing daxue chubanshe, 2000.

———. "A Scene in the Fog: Reading Sixth Generation Films." In *Cinema and Desire: Feminist Marxism and Cultural Politics in the Work of Dai Jinhua*, edited by Jing Wang and Tani Barlow, 71–98. London: Verso, 2002.

Dussel, Enrique. "Beyond Eurocentrism: The World-System and the Limits of Modernity." In *The Cultures of Globalization*, edited by Fredric Jameson and Masao Myoshi, 3–31. Durham, N.C.: Duke University Press, 1998.

"DV, li dianying you duoyuan" DV, 离电影有多远? (DV, How Far Away from Film?) . *Xinmin Zhoukan* 新民周刊, Nov. 20, 2001. www.kpworld.com/xb/news/pn48013.html.

Fang Fang 方方. *Zhongguo jilupian fazhan shi* 中国纪录片发展史 (History of the Development of Chinese Documentary Cinema). Beijing: Zhongguo xiju chubanshe, 2003.

Fenghuang weishi (Phoenix Satellite TV), ed. *DV xin shidai 1* (DV New Generation 1). Beijing: Zhongguo qingnian chubanshe, 2003.

Foucault, Michel. *The History of Sexuality, Vol. 1: An Introduction.* Translated by Robert Hurley. London: Allen Lane, 1979.

Gladney, Dru C. "Tian Zhuangzhuang, the Fifth Generation, and Minorities Film in China." *Public Culture* 8, no. 1 (1995): 161–75.

Green, Andrew. "More Quality, Less Quantity." *China Economic Review* 8, no. 6 (June 1998): 35.

Han Xiaolei 韩小磊. "Guanyu xinyidai qingnian daoyan qun" 关于新一代青年导演群 (About the Newborn Generation of Film Directors). *Beijing dianying xueyuan xuebao*, 1995, no. 1:103–11.

———. "Dui diwudai de wenhua tuwei: houwudai de geren dianying xianxiang" 对第五代的文化突围：后五代的个人电影现象 (A Cultural Breakaway from the Fifth Generation: The Phenomenon of Personal Film in the Post–Fifth Generation). *Dianying yishu*, 1995, no. 2:58–63.

Hardt, Michael, and Anthony Negri. *Empire.* Durham, N.C.: Duke University Press, 2000.

Hei Ding 黑丁 and Feng Hong 封洪. "Zai duoyuan fazhan de geju zhong zouxiang xin shiji: 90 niandai Zhongguo dianying fazhan taishi yantaohui zongshu" 在多元发展的格局中走向新世纪：90年代中国电影发展态势研讨会综述 (Moving toward the New Century amidst a Polycentric Pattern of Development: A Summary of the Roundtable on the State of Chinese Film Development in the 1990s). *Dangdai dianying*, 1994, no. 3:26–28.

Hillier, Jim, ed. *American Independent Cinema: A Sight and Sound Reader.* London: British Film Institute, 2001.

Huang Shixian 黄式宪. "Qingchun dubai: qianweixing yu dazhongxing—Zhongguo dianying xinshengdai jiqi xinzuo *Chaoji chengshi* sumiao" 青春独白：前卫性与大众性—中国电影新生代及其新作《超级城市》素描 (Monologues of the Youth: Avant-gardism and Mass Appeal—A Sketch of the Newborn Generation Film *Super City*). *Dianying shuangzhoukan* 电影双周刊, 1998, no. 7:70–72.

———. "Diliudai bei mingming" 第六代被命名 (Naming the Sixth Generation), *Dianying pingjie* 电影评介, 2000, no. 3:15–19.

———. "Diliudai: laizi bianyuan de chaoxun" 第六代：来自边缘的潮汛 (The Sixth Generation: The Tidal Wave from the Margin). In Chen Xihe and Shi Chuan, *Duoyuan yujing zhong de xinshengdai dianying*, 23–39.

Jaffee, Valerie. "Bringing the World to the Nation: Jia Zhangke and the Legitimation of Chinese Underground Film." *Senses of Cinema* no. 32 (July–Sept. 2004). www.sensesofcinema.com/contents/04/32/chinese_underground_film.html#4 (accessed Feb. 21, 2005).

Jaivin, Linda. "Defying a Ban, Chinese Cameras Roll." *The Wall Street Journal*, Jan. 18, 1995, A12.

Jia Zhangke贾樟柯. "Yeyu dianying shidai jijiang zaici daolai" 业余电影时代即将再次到来 (The Age of Amateur Cinema Will Return). First published in *Nanfang zhoumo* in 1999. In Zhang Xianmin and Zhang Yaxuan, *Yige ren de yingxiang*, 306–8.

———. "Youle VCD he shuma shexiangji yihou" 有了VCD和数码摄像机以后 (Now That We Have VCDs and Digital Cameras). In Zhang Xianmin and Zhang Yaxuan, *Yige ren de yingxiang*, 309–11.

Jin Danyuan金丹元and Ding Ning丁宁. "Zai houyujing zhong qidai tupo: lun Zhongguo xinyidai daoyan de duochong xuanze" 在后语境中期待突破: 论中国新一代导演的多重选择 (Anticipating a Breakthrough in the Post-context: Multiple Choices of the New-Generation Directors). In Chen Xihe and Shi Chuan, *Duoyuan yujing zhong de xinshengdai dianying*, 49–63.

Kleinhans, Chuck. "Independent Features: Hopes and Dreams." In *The New American Cinema*, edited by Jon Lewis, 307–27. Durham, N.C.: Duke University Press, 1998.

Kraus, Richard. *The Party and the Arty: How Money Relaxes Political Control over China's Arts*. Lanham, Md.: Rowman & Littlefield, 2003.

Larsen, Ernest. "Video *vérité* from Beijing." *Art in America* (Sept. 1998). www.findarticles .com/cf_dls/m1248/n9_v86/21268565/p2/article.jhtml?term= (accessed July 17, 2005).

Leary, Charles. "Performing the Documentary, or Making it to the Other Bank." *Senses of Cinema* 27 (July–Aug. 2003). www.sensesofcinema.com/contents/03/27/performing_documentary.html (accessed July 23, 2005).

Lee, Leo Ou-fan. *Shanghai Modern: The Flowering of a New Urban Culture in China, 1930–1945*. Cambridge, Mass.: Harvard University Press, 1999.

Lent, John A., Wang Renying, and Yuheng Bao. "Contemporary Chinese Cinema: A Chronicle of Events, 1978-2000." *Asian Cinema* 11, no. 2 (2000): 172–74.

Leyda, Jay. *Dianying: An Account of Films and the Film Audience in China*. Cambridge, Mass.: MIT Press, 1972.

Li Bin 李彬. "Yingxiang yu zhenxiang: jilupian *DV China* daoyan Zheng Dasheng fangtan" 影像与真相: 纪录片DV China 导演郑大圣访谈 (Image and Reality: An Interview with Zheng Dasheng, Director of the Documentary *DV China*). *Beijing dianying xueyuan xuebao* 北京电影学院学报, 2002, no. 6:67–76.

Li Xiaoping. "Significant Changes in the Chinese Television Industry and Their Impact in the PRC: An Insider's Perspective." Working Paper of the Center for Northeast Asian Policy Studies, the Brookings Institution, Washington, D.C., August 2001. *Columbia International Affairs Online*. www.ciaonet.org/wps/lix01 (accessed Sept. 10, 2002).

Lin, Xiaoping. "New Chinese Cinema of the 'Sixth Generation': A Distant Cry of Forsaken Children." *Third Text* 16, no. 3 (2000): 261–84.

Lin Xudong 林旭东, Zhang Yaxuan 张亚璇, and Gu Zheng 顾峥, eds. *Jia Zhangke dianying: guxiang sanbuqu zhi "Xiao Wu"* 贾樟柯电影: 故乡三部曲之 《小武》 (Jia Zhangke's Films: Hometown Trilogy, *Xiao Wu*). Beijing: Mangwen chubanshe, 2003.

———, eds. *Jia Zhangke dianying: guxiang sanbuqu zhi "Zhantai"* 贾樟柯电影: 故乡三部曲之 《站台》 (Jia Zhangke's Films: Hometown Trilogy, *Platform*). Beijing: Mangwen chubanshe, 2003.

———, eds. *Jia Zhangke dianying: guxiang sanbuqu zhi "Xiao Wu"* 贾樟柯电影: 故乡三部曲之 《任逍遥》 (Jia Zhangke's Films: Hometown Trilogy, *Unknown Pleasures*). Beijing: Mangwen chubanshe, 2003.

Link, Perry, Richard P. Madsen, and Paul G. Pickowicz, eds. *Unofficial China: Popular Culture and Thought in the People's Republic*. Boulder, Colo.: Westview Press, 1989.

———, eds. *Popular China: Unofficial Culture in a Globalizing Society*. Lanham, Md.: Rowman & Littlefield, 2002.

Liu Guangyu刘广宇. "Ziyou de shuxie yu chenzhong de yingxiang: Zhongguo dianying diliudai de jingshen sumiao" 自由地书写与沉重的影像: 中国电影第六代的精神素描 (Free Writing and Loaded Images: A Sketch of the Chinese Sixth Generation Filmmakers). In Chen Xihe and Shi Chuan, *Duoyuan yujing zhong de xinshengdai dianying*, 255–67.

Liu, Joey. "Welcome to the Reel World." *South China Morning Post*, Nov. 2, 2004, C5.

Lu, Tonglin. "Music and Noise: Independent Film and Globalization." *China Review* 3, no. 1 (2003): 57–76.

Lü Xinyu 吕新雨. *Jilu Zhongguo: dangdai Zhongguo xin jilu yundong* 纪录中国: 当代中国新纪录运动 (Documenting China: The New Documentary Movement in Contemporary China). Beijing: Sanlian shudian, 2003.

———. "Ruins of the Future: Class and History in Wang Bing's *Tiexi District*." *New Left Review* 31 (2005): 125–36.

Ma Ning马宁. "Zhongguo dianying keneng cunzai de kunhuo" 中国电影可能存在的困惑 (Some Possible Confusion for Chinese Film). *Dianying yishu*, 2002, no. 1:62–67.

Mast, Gerald, Marshall Cohen, and Leo Braudy, eds. *Film Theory and Criticism: Introductory Readings*. Fourth edition. New York: Oxford University Press, 1992.

Mei Bing 梅冰 and Zhu Jingjiang 朱靖江. *Zhongguo duli jilu dang'an* 中国独立纪录片档案 (Records of China's Independent Documentary Cinema). Xi'an: Shaanxi shifan daxue chubanshe, 2004.

Mian Mian 棉棉. *Tang*糖. Taipei: Shengzhi chubanshe, 2000.

———. *Candy*. Translated by Andrea Lingenfelter. Boston: Back Bay Books, 2003.

Miyoshi, Masao. "'Globalization,' Culture, and the University." In *The Cultures of Globalization*, edited by Fredric Jameson and Masao Miyoshi, 247–70. Durham, N.C.: Duke University Press, 1998.

Nanfang dushi bao. "Daoyan Jia Zhangke fangtan: dui zhuliu de tuoxie" 导演贾樟柯访谈: 对主流的妥协 (Interview with Director Jia Zhangke: Compromise with the Mainstream). *Nanfang dushi bao*, April 14, 2003.

———. "Duli dianying qi junzi lianming shangshu dianying ju: zuotanhui neimu shoudu gongkai" 独立电影七君子联名上书电影局: 座谈会内幕首度公开 (Seven Lords of Independent Film Signed a Petition to the Film Bureau: The Forum's Inside Information Made Public for the First Time." *Nanfang dushi bao*, Dec. 4, 2003.

Nanfang zhoumo. "Dangdai yishu yu dazhong xiaofei de yanhuan" 当代艺术与大众消费的言欢 (Pleasurable Dialogue between Contemporary Art and Mass Consumption). *Nanfang zhoumo*, March 27, 2003.

———. "Gongchang he yishu" 工厂和艺术 (Factory and Art). *Nanfang zhoumo*, March 27, 2003.

Nichols, Bill. *Ideology and the Image*. Bloomington: Indiana University Press, 1981.

———. "Discovering Form, Inferring Meaning: New Cinemas and the Film Festival Circuit." *Film Quarterly* 47, no. 3 (1994): 16–30.

Oushakine, Serguei A. "The Terrifying Mimicry of the Samizdat." *Public Culture* 13, no. 2 (2001): 191–214.

Palmer, Augusta. "Taming the Dragon: Part II, Two Approaches to China's Film Market." *indieWIRE*, Dec. 8, 2000. www.indiewire.com/biz/biz_001208_ChinesePartII.html (accessed July 23, 2005).

Pan Ruojian 潘若简 and Zhuang Yuxin 庄宇新. "Guanyu xinshengdai taolun jiyao" 关于新生代讨论纪要 (A Review of the Discussion about the Newborn Generation of Filmmakers). *Beijing dianying xueyuan xuebao*, 1995, no. 1:168–69.

Pickowicz, Paul G. "Huang Jianxin and the Notion of Postsocialism." In *New Chinese Cinema: Forms, Identities, Politics*, edited by Nick Browne, Paul G. Pickowicz, Vivian Sobchack, and Esther Yau, 57–87. Cambridge, England: Cambridge University Press, 1994.

——. "Velvet Prisons and the Political Economy of Chinese Filmmaking." In *Urban Spaces: Autonomy and Community in Contemporary China*, edited by Deborah Davis, Richard Kraus, Barry Naughton, and Elizabeth Perry, 193–220. Cambridge, England: Cambridge University Press, 1995.

——. "Filme und die Legitimation des Staates im Heutigen China." In *Peking, Shanghai, Shenzhen: Stadte des 21. Jahrhunderts*, edited by Kai Vockler and Dirk Luckow, 402–11 (German), 566–570 (English). Frankfurt: Campus Verlag GmbH, 2000.

Prudentino, Luisa. *Le Regard des ombres*. Paris: Bleu de Chine, 2003.

Qiao, Michelle. "The Metaphysics of Film." *China Daily*, Jan. 14, 2004. www1.chinadaily.com .cn/en/doc/2004-01/14/content_298716.htm (accessed Feb. 25, 2004).

Qu Chunjing曲春景. "Dianying de wenxian jiazhi yu yishu pinwei: tan xinshengdai dianying de chengbai" 电影的文献价值与艺术品位: 谈新生代电影的成败 (Film's Documentary and Artistic Values: Newborn Generation Films' Success and Failure). In Chen Xihe and Shi Chuan, *Duoyuan yujing zhong de xinshengdai dianying*, 189–200.

Reynaud, Bérénice. "New Visions/New Chinas: Video-Art, Documentation, and the Chinese Modernity in Question." In *Resolutions: Contemporary Video Practices*, edited by Michael Renov and Erika Suderburg, 229–57. Minneapolis: University of Minnesota Press, 1996.

——. *Nouvelles Chines: Nouveaux cinema*. Paris: Editions cahiers du cinema, 1999.

——. "Dancing with Myself, Drifting with My Camera: The Emotional Vagabonds of China's New Documentary." *Senses of Cinema* 28 (Sept.–Oct. 2003). www.senseofcinema.com/ contents/03/28/chinas_new_documentary.html (accessed July 23, 2005).

Seid, Steve. "Unofficial China: The New Documentary Movement." Presented in collaboration with *Unofficial China: The New Documentary Movement* at The Pacific Film Archive, March 8–19, 1998. www.naatanet.org/Exhibition/html/sfiaaff98/programs/unofficial.html.

Shen Liang沈亮. "Keai de chuantong: lun diliudai dianying zhong de baoshou qingxiang" 可爱的传统: 论第六代电影中的保守倾向 (A Lovely Tradition: The Conservative Tendency in Sixth Generation Films). In Chen Xihe and Shi Chuan, *Duoyuan yujing zhong de xinshengdai dianying*, 243–54.

Shi Chuan 石川. "Daiqun mingming yu daiqun yuma" 代群命名与代群语码 (The Labels and Linguistic Codes Associated with Generations). In Chen Xihe and Shi Chuan, *Duoyuan yujing zhong de xinshengdai dianying*, 234–42.

"Stainless Steel Mouse that Roared," *Wired News*, Dec. 1, 2003, www.wired.com/news/ politics/0,1283,61420,00.html?tw=wn_story_related (accessed Feb. 20, 2005).

Teo, Stephen. "'There Is No Sixth Generation!': Director Li Yang on *Blind Shaft* and His Place in Chinese Cinema." *Senses of Cinema* 27 (July–Aug. 2003). www.sensesofcinema.com/ contents/03/27/li_yang.html (accessed July 23, 2005).

Tudor, Andrew. "Sociology and Film." In *The Oxford Guide to Film Studies*, edited by John Hill and Pamela Church Gibson, 190–94. New York: Oxford University Press, 1998.

Turner, Graeme, ed. *The Film Cultures Reader*. London: Routledge, 2002.

Voci, Paola. "From the Center to the Periphery: Chinese Documentary's Visual Conjectures." *Modern Chinese Literature and Culture* 16, no. 1 (2004): 65–113.

Wang, Ban. "Documentary as Haunting of the Real: The Logic of Capital in *Blind Shaft*." *Asian Cinema* 16, no. 1 (2005): 4–15.

Wang, Qi. "The Ruin Is Already a New Outcome: An Interview with Cui Zi'en." *Positions* 12, no. 1 (2004): 181–94.

Wang Weici 王慰慈. *Jilu yu tansuo: 1990–2000 dalu jilupian de fazhan yu koushu jilu* 记录与探索: 1990–2000 大陆纪录片的发展与口述记录 (Documentation and Exploration: The Growth of Documentary in Mainland China and Its Related Oral Histories, 1990–2000). Taipei: Guojian dianying ziliao guan, 2001.

Wang Xiaoyu 王晓玉. *Zhongguo dianying shigang* 中国电影史纲 (An Outline History of Chinese Cinema). Shanghai: Shanghai guji chubanshe, 2003.

Wang, Yiman. "The Amateur's Lightning Rod: DV Documentary in Postsocialist China." *Film Quarterly* 58, no. 4 (2005): 16–26.

Wei Hui 卫慧. *Shanghai baobei* 上海宝贝. Taipei: Shengzhi chubanshe, 2000.

———. *Shanghai Baby*. Translated by Bruce Humes. London: Robinson, 2001.

Winston, Brian. *Claiming the Real: The Griersonian Documentary and Its Legitimations*. London: British Film Institute, 1995.

Wood, Ellen Meiksins. *Empire of Capital*. London: Verso, 2003.

Wu Wenguang 吴文光, ed. *Xianchang (di yi juan)* 现场 (第一卷) (Document: The Present Scene, Vol. 1). Tianjin: Tianjin shehui kexue chubanshe, 2000.

———, ed. *Xianchang (di er juan)* 现场 (第二卷) (Document: The Present Scene, Vol. 2). Tianjin: Tianjin shehui kexue chubanshe, 2001.

———, ed. *Jiang hu baogao: yige dapeng wei ge'an er zhankai de tianye diaocha* 江湖报告: 一个大棚为个案而展开的田野调查 (Jiang Hu Report: A Field Investigation Unfolding from the Case of the "Big Tent"). Beijing: Zhongguo qingnian chubanshe, 2001.

———. *Jingtou xiang ziji de yanjing yiyang* 镜头像自己的眼睛一样 (The Lens Is the Same as My Eye). Shanghai: Shanghai yishu chubanshe, 2001.

"Wu Wenguang zuopin yilan" 吴文光作品一览 (Exhibitions of Wu Wenguang's Works). *Xin qingnian* 新青年, May 16, 2001. http://movie.newyouth.beida-online.com/data/data.php3?db=movie&id=wwgzpyl.

Wu Xiaoli 吴小丽 and Xu Shengmin 徐生民. *Jiushi niandai Zhongguo dianying lun* 九十年代中国电影论 (Chinese Films in the 1990s). Beijing: Wenhua yishu chubanshe, 2005.

Xia Dongmei 夏冬梅 and Du Yongli 杜永利. "'Xu . . . xu . . .' Yong xusheng wei xiaoyuan DV guzhang" 嘘 . . . 嘘 . . . 用嘘声为校园DV鼓掌 (Cheering for College DV with Boos and Hisses). *PC Online* 太平洋电脑网, May 6, 2003. http://arch.pconline.com.cn/digital/textlib/dv/dv04/10305/158895.html (accessed July 23, 2005).

Xu Guangchun 徐光春, ed. *Zhonghua renmin gongheguo guangbo dianshi jianshi, 1949–2000* 中华人民共和国广播电视简史, 1949–2000 (A Concise History of Radio and Television in the People's Republic of China, 1949–2000). Beijing: Zhongguo guangbo dianshi chubanshe, 2003.

Xu, Jian. "Representing Rural Migrants in the City: Experimentalism in Wang Xiaoshuai's *So Close to Paradise* and *Beijing Bicycle*." *Screen* 46, no. 4 (2005): 433–49.

Yan Jun 颜峻. "Kan dianying, ting yinyue, guang gongyuan" 看电影, 听音乐, 逛公园 (Watching Films, Listening to Music, and Visiting Parks). *Xin qingnian* 新青年, April 15, 2002. http://xueshu.newyouth.beida-online.com/data/data.php3?db=xueshu&id=kandianying (accessed Feb. 20, 2004).

Yang, Mayfair Mei-Hui. "Film Discussion Groups in China: State Discourse or a Plebeian Public Sphere?" *Visual Anthropology Review* 10, no. 1 (1994). 112–25.

Yang Ping. "A Director Who Is Trying to Change the Audience: A Chat with Young Director Tian Zhuangzhuang." In *Perspectives on Chinese Cinema*, edited by Chris Berry, 127–30. London: British Film Institute, 1991.

Yin Hong 尹鸿. "Diwudai yu xinshengdai dianying shidai de jiaocha yu guodu" 第五代与新生代电影时代的交叉与过渡 (The Cross-Over between and Transition from the Fifth Generation to the Newborn Generation Film). *Dianying yishu*, 1998, no. 1:23–27.

———. "Zai jiafeng zhong zhangda: Zhongguo dalu xinsheng dai de dianying shijie" 在夹缝中长大: 中国新生代的电影世界 (Growing Up between the Fissures: The Film World of the Newborn Generation). *Ershiyi shiji* 49 (Oct. 1998): 88–93.

———. *Yin Hong yingshi shiping* 尹鸿影视时评 (Film and Television Criticism in the Work of Yin Hong). Henan: Henan daxue chubanshe, 2002.

Ying Xiong 应雄. "Tianjiang daren: diliudai de jiyu yu wenti" 天降大任: 第六代的机遇与问题 (An Immense Responsibility: Opportunities and Problems Faced by the Sixth Generation). *Beijing dianying xueyuan xuebao*, 1995, no. 1:126–27.

Yu Aiyuan 余爱鱼. "Guanyu Zhongguo 'dixia dianying' de wenhua jiexi" 关于中国"地下电影"的文化解析 (Cultural Analysis of "Underground Film" in China). *Shiji Zhongguo* 世纪中国, Aug. 9, 2000. www.cc.org.cn/zhoukan/shidaizhuanti/0208/0208091002.htm (accessed Feb. 20, 2004).

Zhang Fu 张蚨. "Yige fengge zhuyi de shidai: 90 niandai Zhongguo dianying de tuwei biaoyan" 一个风格主义的时代: 90年代中国电影的突围表演 (An Era of Stylism: Breakthrough Performances of Chinese Films in the 1990s). *Beijing dianying xueyuan xuebao*, 1995, no. 1:118–20.

Zhang Ming章明. *Zhaodao yizhong dianying fangfa* 找到一种电影方法 (Discovering a Film Method). Beijing: Zhonggguo guangbo dianshi chubanshe, 2003.

Zhang Xianmin 张献民. "Meiyou gongkai de guangying: dalu 1990 nian hou de jinpian shi" 没有公开的光影: 大陆1990年后的禁片史 (The Unexposed Films: A History of Banned Films in Mainland China after 1990). *Fenghuang zhoukan* 34 (2002).

———. "A History of 'Forbidden Films' after 1990." In *Cinema on the Borderline: Chinese Independent Films*, 30–53. Pusan, South Korea: Eighth Pusan International Film Festival, 2003.

———. *Kanbujian de yingxiang* 看不见的影像 (Films Banned from Watching). Shanghai: Sanlian shudian, 2004.

Zhang Xianmin 张献民 and Zhang Yaxuan 张亚璇. *Yige ren de yingxiang: DV wanquan shouce* 一个人的影像 (All About DV: Works, Making, Creation, Comments). Beijing: Zhongguo qingnian chubanshe, 2003.

Zhang, Yingjin. *Screening China: Critical Interventions, Cinematic Reconfigurations, and the Transnational Imaginary in Contemporary Chinese Cinema.* Ann Arbor: Center for Chinese Studies, University of Michigan, 2002.

———. *Chinese National Cinema.* London: Routledge, 2004.

———. "Styles, Subjects, and Special Points of View: A Study of Contemporary Chinese Independent Documentary." *New Cinemas* 2, no. 2 (2004): 119–35.

———. "Rebel Without a Cause? China's New Urban Generation and Postsocialist Filmmaking." In Zhen Zhang, *The Urban Generation.*

Zhang, Zhen, ed., *The Urban Generation: Chinese Cinema and Society at the Turn of the Twenty-first Century.* Durham, N.C.: Duke University Press, 2006.

Zhao Shi 赵实. "He qingnian pengyou tanxin" 和青年朋友谈心 (A Heart-to-Heart Talk with Young Friends). *Dianying yishu*, 2000, no. 1:4–7.

Zheng Dongtian 郑洞天. "Diliudai dianying de wenhua yiyi" 第六代电影的文化意义 (The Cultural Significance of the Sixth Generation Film). *Dianying yishu*, 2003, no. 1:42–43.

Zheng Wei 郑伟. "'He' zhong de rizi" "盒"中的日子 (Days Spent in the "Box"). *Dushu*, 2003, no. 6:105–9.

———. "Jilu yu biaoshu: Zhongguo dalu 1990 niandai yilai de duli jilupian" 记录与表述: 中国大陆1990年代以来的独立纪录片 (Documentation and Expression: Mainland Chinese Independent Documentary since 1990). *Dushu*, 2003, no. 10:76–86.

Zheng Xianghong 郑向虹. "Duli yingren zai xingdong: suowei Beijing dixia dianying zhenxiang" 独立影人在行动: 所谓北京"地下电影"真相 (Independent Filmmakers in Action: The Truth about Underground Film in Beijing). *Dianying gushi*, 1993, no. 5:4–7.

———. "Zhang Yuan fangtan lu" 张元访谈录 (An Interview with Zhang Yuan). *Dianying gushi*, 1993, no. 5:8–9.

Zhong Dafeng 钟大丰. "Tizhi nei de caihua" 体制内的才华 (The Talents within the System). *Dianying yishu*, 2000, no. 1:17–18.

Zhou Xing 周星. *Zhongguo dianying yishu shi* 中国电影艺术史 (A History of Chinese Film Art). Beijing: Beijing daxue chubanshe, 2005.

Zhu Chuanming 朱传明. "Zhu Chuanming zishu: naxie wo yuanyi zhushi de ren: guanyu wo de liangbu jilupian" 朱传明自述: 那些我愿意注视的人: 关于我的两部纪录片 (Zhu Chuanming in His Own Words: The People I am Willing to Pay Attention to: My Two Documentaries). *PC Online* 太平洋电脑网, April 28, 2003. http://arch.pconline.com.cn/digital/textlib/other/buy/10304/156657.html (accessed July 23, 2005).

Zhu Jingjiang 朱靖江. *DV baodian: cong 'Haolaiwu' dao duli zhipian ren* DV 宝典: 从"好莱坞"到独立制片人 (The DV Bible: From "Hollywood" to Independent Filmmakers). Beijing: Beijing bianyi chubanshe, 2003.

Zhu, Yan. *798: A Photographic Journal by Zhu Yan*. Beijing: Timezone 8, 2004.

Zhu, Ying. *Chinese Cinema during the Era of Reform: The Ingenuity of the System*. Westport, Conn.: Praeger, 2003.

Žižek, Slavoj. *The Sublime Object of Ideology*. London: Verso, 1989.

Internet Resources

Note: The following include Internet resources that feature substantial information regarding Chinese underground and independent film, contain useful research material on Chinese cinema, or provide entry points to online film forums in China.

Allmov.com 互联影库 (Internet film database), Shanghai, China:
www.allmov.com

Asian Cinema Connections, University of Southern California, United States:
www.asianfilms.org/china

Chinese Cinema: An Annotated Directory of Internet Resources, University of Redlands, California, United States:
http://newton.uor.edu/Departments&Programs/AsianStudiesDept/china-film.html

Chinese Cinema Links, by Yomi Braester, University of Washington, Seattle, United States:
http://faculty.washington.edu/yomi/fun.html

A Chinese Cinema Page, by Shelly Kraicer, Toronto, Canada:
www.chinesecinemas.org

Chinese Movie Database 中文电影资料库, China:
www.dianying.com

Chinese Underground Film Collection, University of California, San Diego, United States:
http://gort.ucsd.edu/EAFC/ChinUnderIndeFilm.html

Chinese Underground Film Festival, University of California, San Diego, United States:
http://cuff.ucsd.edu

Documentary Box, Yamagata International Documentary Film Festival, Japan:
www.city.yamagata.yamagata.jp/yidff/docbox/docbox.html

DV China, DV 中国技术推广中心, Beijing, China:
http://new.dvchina.cn

Fanhall Studio 现象工作室, Beijing, China:
www.fanhall.com

Internet Movie Database (IMDb), United States:
www.imdb.com

Jilu Zhongguo 记录 · 中国 (document-China), Communication University of China 中国传媒大学, Beijing, China:www.chinadocu.com

Modern Chinese Literature and Culture Resource Center, Ohio State University, United States:
  http://mclc.osu.edu/rc/filmbib.htm
Movie Peaks Movie Forum 电影艺术论坛 (Film art forum), Shanghai, China:
  http://moviepeaks.joyren.com/bbs
Movie Youth 影养青年, Beijing, China:
  www.movieyouth.com
Naoteng 闹腾电影 (Lively film), China:
  www.naoteng.com
Reel China, R.E.C. Foundation, New York:
  www.reelchina.net
Senses of Cinema, an online journal, University of Melbourne, Australia:
  www.sensesofcinema.com
Xin qingnian 新青年 (New youth), Beijing University, Beijing, China:
  http://newyouth.beida-online.com/index.htm

Index

Note: This index excludes items in appendixes.

A Nian (Xu Hongyu), 210; *Chengshi aiqing* (see *Love in the City*)
Along the Railroad (*Tielu yanxian*), 36, 45n54, 68–69, 107n39, 182
amateurism, x, 24, 33–34, 61, 66, 70, 77–104. *See also* DV (digital video) filmmaking
Antonioni, Michelangelo, 165
Artisan Pickpocket (*Xiao Wu*), 1, 24, 37–39, 62, 79, 125–29
Ashes of Time (*Dongxie xidu*), 154
At Home in the World (*Sihai weijia*), 16, 55, 60–61
audience, x, 1, 34–39, 56, 70, *166–69*, 183
avant-garde, 24, 33, 145, 181
awards, 10, 20n2, 35–37, 45n54, 57, 62, 115, 149–50

Bazin, André, 28, 126–27
Beijing Bastards (*Beijing zazhong*), 2, 29, 48, 77–79, 102, 108n48, 145, 150–53
Beijing Bicycle (*Shiqi sui de dan danche*), 1, 141n17, 176
Beijing Cotton-Fluffing Artisan (*Beijing tanjiang*), 62, 68, 96, 182
Bergman, Ingmar, 169
Blind Shaft (*Mangjing*), viii, 10, 104n6
Blue Kite, The (*Lan fengzheng*), 4–5, 8, 11–12
Bourdieu, Pierre, 161–63, 185
Box, The (*Hezi*), 6, 36
Brighter Summer Day, A (*Gulingjie shaonian sharen shijian*), 169

Bumming in Beijing: The Last Dreamers (*Liulang Beijing: zuihou de mengxiangzhe*), 16, 31, 47–61, 66, 83–88, 102, 107n39, 108n48, 110, 149–51
Bunuel, Luis, 169

CCTV (Chinese Central Television), 51, 58–61, 97–98, 117–18
censorship, xi, 5, 11–13, 23, 31, 38, 41n1, 44n44, 106n26, 113–15, 127–28, 140n4, 150, 172, 213n2; self-censorship, 1, 6. *See also* state (government), the; system (*tizhi*), the
Chen Kaige, 25, 140n15, 184; *Huang tudi* (see *Yellow Earth*)
Chen Miao (Michelle Chen), 16; *Shanghai nanhai* (see *The Snake Boy*)
Chunking Express (*Chongqing senlin*), 154
Conjugation (*Dongci bianwei*), 24
consumption, xi, 161–86
Crazy English (*Fengkuang yingyu*), 69
Cui Zi'en, 8, 34–37, 41, 43n28, 145, 151, 210, 213n3; *Choujue dengchang* (see *Enter the Clowns*); *Jiuyue* (see *Old Testament*)
Cultural Revolution, 25, 54, 106n31, 125

Dance with Migrant Workers (*He mingong yiqi tiaowu*), 66
Dancing with Myself (*He ziji tiaowu*), 118
Daughter of the Party (*Dang de nü'er*), 100

Days, The (*Dong Chun de rizi*), 30, 79, 102, 145, 150, 153, 182
Delamu, 121n5
Devils on the Doorstep (*Guizi laile*), 8, 11–12, 27
Dirt (*Toufa luanle*), 153
distribution, 1, 11–13, 35–39, 49, 91, 161
documentary film, vii, x–xi, 16, 27–36, 124, 182. *See also vérité*
Drowned Youth, The (*Yanmo de qingchun*), 153
Du Haibin, 36, 45n54, 68–70, 107n39, 182; *Tielu yanxian* (see *Along the Railroad*)
DV (digital video) filmmaking, 34, 43n35, 65–70, 97–103. *See also* amateurism
DV China (*DV Zhongguo*), 66, 79, 97–103

East Palace, West Palace (*Donggong xigong*), 7, 30, 174
Einsenstein, Sergei, 170
Enter the Clowns (*Choujue dengchang*), 43n28
exhibition, 11–13, 35–39, 61, 97, 161–87. *See also* film club
experimental film, 49, 104n6
Extras (*Qunzhong yanyuan*), 66, 79, 90–98, 102–3, 105n14

Fassbinder, R. W., 82
Fei Mu, 29
Fellini, Federico, 169
festival. *See* film festival
fifth generation, 5, 25–27, 54, 59, 78–80, 101, 140n6, 150
film club, xi, 12, 44n47, 161–86. *See also* exhibition
film festival, 10–12, 23–24, 31, 35–38, 41n1, 55–57, 62–63, 69–71, 115, 150–51, 180–82
Fish and Elephant (*Jinnian xiatian*), 24, 104n6, 174
Five-Tune Big Drums (*Wuyin dagu*), 184
Forever Young (*Qingchun wansui*), 187n15
For Fun (*Zhaole*), 184
Frozen (*Jidu hanleng*), 30
Fuck the Movies (*Cao tama de dianying*), 66

globalization, 17, 114–15, 123–39
Godard, Jean-Luc, 82, 169

Go for Broke (*Heng shu heng*), 30
government. *See* state, the
Green Tea (*Lücha*), 44n44, 156
Guan Hu, 41n3, 144, 153, 156; *Toufa luanle* (see *Dirt*)

He Jianjun (He Yi), 26, 28–29, 45n54, 106n26, 144, 153, 180–82, 210; *Manyan* (see *Pirated Copy*); *Xuanlian* (see *Red Beads*); *Youcai* (see *Postman*)
He Yi. *See* He Jianjun
Hero (*Yingxiong*), 20
Horse Thief (*Daoma zei*), 121n5
Hou Hsiao-hsien (Hou Xiaoxian), 29, 43n24, 62
Hou Xiaoxian. *See* Hou Hsiao-hsien
House of the Flying Daggers (*Shimian maifu*), 20
Hu Shu, 36, 68, 107n39; *Wo bu yao ni guan* (see *Leave Me Alone*)
Hu Xueyang, 41n3, 144, 153; *Yanmo de qingchun* (see *The Drowned Youth*)
Huang Jianxin, 150
Huang Shuqing, 187n15; *Qingchun wansui* (see *Forever Young*)
Huo Jianqi, 177, 184; *Nashan, Naren, Nagou* (see *Postman in the Mountains*); *Nuan* (see *Nuan*)

I Love You (*Wo ai ni*), 44n44
In Expectation (*Wushan yanyu*). See *Rainclouds over Wushan*
In the Heat of the Sun (*Yangguang canlan de rizi*), 27, 54, 177
independent film, vii–xi, 3–6, 23–41, 50–65, 77, 109–20, 124–25, 140n4, 143–56, 209–13; "in dependence," vii, xi, 111. *See also* underground film
Infernal Affairs III (*Wujian dao III*), 177
I've Graduated (*Wo biye le*), 48, 55
Ivens, Joris, 53

Jia Zhangke, viii, 1–6, 12, 23–39, 43n35, 47, 62, 66–68, 78–84, 96, 102, 116, 123–39, 146–47, 156, 172, 180–82, 210; *Ren xiaoyao*, (see *Unknown Pleasures*); *Shijie* (see *The World*); *Xiao Wu* (see *Xiao Wu*, aka *Artisan Pickpocket*); *Zhantai* (see *Platform*)

Jiang Hu: Life on the Road (Jiang Hu), 31–36, 47–48, 66–72, 79, 83–90, 95–103, 105n14, 182

Jiang Wen, 8, 24, 27, 54, 146, 156, 177; *Guizi laile* (see *Devils on the Doorstep*); *Yangguang canlan de rizi* (see *In the Heat of the Sun*)

Jiang Yue, x, 48, 53, 59–60, 65, 83, 109–20; *Bi an* (see *Other Bank, The*); *Xingfu shenghuo* (see *This Happy Life*)

Ju Anqi, 36–37, 107n39, 180–82; *Beijing de feng henda* (see *There's a Strong Wind in Beijing*)

Kang Jianning, 71
Kieslowski, Krzysztof, 81
Klassen, Solveig, 24, 213n2; *Wode sheyingji bu sahuang* (see *My Camera Doesn't Lie*)
Kurosawa, Akira, 81

Lau, Wai Keung. See Liu Weiqiang
Leave Me Alone (Wo bu yao ni guan), 36, 68–69, 107n39
Lee, Ang (Li An), 62
Li An. See Lee, Ang
Li Dan, 70; *Laorenmen* (see *Old People*)
Li Hong, 36, 53, 71, 109–19; *He ziji tiaowu* (see *Dancing with Myself*); *Huidao Fenghuang qiao* (see *Out of Phoenix Bridge*)
Li Xin, 41n3, 147
Li Yang, viii, 10, 104n6; *Mangjing* (see *Blind Shaft*)
Li Yu, 24, 104n6, 174; *Jinnian xiatian* (see *Fish and Elephant*)
library collection, viii, xi, 209–13
Life on the Road. See *Jiang Hu*
Lin Nong, 100; *Dang de nü'er* (see *Daughter of the Party*)
Liu Weiqiang (Andrew Lau, Wai Keung Lau), 177; *Wujian dao III* (see *Infernal Affairs III*)
Lou Ye, 23–24, 29, 39–40, 106n31, 144–46, 153, 180–83; *Suzhou he* (see *Suzhou River*); *Zhoumo qingren* (see *Weekend Lovers*)
Love in the City (Chengshi aiqing), 210
Lu Xuechang, 24, 35, 144–46; *Zhangda chengren* (see *The Making of Steel*)

Lü Yue, 29; *Zhao xiansheng* (see *Mr. Zhao*)
Lunar Eclipse (Yueshi), 39–40

Mai Zhaohui (Alan Mak, Siu Fai Mak), 177
Making of Steel, The (Zhangda chengren), 35, 44n42
Mama (Mama), 30, 145, 149
media, xi, 12, 23, 31, 38–40, 60–61, 117–19
migrant workers, 10, 31
minjian (unofficial), 25–26
Miss Jin Xing (Jin Xing xiaojie), 69
modernity, xi, 18, 123
Mr. Zhao (Zhao xiansheng), 29
My Camera Doesn't Lie (Wode sheyingji bu sahuang), 24, 213n2

1966, My Time in the Red Guards (1966, Wo de hong weibing shidai), 54–55, 66
Ning Dai, 106n26, 150; *Tingji* (see *Shutting Down*)
Ning Ying, 184; *Zhaole* (see *For Fun*)
No. 16 South Barkhor Street (Bakuo nan jie 16 hao), 48, 55, 61, 110–15
Nuan, 177

occidentalism, 13–18
Old Men (Laotou), 36, 45n52, 62, 68, 107n39, 182
Old People (Laorenmen), 70
Old Testament (Jiuyue), 8, 43n28
Orphan of Anyang, The (Anyang yinger), 31–32
Other Bank, The (Bi an), 48, 55, 60, 83, 105n12, 110
Out of Phoenix Bridge (Huidao Fenghuang qiao), 36, 45n52, 53, 110–15

performance, 66–67, 87–90
personal filmmaking, ix, 26–28, 33, 67, 102
Pirated Copy (Manyan), 45n54
Platform (Zhantai), 1, 25, 79–81, 126–28, 172
Polanski, Roman, 82
politics, ix–x, 1–20, 26, 38–39, 56, 69, 171–72, 186n13
Postman (Youcai), 28, 182, 210
Postman in the Mountains (Nashan, Naren, Nagou), 177

private filmmaking, 3–4
prostitution, 13, 31, 69, 136–37

Quitting (Zuotian), 30

Rainclouds over Wushan, aka *In Expectation (Wushan yunyu)*, 23–27, 182
realism, 27–29, 38–39, 125–27; Italian neorealism, 28
Red Beads (Xuanlian), 153
Resisting Eminent Domain (Dingzi hu), 69
Road Home, The (Wo de fuqin muqin), 155
Runaway (Daibi), 182

Schneidere-Roos, Katharina, 24, 213n2
Seafood (Haixian), 36
Secret of My Success, The (Linqi da shetou), 118
self, 14–18, 33–34, 66, 102–3
Seventeen Years (Guonian huijia), 35, 156
sexuality, 7, 90–97, 130–32
Shi Jian, 48, 51–60, 65; *Tiananmen*, 48, 51–52, 55, 58; *Wo biye le* (see *I've Graduated*)
Shi Runjiu, 41n3, 104n6
Shinsuke, Ogawa, 48, 53
Shower (Xizao), 155
Shutting Down (Tingji), 150
Sister Jiang, a Revolutionary Martyr (Jiang Jie), 156
Siu Fai Mak. *See* Mai Zhaohui
sixth generation, viii–ix, 5, 24–26, 37, 47, 77–80, 104n6, 106n31, 144–56
Snake Boy, The (Shanghai nanhai), 16
So Close to Paradise (Biandan guniang), 182
Springtime in a Small Town (Xiaocheng zhi chun), 8
Square, The (Guangchang), 48, 55, 110, 114–15
state (government), the, 1–17, 25–26, 33, 47, 165, 170–76, 180. *See also* censorship; system (*tizhi*), the
style, x, 8, 26–38, 52, 58, 99
subjectivity, x, 24–29, 151
Suzhou River (Suzhou he), 39–40, 45n59, 182
system (*tizhi*), the, 1–17, 25, 33, 47–72, 109–20; three-legged system, 109, 115–17. *See also* censorship; state (government), the

Tang Xiaobai (Emmy Tang), 24; *Dongci bianwei* (see *Conjugation*)
Tarantino, Quentin, 82, 130
Tarkovsky, Andrei, 169
There's a Strong Wind in Beijing (Beijing de feng henda), 36–37, 107n39, 182
This Happy Life (Xingfu shenghuo), 118
Tian Zhuangzhuang, 4–5, 8, 106n26; *Daoma zei* (see *Horse Thief*); *Delamu* (see *Delamu*); *Lan fengzheng* (see *Blue Kite, The*); *Xiaocheng zhi chun* (see *Springtime in a Small Town*)
Tiananmen, 48, 51–52, 55, 58
truth, x, 23–27, 38–41, 56–59

underground film, vii–xi, 1–20, 26, 35, 41n3, 48, 77–79, 102–4, 112, 143–56, 209–13. *See also* independent film
Unhappiness Doesn't Stop at One (Bu kuaile de bu zhi yige), 70
Unknown Pleasures (Ren xiaoyao), viii, 1, 12, 79, 124–39

vérité (cinéma vérité), 47–72, 99, 110, 121n1. *See also* documentary
von Tier, Lars, 169

Wang Bing, viii, 68; *Tiexi qu* (see *West of the Tracks*)
Wang Chao, 24, 31–34, 105n6, 146; *Anyang yinger* (see *The Orphan of Anyang*)
Wang Fen, 70; *Bu kuaile de bu zhi yige* (see *Unhappiness Doesn't Stop at One*)
Wang Guangli, 30, 41n3, 106n26, 147; *Heng shu heng* (see *Go for Broke*)
Wang Jiawei. *See* Wong Kar-Wai
Wang Quan'an, 39–40, 41n3; *Yueshi* (see *Lunar Eclipse*)
Wang Rui, 144
Wang Xiaoshuai, viii, 1–3, 24–30, 47, 79, 102, 106n26, 141n17, 144–53, 176, 180–82, 210; *Biandan guniang* (see *So Close to Paradise*); *Dong Chun de rizi* (see *The Days*); *Jidu hanleng* (see *Frozen*); *Shiqi sui de dan danche* (see *Beijing Bicycle*)
Weekend Lovers (Zhoumo qingren), 153
Wei Ating, 184; *Wuyin dagu* (see *Five-Tune Big Drums*)

West of the Tracks (*Tiexi qu*), viii, 68–69
What Is Film? (*Dianying shi shenme*), 47
Wiseman, Frederick, 48, 53
Wong Kar-Wai (Wang Jiawei), 154; *Chongqing senlin* (see *Chunking Express*); *Dongxie xidu* (see *Ashes of Time*)
World, The (*Shijie*), viii, 104n6, 126–28, 139, 156
Wu Wenguang, x, 16, 23, 29–37, 41n1, 47–72, 79, 83–90, 95–96, 102, 109–10, 116, 149–51, 182; *Cao tama de dianying* (see *Fuck the Movies*); *Dianying shi shenme* (see *What Is Film?*); *He mingong yiqi tiaowu* (see *Dance with Migrant Workers*); *Jiang Hu* (see *Jiang Hu: Life on the Road*); *Liulang Beijing* (see *Bumming in Beijing*); *1966, Wo de hong weibing shidai* (see *1966, My Time in the Red Guards*); *Sihai weijia* (see *At Home in the World*)

Xiao Wu. See *Artisan Pickpocket*
Xie Fei, 39, 146

Yang Chao, 182; *Daibi* (see *Runaway*)
Yang Dechang. *See* Yang, Edward
Yang, Edward (Yang Dechang), 169; *Gulingjie shaonian sharen shijian* (see *A Brighter Summer Day*)
Yang Lina. *See* Yang Tianyi
Yang Tianyi (Yang Lina), 36, 62, 68, 107n39, 182; *Laotou* (see *Old Men*)
Yang Zi, 68
Yellow Earth (*Huang tudi*), 140n15, 184

Ying Weiwei (Echo Y. Windy), 6, 36; *Hezi* (see *The Box*)

Zhang Ming, 23–25, 28, 31, 33, 35, 105n6, 146, 182–83; *Wushan yunyu* (see *Rainclouds over Wushan*)
Zhang Yang, 30, 41n3, 104n6, 125, 147, 151, 155; *Xizao* (see *Shower*); *Zuotian* (see *Quitting*)
Zhang Yimou, 20, 25, 39, 54, 105n14, 150–51, 155; *Shimian maifu* (see *House of the Flying Daggers*); *Wo de fuqin muqin* (see *The Road Home*); *Yingxiong* (see *Hero*)
Zhang Yuan, viii, x, 2–3, 7–10, 24–30, 35–37, 41n1, 44n44, 47–48, 68–69, 78–79, 102, 106n26, 110, 114–16, 144–56, 174; *Beijing zazhong* (see *Beijing Bastards*); *Dingzi hu* (see *Resisting Eminent Domain*); *Donggong xigong* (see *East Palace, West Palace*); *Fengkuang yingyu* (see *Crazy English*); *Guonian huijia* (see *Seventeen Years*); *Jin Xing xiaojie* (see *Miss Jin Xing*); *Lücha* (see *Green Tea*); *Mama* (see *Mama*); *Sister Jiang, a Revolutionary Martyr* (see *Jiang Jie*); *Wo ai ni* (see *I Love You*)
Zheng Dasheng, x, 66, 79, 97–103; *DV Zhongguo* (see *DV China*)
Zhu Chuanming, x, 62, 66–68, 79, 90–97, 102, 182; *Beijing tanjiang* (see *Beijing Cotton-Fluffing Artisan*); *Qunzhong yanyuan* (see *Extras*)
Zhu Wen, 36, 41n3, 42n18; *Haixian* (see *Seafood*)

About the Contributors

Chris Berry holds a PhD degree in cinema studies from UCLA and is currently professor of film and television studies in the Department of Media and Communications at Goldsmiths College, University of London. Among other publications, he is the author of *Postsocialist Cinema in Post-Mao China* (2004); the coauthor of *Cinema and Nation* (2006); the editor of *Perspectives on Chinese Cinema* (1991) and *Chinese Films in Focus* (2003); the coeditor of *Island on the Edge: Taiwan New Cinema and After* (2005); and translator of Ni Zhen's *Memoirs from the Beijing Film Academy* (2002).

Chen Mo is a senior researcher and a prolific scholar at the China Film Archive, Beijing. Among other publications, he is the author of *Zhang Yimou dianying lun* (On Zhang Yimou's Films, 1995), *Daoguang xiaying mengtaiqi: Zhongguo wuxia dianying lun* (Montages of Swords and Knights-Errant: On Chinese Martial Arts Films, 1996), *Chen Kaige dianying lun* (On Chen Kaige's Films, 1998), *Bainian dianying shanhui* (A Hundred Years of Cinema in Flashback, 2000), and *Yingshi wenhua xue* (A Study of Film and Television Culture, 2001).

Jim Cheng holds an MA in comparative literature and an MLS in library and information science, both from the University of Washington, Seattle. He is the head of the International Relations and Pacific Studies Library and East Asia Collection at the University of California, San Diego, and has published *An Annotated Bibliography for Chinese Film Studies* (2004) and articles in *Journal of East Asian Libraries* and *Portal: Libraries and the Academy*.

Valerie Jaffee earned her MA in modern Chinese literature from Columbia University and is currently a student at the Yale Law School. She recently spent a year at the Beijing Film Academy on a Fulbright fellowship, researching underground and independent Chinese cinema. She has published articles on Jia Zhangke in the journal *Senses of Cinema*.

Matthew David Johnson is a PhD candidate in Chinese history at the University of California, San Diego. He conducted two years of field research in China and is completing a dissertation on cultural policy, "propaganda" filmmaking, and cinematic culture in socialist China, 1949–1969. He has contributed to such academic publications as *The China Journal*.

Tonglin Lu holds a PhD in comparative literature from Princeton University and is currently professor of Chinese literature in the Department of Comparative Literature at the University of Montréal, Canada. Among other publications, she is the author of *Rose and Lotus* (1991); *Misogyny, Cultural Nihilism, and Oppositional Politics* (1995); and *Confronting Modernity in the Cinemas of Taiwan and Mainland China (2002)* and the editor of *Gender and Sexuality in Twentieth-Century Chinese Literature and Society* (1993).

Seio Nakajima is a PhD candidate in sociology at the University of California, Berkeley. He has contributed research articles on Japan, China, and Taiwan in *Urban Symbolism and Rituals* (ed. Bozidar Jezernik, 1999) and *Issues in Social Stratification in East Asia in Comparative Perspective* (ed. Shigeto Sonoda, 1995).

Paul G. Pickowicz is professor of history and Chinese studies at the University of California, San Diego. Among other publications, he is the author of *Marxist Literary Thought in China* (1981); coauthor of *Chinese Village, Socialist State* (1991) and *Revolution, Resistance, and Reform in Village China* (2005); and a coeditor of *Unofficial China* (1989), *New Chinese Cinemas* (1994), *Popular China* (2002), and *The Chinese Cultural Revolution as History* (2006).

Zhiwei Xiao holds a PhD in Chinese history from the University of California, San Diego, and is associate professor of history at California State University, San Marcos. He is the coauthor of *Encyclopedia of Chinese Film* (1998) and has contributed to academic journals (e.g., *Asian Cinema, China Review International, Chinese Historical Review*, and *Twentieth-Century China*) and such critical volumes as *Transnational Chinese Cinemas* (ed. Sheldon Lu, 1997) and *Cinema and Urban Culture in Shanghai* (ed. Yingjin Zhang, 1999).

Yingjin Zhang holds a PhD in comparative literature from Stanford University and currently serves as director of the Chinese Studies Program and professor of Chinese literature and cultural studies at the University of California, San Diego. Among other publications, he is the author of *The City in Modern Chinese Literature and Film* (1996), *Screening China* (2002), and *Chinese National Cinema* (2004); the coauthor of *Encyclopedia of Chinese Film* (1998); and the editor of *China in a Polycentric World* (1998) and *Cinema and Urban Culture in Shanghai, 1922–1943* (1999).